TRANSPORT POLICY AND RESEARCH: WHAT FUTURE?

Transport Policy and Research: What Future?

Edited by

LIANA GIORGI and RONALD J. POHORYLES
Interdisciplinary Centre for Comparative Research in the Social Sciences

Routledge
Taylor & Francis Group
LONDON AND NEW YORK

First published 2001 by Ashgate Publishing

Reissued 2018 by Routledge
2 Park Square, Milton Park, Abingdon, Oxon, OX14 4RN
711 Third Avenue, New York, NY 10017, USA

Routledge is an imprint of the Taylor & Francis Group, an informa business

A Library of Congress record exists under LC control number: 00054304

ISBN 13: 978-1-138-71711-4 (hbk)
ISBN 13: 978-1-138-71710-7 (pbk)
ISBN 13: 978-1-315-19650-3 (ebk)

Contents

Notes on Contributors

Barbara Adam is Professor of Sociology, Cardiff University; Max Weber Professor, LMU Münich (1999-2000). Founder Editor (1992-1998), Consulting Editor (1999 to present) of *Time and Society*. Award-winning author of 100+ publications, including three monographs and four edited books. Internationally renowned specialist in the study of social time. Research interests: time with reference to the environment, globalisation, risk, science and technology and transport. Keynote addresses across Europe as well as North and South America. Previous projects of relevance include an ESRC Fellowship of the 'Global Environmental Change Initiative' on the temporal and spatial problems for the social sciences (1994-1996); participation at the project TENASSESS of the 4th Framework Transport RTD Programme (1996-1999); and an ESRC pilot project on bridging time theory and practice and the exploration of time politics for the food system (1999).

David Banister is Professor of Transport Planning at the University of London and Director of Research at the Bartlett School of Planning at University College London. Over the past twenty years he has built up an international reputation as one of the leading UK researchers in transport and planning analysis, and in particular the contribution that the social scientist can make to the investigation of these problems. This research has been extensively reported in 16 authored and edited books, some 20 research monographs, and over 200 papers published in journals or as contributions to books.

Mark Brown is a transport economist and a director of Halcrow Rail, a major UK multi-disciplinary consultancy. Over the past 15 years, he has worked on highway, rail and urban transport schemes in Europe, South-East Asia, Australia and the Caribbean. His research interests include project and policy appraisal within the transport sector and he has written and published widely on this subject. He has recently led research projects for the UK Government and European Commission on the appraisal of the Trans-European network, railway competitiveness and the economics of transport law enforcement. He is currently working with Government Agencies and the private sector to establish effective public-private partnerships to deliver major transport infrastructure projects.

Emily Bulman has degrees in mathematics from Cambridge University and transport economics from the University of Leeds. She has worked as an economist in the transport and water sectors, specialising in developing policy and project appraisal. Emily is working at Halcrow Fox and will soon begin working as a consultant at National Economic Research Associates, based in London.

Paul Freudensprung is currently studying at the Institute of Transport Studies at the University of Sydney. He worked for the ICCR from 1996-1998 on the TEASSESS project.

Liana Giorgi is Vice-Director of the ICCR and responsible for a number of international projects run by the institute in the departments of *Social Policy Analysis* and *Transport Policy Analysis and Evaluation*. She is co-editor of the ICCR book series *Contemporary Trends in European Social Sciences*; and of *Innovation - The European Journal of Social Sciences*. She previously worked at the Institute of Women's Studies at the University of Amsterdam and received her degrees in social and political sciences at the University of Cambridge; and a degree in cognitive science from MIT (USA). She was national co-ordinator of the European Community Household Panel (ECHP) in Austria between 1994-1998; scientific co-ordinator of the project CODE-TEN 'Strategic Assessment of Corridor Developments' (1998-1999) and research manager of the Thematic Network 'Policy and Project Evaluation' (1999-2000). She is the author of *The post-socialist media: What power the West?* (Avebury, 1995), and co-editor of *European Transformations: Five decisive years at the turn of the century* (Avebury, 1995) in addition to numerous journal articles on the above topics.

Simon Milner is currently an Associate with Halcrow Fox in its London office. Since originally joining the company in 1995 he has been responsible for a large part of the company's policy research work on behalf of the European Commission. As well as strategic policy research at the Trans-European level, he has been involved in several EC-funded studies that focus on urban public transport policy and best practice guidelines.

Steven Ney is a Research Fellow at the ICCR. He has a BSc. in Econ. Hons (Economics and Politics) from QMW, London, an MSc. Econ (Public Policy) from QMW, London, and is a Doctoral Candidate at the University of Bergen, Norway. Previous research appointments include St. Anne's College, Oxford; NOP Market Research; Technische Universität Wien; and IIASA, Laxenburg. His main research interests are Public Sector Management, Science and Technology Policy, Social Security Reform, Environmental Policy, Democratic Theory.

Marianne Ollivier-Trigalo is a researcher at INRETS (National Research Institute on Transport and Safety, France), analysing the decision-making processes in the fields of transport policy with a particular focus on major infrastructure projects. Her research problematic, based on public policy analysis and political sociology concepts, pays attention on conflicts and problems of co-ordination between actors, notably in terms of territorial and public participation dimensions. She is currently researching on the question of the codification of public debate in the fields of major projects in France.

Ronald J. Pohoryles is director of the ICCR Vienna, president of the ICCR International, senior lecturer for comparative political systems at the University of Innsbruck, and president of the European Association for the Advancement of Social Sciences. He is co-editor of the book series *Contemporary Trends in European Social Sciences* and of the journal *Innovation - The European Journal of Social Sciences*, both of which he launched. His research expertise covers European integration emphasising public policy analysis, science and technology with emphasis on internationalisation, East-West relations and the process of accession, environmental sociology and technological integrated assessment, as well as social policy and multiculturalism. His publications include numerous articles and books on the above topics. Ronald Pohoryles is head of research of the ICCR research areas Environment and Sustainability, Society, Technology and Research as well as European Developments – Policies and Politics.

Christian Reynaud is director of the Transport Economics and Sociology department of INRETS. He is a member of different international, European (ECMT, ECE, Cost Committee) and French transport committees. Research interests include transport and the enlargement process (ITIS project with UNDP, Barbizon, ECMT); as well as the transport specific problems of the Mediterranean region (CORRIMED, INFRAMED, RETRAMED projects).

Sandrine Rui After having worked as a research fellow at the department of economy and sociology of transports at the National Research Institute on Transport and Safety (INRETS, Paris), she is now teaching sociology at the University of Pau (université de Pau et des pays de l'Adour). She works with the Institute of Research on Societies and Land use planning (IRSAM, Pau). She is finishing a thesis on the conditions of producing public spaces of discussion, based on the observation of the procedures of public debate concerning the implementation of infrastructures of transport.

Dominic Stead is Research Fellow in the Bartlett School of Planning, University College London. He has qualifications in environmental science and town planning and his research interests focus on the relationships between transport, land use planning and the environment. Since joining University College London in 1996, Dominic has been actively involved in a number of European funded research projects.

Annuradha Tandon is a Scientific Researcher with the ICCR. She is an Economist from the Delhi University and a Post Graduate in Business Administration. Her research interests focus on Transport Policy Analysis and Evaluation and Urban Transport. She has been actively involved in a number of projects under the Fourth and Fifth Framework programme of the DG Transport.

Foreword

What is the meaning of 'sustainable mobility'? Is there a European common transport policy? To what extent is policy relevant for transport developments? What is the contribution of European transport research? These are some of the questions and themes addressed by this new book in the ICCR book series *Transport Policy and Research: What Future?*

At the eve of the millennium and as the twin processes of European integration and enlargement gain momentum, it is necessary to develop and elaborate strategic visions for the future that can assist the formulation and implementation of relevant measures towards sustainable mobility. To do this it is important to understand the dynamics surrounding policy formulation and implementation, the conflicts of interest underlying these processes at the regional, national and supra-national levels, the inherent contradictions of the ecological modernisation discourse as it applies to transport, and the role of the public or the citizen in determining trajectories for future developments. In addition it is important to examine the dynamics of the science-policy interaction in the field of transport.

The book distils the results of three projects that have recently been completed with the support of the European Commission under the Fourth Framework Transport RTD Programme, namely the TENASSESS, CODE-TEN and POSSUM projects. The majority of the contributions derive from the TENASSESS project.

The TENASSESS project was co-ordinated by 'The Interdisciplinary Centre for Comparative Research in the Social Sciences' (ICCR) and carried out by a consortium of 16 partners across Europe. The TENASSESS consortium had members from HALCROW (UK), INRETS (France), PLANCO (Germany), SYSTEMA (Greece), GRUPO CLAS (Italy), TRT (Italy), the Technical University of Denmark, the European Rail Institute, the University of Cologne, NEA (Netherlands), the University of Catalunya and the University of Cardiff.

The editors would like to thank the European Commission (DG-TREN) for contributing to the financing of the TENASSESS project. We are particularly grateful to Catharina Sikow-Magny and Keith Keen of DG-TREN for their support and for their comments throughout the project. These have been very valuable and have significantly contributed to the quality of our work.

The Editors
Liana Giorgi &
Ronald J. Pohoryles

Vienna, March 2001

1 The Europeanisation of Transport Policy

PAUL FREUDENSPRUNG AND LIANA GIORGI

In the past transport policy has almost exclusively been a national issue. Despite the increasing number of common European initiatives, progress towards a common European action programme has been slow.

The legal basis for the creation of a common transport policy is provided in the Treaty establishing the European Economic Community, signed in March 1957 (Title IV, articles 74-84). Until 1985 the European Conference of Transport Ministers (ECMT) was the main institution to co-ordinate pan-European transport policy initiatives.

In 1961 the Schaus Memorandum presented first general guidelines of a common transport policy. These were followed by an action programme for regulations, and a first outline for a Community-wide transport network. Due to unfavourable reactions of the Member States those initiatives showed little effect. In 1975 the Commission suggested a shift from regulating the transport market to seeking a balance between market forces without interventions.

The *White Paper on the Completion of the Internal Market* published in 1985 emphasised that restrictions on the provision of transport services were one of the main barriers to open trade. The removal of these barriers necessitated the intervention of the European Court of Justice upon the initiative of the Parliament: called upon to interpret the application of the directives of the Treaty of Rome in relation to transport, the European Court of Justice declared European inland freight and passenger transport open to all firms within the Community without any discrimination for place of establishment. This was the first European-wide action to liberalise the access to the national transportation markets.

In the following years the Member States could agree on several actions to be launched at the Community level, including the DRIVE and the EURET programmes. Specific initiatives where prepared regarding road safety (seat-belts, alcohol), waterborne transport (1101/89/EEC), the separation of rail infrastructure and service provision (440/91/EEC), as well as the liberalisation of air transport in 1987, 1990 and 1992. The majority of the measures brought forward between 1985 and 1992 aimed at eliminating regulatory barriers to the internal market.

With the publication of the *White Paper on the Future Development of the Common Transport Policy* in 1993 the common transport policy approach came to delineate a more comprehensive framework, covering a broad range of additional fields, including environmental protection and conservation, social impacts as well as the relation to third countries. In total seven pillars were identified for a successful European transport policy:

- an efficiently working internal market, facilitating free movement of people and goods;
- a coherent, integrated transport system using the most appropriate technologies;
- a trans-European transport network which interconnects national networks, makes them interoperable and links the peripheral regions with the central ones;
- transport systems helping to resolve major environmental problems;
- promotion of the highest possible safety standards;
- social policies to protect and promote the interests of both transport workers and users;
- developing relations with third countries.

The Maastricht Treaty of the European Union (Title XII) underlined the importance of transport and in particular of the trans-European network. Furthermore, articles 75 to 81 of the Treaty extended the competencies of the European Council of Ministers to cover common regulations for international transport; market access; transport safety; fiscal harmonisation including customs duties and cross-border charges; transport pricing; and state subsidies. Relevant proposals were submitted to the Council by the European Commission. Feedback had since been obtained by the Economic and Social Committee, the Committee of the Regions and the European Parliament.

Subsidiarity is the Union's guiding principle in realising the objectives set out in its Common Transport Policy. Therefore partnerships between the Union's institutions and the Member States are necessary at all levels, that is at the highest political and official levels, as well as among operators, users, investors and environmental organisations. In the framework established by the principle of subsidiarity, it is the Union's task to promote the interconnection and interoperability of national transport networks as well as the access to those networks. The planning of transport infrastructure remains with the Member States, however Union priorities have to be taken into account. It is likewise the task of the Member States to decide the timing of realisation of projects and to determine financing strategies.

The Union fulfils its tasks through publishing guidelines which identify measures and projects of common interest, indicating also their priority in terms of realisation. It also issues guidelines for the technical harmonisation process of the national transport systems. All guidelines proposed by the Commission have to be adopted by the Council and the European Parliament in accordance with the co-decision procedure. In a consultation process the opinions from the Economic and Social Committee and from the Committee of the Regions are sought. Financial support is granted for feasibility studies; loan guarantees and interest subsidies are available for projects. In targeted regions up to 90 per cent of project costs may be funded through the instrument of the Cohesion Fund.

In the course of the first months of 1994 and in accordance with Article 129 C of the Maastricht Treaty of the European Union, the Commission brought forward various policy proposals in the fields of energy and transport (COM(93)685 and COM(94)116), the interoperability of high-speed trains (COM(94)107) and the financial regulation of the trans-European networks (COM(94)62). The concept of the trans-European networks was elaborated during the formulation of the Maastricht Treaty, which specified a network of transport corridors forming the backbone of the European transport system. Also in 1994, specifically at the Essen Council Meeting in December, the 14 TEN priority projects as suggested by the Group of Personal Representatives (Christophersen Group) were accepted. Essen also established the backbone for the extension of the TEN to Central and Eastern Europe as well as to the CIS. What came to be known as the pan-European corridors have recently been adopted into the relevant TEN directive of the European Commission. The Action Programme to the White Paper specifying the medium term perspective of the transport policy actions until 2000 was adopted by the Council in July 1995.

In order to stimulate discussion regarding the environmental aspects and impacts of transport, the Commission published two Green Papers in 1995: the Green Paper *Citizens' Network* and the Green Paper on *Fair and Efficient Pricing in Transport*. The Green Paper *Citizens' Network* has an additional significance: with it, the Commission for the first time addresses officially the problems inherent in urban and regional transport. Until this time, these issues were only addressed indirectly through research carried out in the framework of the Fourth Framework Programme. In 1996 another White Paper followed on the *Revitalisation of European Railways*, which focused on liberalising the market of railway operations in Europe. In 1997 and 1998 various communications of the Commission for promoting the actions outlined by the various policy documents were published. Among these the most important are: the *Communication of the Commission on the Common Transport Policy* (1998); the *Communication of the Commission on How to Promote Good Local and Regional Public Transport* (1998); and the *Communication of the Commission on Intermodal Transport* (1997).

Throughout the past decade, the Member States played different roles in the process of developing and shaping transport policies at Community level. Deregulation, liberalisation and privatisation were for a certain time very fiercely discussed and opposed to. Today they are broadly accepted as efficiency principles, whereby the procedures and details of implementation as well as their implications about the role of the state as regulator remain, as we will see, under debate. Certain is that the orientation of the Common Transport Policy has changed following the input of the Member States.

With the European Monetary Union Treasuries have gained a major influence on all aspects of transport investments which involve some measure of public involvement. The promotion of private-public partnerships for funding transport projects is a main issue in all countries, but very few implemented cases have been documented. The success in attracting private investors is generally still moderate. In turn this continues to strengthen the role of national governments in European transport policy-making.

National Regulatory Environments in Comparative Perspective

The increasing role of the Treasury in determining public investment in the field of transport is not the only reason for investigating national transport policies. Many of the problems encountered in implementing the European Common Transport Policy relate to the variation in the regulatory environments in the field of transport across Member States. The following were identified as of specific importance:[1]

- the variation in the distribution of administrative responsibility and competencies at the national level;
- the variation in the degree of planning of transport policy in the form of master plans but also assessment and/or evaluation frameworks;

- the variation in the degree of centralisation or decentralisation, especially with respect to the role assigned to the regions, hence the process of territorialisation; and
- the variation in the degree of negotiation with relevant actors, including citizens' movements or the public at large.

At the same time there are some general harmonising trends across all four dimensions which can, in part, be attributed to the influence of the European Union: i.e. towards greater sharing of responsibility and stronger co-ordination at the national administrative level; towards the development of a planning structure that fits the requirements of the European CTP; towards the devolution of power to the regions, that is, decentralisation; and towards a stronger emphasis on negotiation at all levels. Whether the differences or the similarities along these dimensions are more relevant for understanding the development of CTP is a subject we return to at the end of this chapter.

Distribution of Administrative Competencies at National Level

In most countries, the responsibility for drawing out and co-ordinating transport policy at national level rests with a single ministry. The implementation of transport policy rests with numerous agencies or departments, of which some are independent, some are under the direct jurisdiction of the ministry in charge of transport. In some countries however, notably in Italy, Spain and Austria, strategic policy planning is itself divided as a task: thus in Spain and Italy infrastructure planning is separated from transport policy more generally; whereas in Austria, until recently, road and rail competencies were separated with the Ministry of Science and Transport being in charge of rail and the Ministry of Economic Affairs being in charge of road.

As a result of the increasing emphasis laid on consensus on the one hand, and the achievement of integration across policy areas on the other, other actors come increasingly to play a stronger role in the formulation and implementation of transport policy. The most important among these actors is the ministry responsible for environmental affairs (and/or public works or spatial planning): currently this is especially the case in those countries like Denmark, Germany, Sweden and the Netherlands, where transport planning is incorporated in the larger framework of spatial and environmental planning and where, subsequently, such consultations are already part of the regular process of policy formulation.

Finally, due to the heavy involvement of public funds in transport investments, the respective national ministries of finance influence heavily the realisation of transport policies and projects. This has always been the case; currently, it is compounded by first, the budgetary restrictions imposed on both the national and the European budgets and second, the slow pace of development of the envisaged public-private partnerships.

Transport Planning

Most European countries have elaborated specific master plans for transport, others provide in addition very specific assessment frameworks for transport investments and policy progress. Depending on the structure of the country such master plan concepts are available for the national, regional and in some cases for the local levels. Often they are accompanied by detailed infrastructure master plans. In some cases, such as in Denmark, the Netherlands, Sweden and Germany, they are embedded in a wider frame for future planning and development covering socio-economic, environmental and spatial aspects; Austria and partly also France are in the process of elaborating such a set of interconnections. Not surprisingly these set of countries also displays quite comprehensive environmental plans or laws that make specific references to transport.

Only two European countries, namely, Greece and Luxembourg, have no form of general transport policy documents. Spain has merely an infrastructure development plan but no transport master plan; in Italy, the general plan for transport, dating back to 1986, has shown little relevance for transport development in the past two decades.

In Belgium, transport infrastructure plans were prepared separately for the two main regions, i.e. Walloonia and Flanders respectively. In Sweden, the 1988 ten-year plan on transport is in the process of being revised; in France, the transport framework law LOTI of 1982 is relevant only in relation to the annual reports on transport development and stands in close relation to the framework law on physical planning.

These overarching policy documents, where they exist, do not always carry the same weight in terms of implementation. With the exception of Denmark, the Netherlands, Germany, and Sweden, they for the most part only set general orientation guidelines or define general objectives or assessment criteria. More specific on actual instruments or measures of implementation are the infrastructure investment plans; however here also, it is increasingly becoming common practice that the goals set out are not met within the time framework originally specified.

Related to the incidence of general planning documents, but not necessarily dependent on it, is the scope of planning activities, what we call 'planning culture'. This characterises especially France and Germany and is closely linked to a 'technocratic' orientation.

In those countries without general guiding policy documents, and especially in Greece, Italy and Spain, there was for several years little in the sense of a proactive approach in the field of the elaboration of transport policy. In these countries the elaboration of the European Common Transport Policy has provided a lever for upgrading and/or structuring national transport policy as well as for levelling conflicts and speeding-up decision-making procedures. In other words, the non-existent or hardly elaborated national transport plans were here replaced by the Community's Transport Acquis.

Degree of Centralisation and the Process of Territorialisation

The third major discriminatory variable in comparing national transport policies is the degree of centralisation, especially with regard to the role assigned to the regions – hence also the process of territorialisation.

At the most obvious level, competencies among the state's territorial authorities are distributed in different ways depending on the degree and character of federalisation as established in the respective State Constitutions. Variation exists according to the specific fields of application and with regard to the role of the state as co-ordinator or planner of specific activities.

Typically in the transport field regions are responsible for urban as well as regional transport networks, and especially national or secondary road infrastructure, regional rail services and urban public transport. By reason of their jurisdiction over physical planning and/or land use designation, they are also involved in the planning of international routes. In most countries the relationship between the state and the regions is hierarchical – also regarding financing. Only in Germany and Belgium (as of recently) can the state be said to have more the role of co-ordinator.

However, there are two parallel phenomena that in many countries, and most notably, in France, Italy and Spain, are causing major re-orientations: the first is the growing demand of the regions to have more autonomy and, hence, reverse the top-down approach; the second is the wish of the state to more actively involve the regions in the financing of major infrastructure investments. Not least important is that many problems in the transport area are caused by the uncoordinated sprawl of human activities (housing, working, education, leisure activities, shopping). Co-ordination would therefore appear necessary both at the national level and at the European level in relation to the regions.

Culture of Negotiation in Decision-Making

The description of decision-making processes represents a complex task by reason of the increasing number of relevant actors. Not all of these actors are organised as lobbies or interest groups. At times and in some contexts, this renders the decision-making process informal or little transparent. This is especially the case in countries not displaying a formalised decision-planning procedure or elaborated policies in the form of documents.

Economic actors and the interests they represent play an important role. In the sector of transport, economic actors are often institutional players who till recently represented the state, but which now are called upon to represent 'private' or 'independent and market-oriented' interests. Under the framework of liberalisation and privatisation the status of the state-owned transport industry has changed: in the airline sector all flag carriers and most of the major European airports have been transformed into public limited companies, though in all cases the state or other public entities remain the major or exclusive shareholders. The restructuration of the railways has started in some countries (Sweden, Denmark, Germany, Greece, Italy) but is still outstanding in most. Great Britain has been the most advanced on this path, having completely privatised both the air and the rail transport markets in the recent past.

Apart from transport service and infrastructure operators, interest groups play a major role in transport policy. Trade unions have traditionally had a strong influence on the public transport sector, but especially in Italy, France, Austria and Sweden. Representative organisations of the employers and operators are active in all the countries. The supply industry has gained major influence in transport policy as being one of the most important employers in some of the Member States.

With regard to direct public participation in decision-making processes, these have evolved differentially throughout the Union: in Germany, the Netherlands, Denmark and Sweden there are structures for giving each single citizen the possibility to comment on transport infrastructure projects or policies, and the comments have to be taken into account or responded to; in Italy there are such procedures only for specific types of projects, whilst in Austria more emphasis is laid on encouraging citizens to become involved in decision-making processes through public hearings and information campaigns. In most countries direct public participation is not far developed: in Greece, for instance, grassroots' movements are considered to have no political power at all.

Some prototypical models are summarised below:

In the *Netherlands*, the Planning Central Decision (PKB) represents probably the most advanced system for direct public participation; the

Netherlands, like Denmark and Sweden is characterised by a strong negotiation model in decision-making, involving all actors, including the public.

Germany displays by far the most elaborate operationalised framework of federalism: the *Länder* and the federal government are co-operating on the basis of the principle of subsidiarity.

Decision-making in *Austria* is characterised best as proceeding according to a negotiated compliance model, and involving social partners, that is the Chambers of Labour and Commerce, trade unions and the Agricultural Chamber. Representatives of relevant actors comment on the government's proposals for policy and legislation prior to the latter's submission to the Parliament.

In *France* decision-making has traditionally been very centralised and technocratic. However, as a result of the decentralisation laws of 1982 and 1986, there are currently serious attempts to establish a decision-making framework which is based on negotiation and decentralisation, including revisions in the structure and form of public audits. Problems still exist with regard to the degree and scope of competency to be achieved by regions, especially given that the various regions have different views on this matter.

The transformation of *Belgium* into a federal state with autonomous regions from 1974 to 1995, has affected the decision-making process through the overall shift of competencies at the regional level.

In *Italy*, trade unions have a specifically strong impact on policy and decision-making. Due to the notorious instability of governments and the frequent changes of ministers and of other relevant actors at the administrative level, some actors, such as the directorate of the national railways, have a very strong influence on policy making.

Finally, in *Greece*, policy and decision-making depends very much on personal initiative, which can be considered as stronger and more important than formalised procedures.

Conflict Areas in Transport Policy

Three general conflict areas which are common to all European countries can be identified. They comprise:

- conflicts about competencies;
- thematic conflict 'environment vs. economic development';
- conflicts related to the re-structuring of the transport market.

Conflicts About Competencies

The European Union as currently developing represents a specific form of multi-level governance. Despite the principle of subsidiarity, the borders between the four established political levels – local, regional, national and European – remain diffuse, giving rise to conflicts about competencies. Two developments are at the root of these conflicts: the rise of a new supranational European level, and the demand of regional and local governments for more participation in decision-making.

Disagreements still persist regarding the extent of harmonisation - there are still serious disagreements about which issues and areas are legitimately to be dealt with at the European level. Examples include the common environmental threshold levels, safety regulations or negotiation mandates with third countries.

Regional authorities, especially in those Member States where they still have no or a low participation in decision-making, try to increase their influence within the Member States as well as directly on the European Union. The same is true of local authorities which have the least competence in transport policy, yet are often the most affected by large-scale infrastructure projects. In some cases such as in Greece and Italy the policy initiatives of the European Commission have helped levelling such problems.

Problems in co-ordination arise by the fact that the European Commission represents neither the sole, nor the first, attempt at harmonisation at policy level – the European Conference of Ministers of Transport or the International Union of Railways are two other major European institutions dealing with transport. Within the European Commission the transport agenda is shared between different General Directorates. Despite the fact that over the years there have gradually emerged co-ordination or consultation procedures facilitated by a narrowing down of institutional agendas, be it in terms of geographical scope (thus for instance the European Conference of Ministers of Transport dropped the TEN from its policy agenda in 1994), in terms of mode or in terms of types of impacts, problems remain as agendas unavoidably overlap. Co-ordination represents itself a long process of institutional learning.

Thematic Conflict 'Environment vs. Economic Development'

The conflicts within transport policy can basically be reduced to one pair of contrasting arguments. On the one hand, there are policies concerned with reducing the negative impacts of traffic for the environment and society and even with reducing transport volume per se; on the other hand, there are policies to improve transport flows in order to further enhance economic development. Objectives are generally set in both directions, but the incompatibility or lack of direct congruence displayed between the two is often the source of fierce debate about effectiveness and equity in the medium- to long-term.

What is especially interesting about this type of conflict is that it cuts vertically across all dimensions and/or levels of political decision-making or action, and that it also concerns the industry. This principal conflict about, essentially, the future orientation of transport, only partly overlaps with the conflicts about competencies described above; for the most part it adds on an additional dimension.

The specific instances of enactment of this type of conflict varies greatly among Member States, covering all kinds of environment-related concerns, such as noise abatement, air pollution, safety, pricing of external costs, the extension of transport infrastructure and telematics applications.

Conflicts Related to the Restructuring of the Transport Market

Currently, and with very few exceptions, deregulation and the privatisation of the transport market is a generally agreed-upon policy agenda. Nevertheless a distinction can be drawn between those actors in favour of a swift transformation towards an open market system, and those supporting a slower pace and longer phase-out periods. These conflicts can for the most part be explained by considering the competition patterns among modes. The continuing direct and indirect subsidising of operators in the road, airline and railway business is not welcomed by competitors. Furthermore fair pricing for infrastructure use and service operations is claimed for all modes. Market entry for new transport operators empirically turns out to be very difficult. Conflicts about whether and how to re-regulate the transport markets have, subsequently, become more important.

The re-structuring of the transport market is also connected with some significant labour re-structuring processes. These are the seedbed of conflicts and feed into the decline of trust in the state apparatus. The liberalisation of the transport market has involved, at worst, a number of lay-off in parts of the transport industry and, at best, a status change along with the decline of job security. Along the same lines, the working conditions comprise a major source of debate as they affect the personal situation of the individual employees, but also safety and competition issues.

Transport Policy or Transport Policies?

This chapter outlined the main patterns of conflicts characterising national transport policies in relation to the Common Transport Policy (CTP). To reiterate, these concerned: first, disagreements regarding the share of responsibilities and the distribution of competencies among the European, national and regional levels in connection to the principle of subsidiarity; second, the perceived incompatibility or lack of congruence between economic and environmental goals in the field of transport; and, third, problems arising with regard to the ongoing reform of the transport market, characterised by the twin processes of privatisation and/or de-regulation.

We also discussed the main factors explaining the variation of the regulatory framework across European countries; this variation is itself a reason that explains the difficulties encountered in implementing CTP directives. The four discriminating variables in this connection were identified as: first, the variation in the distribution of administrative responsibilities at national level; second, the variation in the degree and scope of transport planning; third, the variation in the degree of decentralisation and fourth, the differences in the type of negotiation procedures implemented in relation to policy formulation and decision-making.

But how different are the national transport policies from each other and from what is gradually emerging as the Common Transport Policy? As we saw, despite differences in the regulatory frameworks there are also several harmonising trends: there is a significant degree of agreement on the necessity to democratise the decision-making process; on the role of regions in transport planning; on the importance of the integration of environmental concerns in transport planning; and on the significance of privatisation and liberalisation for increasing the efficiency and accountability of the transport sector.

The differences among national transport policies are reflected in the prioritisation of specific policy goals. For instance: the increase of cross-border or international traffic is a highly valued policy goal in most countries by reason of the close association between international traffic flows, trade and economic growth. In most countries, however, it is also important to reduce local road traffic especially in residential areas. How important this second goal is has implications on infrastructure investment and on the solutions found to deal with congestion problems: thus, in Austria, the attachment of this goal to environmental concerns has led to a practical 'construction stop' for new international road projects; in Germany, on the other hand, such problems are more often than not resolved through the construction of bypasses. This is not to say that the reduction of local road traffic is not granted any importance in Germany; rather that it is not as important, or at least not as explicitly associated with environmental pollution.

The potentially contradictory nature of some or several of the CTP objectives is something which is recognised by the Commission itself when it talks about the barriers to CTP implementation (EC, 1993). In fact, the various goals are only contradictory because they are interpreted or valued differently by different actors. Any one actor is absolutely in the position to combine these in a consistent manner and use them to guide policy making. Following this logic, it is possible to distinguish four 'ideal type' transport policy frameworks (cf. Ney, in this volume):

- The traditional transport planning approach assumes that transport is primarily there to serve structural inequalities in particular at the regional level. For this policy framework, the goals of regional cohesion and development are of particular relevance and guide transport policy-making, primarily infrastructure investment.
- A 'modern' variant of the transport planning approach emerged with the onset of privatisation. Under this approach, planning and infrastructure investment are still important, only the planner ought to be the private economic actor, less so the state for which within-sector efficiency becomes of utmost significance.
- The liberal market approach to transport development considers it important to regulate the transport sector through primarily economic instruments. Pricing instruments and taxation are under this scheme of particular relevance. So is liberalisation and privatisation when associated with greater accountability and transparency in operations.
- The ecological approach to transport, considers transport development at best a necessary evil. Transport is considered one main source of pollution, therefore infrastructure investment is considered 'bad' - instead what is called for are measures for making it less necessary to travel and strict environmental regulation.

No one national transport policy can be mapped clearly against the above four-fold typology. This is why we talk of 'ideal' type policy frameworks or policy lenses and not of real policy environments. Nevertheless the above policy packages could be said to describe the main rupture points or cleavages within national transport policy environments as well as at the European level.

In all of the countries under investigation, transport policy has experienced major changes during the past five to ten years. Some countries embarked on a comprehensive (re-)formulation of transport policy objectives and measures; others have relied on the Commission's directives for structuring their transport policies. Regardless of the degree and scope of planning, substantial changes have been embedded in a series of reforms: on the one hand, of the political and policy framework of decision-making with the trend pointing in the direction of decentralisation and greater transparency; on the other hand, of the transport market with privatisation and de-regulation setting the agenda.

With these changes a new terminology has also made its way into transport policy: the new structuring terms are sustainable transport systems, intermodality and interoperability. However, whilst the underlying objectives or general goals – reduction of negative impacts, integration of transport services – are quite clear in general terms, the pragmatic implications of these new transport concepts still remain vague or little elaborated across all levels. One difficulty in terms of operationalisation results from the fact that whilst integrated thinking is accepted as the primary point of departure, this is difficult to put into practice by reason of the still fragmented character of policy formulation within national boundaries and at the supra-national level. The absence of measures of performance relating to transport policy objectives also reflects the indecision that still reigns as to whether these objectives reflect the direction transport policy ought to take: there is still disagreement as to the role of the market; the role of the state; the role of the citizen; and not least important the value of mobility in relative terms.

It will be the answers to the above questions that will determine the direction of transport policy and in particular of the Common Transport Policy in the future. The choice or prioritisation of any particular mode or their systematic integration, whilst not unimportant is not as significant, not least because of technological advances. Understanding this can help achieve a new way of policy formulation and implementation in the field of transport.

Note

1 The details of the national transport policies reviewed in the paper are detailed in Working Papers (1) to (16) produced by the TENASSESS project. See also www.iccr-international.org/tenasses.

References

European Commission (1990), *The European High-Speed Train Network*, Report to the High-Level Group, European Commission, Brussels.

European Commission (1992), *The Future Development of the Common Transport Policy - A Global Approach to the Construction of a Community Framework for Sustainable Mobility*, COM(92) 494, European Commission, Brussels.

European Commission (1993a), *European Transport Policy in the 90's*, European Commission, Brussels.

European Commission (1993b), *The Future Development of the Common Transport Policy. A Global Approach to the Construction of a Community Framework for Sustainable Mobility.* Bulletin of the European Communities, Supplement 3/93, European Commission, Brussels.

European Commission (1993c), *Action Programme for Road Safety*, COM(93) 246 final, European Commission, Brussels.

European Commission (1994a), *The Trans-European Transport Network*, European Commission, Brussels.

European Commission (1994b), *Community Guidelines for the Development of the Trans-European Transport Network*, COM(94) 106, European Commission, Brussels.

European Commission (1994c), *Trans-European Networks*, The group of personal representatives of the heads of state and government, Report to the Corfu European Council, European Commission, Brussels.

European Commission (1994d), *Strategic Environmental Assessment - Existing Methodology*, European Commission, Brussels.

European Commission (1995a), *The Common Transport Policy Action Programme 1995-2000*, European Commission, Brussels.

European Commission (1995b), *The Trans-European Transport Network; Transforming Patchwork Into a Network*, European Commission, Brussels.

European Commission (1995c), 'Amended Proposal for a European Parliament and Council Decision on the Community Guidelines for the Development of the Trans-European Transport Network', *Official Journal* C97, Vol.38.

European Commission (1995d), *Towards Fair and Efficient Pricing in Transport*, Green Paper, COM(95)-691, European Commission, Brussels.

European Commission (1995e), *The Citizens' Network – Fulfilling the Potential of Public Passenger Transport*, COM(95) 601, European Commission, Brussels.

European Commission (1996a), *Strategies for the Revitalisation of the European Railway Companies*, White Paper, COM(96) 421, European Commission, Brussels.

European Commission (1997a), *Case Studies on Strategic Environmental Assessment; Final Report: Volumes 1 & 2*, European Commission, Brussels.

European Commission / ISPRA (1997b), *A Study to Develop and Implement an Overall Strategy for EIA/SEA Research in the EU*, European Commission, Brussels.

European Commission (1998), *Communication from the Commission: Developing the Citizens' Network: Why Good Local and Regional Passenger Transport is Important and How the European Commission is Helping to Bring it About*, COM (98) 431 final, European Commission, Brussels.

European Commission (1999), *Commission Communication to the Council, European Parliament, Economic and Social Committee and Committee of the Regions: The Common Transport Policy; Sustainable Mobility: Perspectives for the Future*, European Commission, Brussels.

High-Level Group Brussels (1997) *Public-Private Partnership Financing of TEN Projects*, Final report, VII/321/97, European Commission, Brussels.

TENASSESS Deliverable R(1), *Policy Issues and National Transport Policies*, 1996, ICCR, Vienna.

TENASSESS Working Paper (1), *National Transport Policy Belgium*, 1996, ICCR, Vienna.

TENASSESS Working Paper (2), *National Transport Policy France*, 1996 (& Update 1998), ICCR, Vienna.
TENASSESS Working Paper (3), *National Transport Policy Germany*, 1996, ICCR, Vienna.
TENASSESS Working Paper (4), *National Transport Policy Luxembourg*, 1996, ICCR, Vienna.
TENASSESS Working Paper (5), *National Transport Policy Finland*, 1996, ICCR, Vienna.
TENASSESS Working Paper (6), *National Transport Policy Italy*, 1996, ICCR, Vienna.
TENASSESS Working Paper (7), *National Transport Policy U.K.*, 1997, ICCR, Vienna.
TENASSESS Working Paper (8), *National Transport Policy Denmark*, 1996, ICCR, Vienna.
TENASSESS Working Paper (9), *National Transport Policy Spain*, 1996, ICCR, Vienna.
TENASSESS Working Paper (10), *National Transport Policy Sweden*, 1996, ICCR, Vienna.
TENASSESS Working Paper (11), *National Transport Policy The Netherlands*, 1996, ICCR, Vienna.
TENASSESS Working Paper (12), *National Transport Policy Greece*, 1996, ICCR, Vienna.
TENASSESS Working Paper (13), *National Transport Policy Austria*, 1996, ICCR, Vienna.
TENASSESS Working Paper (14), *List of Relevant Policy Documents: National Transport Policies*, 1996, ICCR, Vienna.
TENASSESS Working Paper (15), *List of Relevant Actors: National Transport Policies*, 1996, ICCR, Vienna.
TENASSESS Working Paper (16), *List of National Transport Policy Objectives and Measures*, 1996, ICCR, Vienna.

2 The Implementation of Major Infrastructure Projects: Conflicts and Co-ordination

MARIANNE OLLIVIER-TRIGALO

Everyone agrees that decision-making is complex. Public policies are now defined by many actors who interact in order to reach several objectives, most often contradictory. Transport policy does not depart from these rules and the implementation of the Common Transport Policy (CTP) is the theatre of many conflicts and decision-making crises.

The construction of major infrastructures constitutes an important part of the CTP. This is reflected in national master plans as well as in the concept of the Trans-European Networks (TEN), the explicit objective of which is to contribute to the European integration principle.[1] Conflicts surrounding major infrastructure projects, like the TEN, have gradually brought about a re-thinking in this field. Indeed, the direction of CTP, both in terms of contents and in terms of organisation can at present best be judged at the 'local' level of implementation of major infrastructure projects. Such projects raise the questions of equity and representation, be it of regions or of specific social groups in relation to either socio-economic advantage or environmental protection.

These conflicts highlight in addition how currently there is no one sole legitimate bearer of a measure or a project able to co-ordinate and integrate the strategies of the different players. The increase in the number of relevant actors creates a problem in co-ordination which is more than just an organisational problem, which does not mean that organisational problems are to be underestimated.

The problem of co-ordination makes clear three important aspects: first, that the contents of policy are closely inter-linked to the decision process; second that the 'ideology' or the value frameworks within which decision-makers and stakeholders operate influence the operationalisation of policy goals; and third that conflict analysis is fundamental to policy analysis as much as it is to policy implementation. Co-ordination is in other words a problem because there are conflicting or contradictory goals that need to be overcome or balanced in a consistent, transparent and, more importantly, in a legitimate way to make implementation possible.

The need of co-ordination has created a new arena of politics: the role of the 'co-ordinator' or of the '*metteur en oeuvre*' ought not to be confused with that of the decision-maker which still remains the prerogative of the central states. This new role constitutes a rule for the contemporary public decision arena.

Ten case studies[2] were carried out to analyse the above processes of implementation and the problems and conflicts they produce in different national contexts:

- the Øresund link between Denmark and Sweden, one of the few successfully implemented TEN priority projects;
- the Brenner axis, likewise a major focus of the TEN – the part of the axis identified as priority, namely the tunnel, has still to be built;
- the Betuwe railway line between Germany and the Netherlands which is of potential significance for the North European ports in relation to the opening to the East;
- the Twente Central Canal Connection in connection with the Betuwe Line;
- the Inter-island passenger transport system, a programme approved under INTERREG which aims at establishing a helicopter network to increase the accessibility of the Greek islands;
- the Barcelona-Montpellier link, another TEN project and a major TGV project for Spain, and in particular Catalunia, which aims to effect a fast train connection between Spain and France with important implications for the port of Barcelona;
- the Lyon-Turin link Transalpine Railway Connection a project made up of numerous split projects covering the whole regional network;
- the Eastern TGV towards Strasbourg and Luxembourg, a project which for the first time raised doubts about the high-speed rail project;
- the TGV PBKAL Brussels-Amsterdam/Köln the implementation of which represents a serious re-formulation of the high-speed rail towards an integration of regional concerns;

- the Skaramanga Interchange out of Athens, a project of national relevance but displaying conflicts typical of major infrastructure projects, albeit experienced for the first time in the Greek context.

The case studies focused on *the decision process* characterising the implementation process. Any public policy can be considered and approached as a social system (Thoenig, 1985). It is shaped by a system of interacting actors who employ certain practices or activities to reach their objectives. A public policy combines in an interdependent way and through action a process of content definition and implementation (Padioleau, 1998). The players involved in the process configure the relevant issues and, through their interaction, the rules of the decision-making process.

The method employed here to specify this social system drew from *the field of political sociology and the sociology of organised action*. It was based on the concept of 'concrete systems of action' (Crozier and Friedberg, 1977; and Friedberg, 1993) which allowed to characterise the decision process through the actors involved, their objectives, strategies and alliances, paying particular attention to their interplay over time. A guiding principle was *to explore conflicts* and how these constituted the definition and implementation of the project.

The weight of the institutions and of the political systems is significant in public action (Padioleau, 1982). The comparison of the case studies sets the question, how and to what extent national differences with respect to institutions and the political systems are important, where do these converge and how are the differences managed.[3]

In order to characterise the decision-making processes specific to each case, the following data and information were systematically collected: the technical and socio-economic description of the project; the chronology of the decision-making; the political, technical, socio-economic and legal context; the actors involved. After this first documentary work, a set of interviews was undertaken. As a methodological principle, we considered as prior the protagonists' viewpoints and their own perception of the decision-making process, their role, their action and their interrelationships. We assumed that actors in any specific situation determine and through their interaction what constitutes a problem.

Actors were classified according to spheres of action: civil, socio-economic, technical, administrative and political. What primarily distinguishes them is their level of organisation and the role assigned to them in the decision-making process. The analysis of their mobilisation allows us to distinguish between the promoters and the opponents to a project. Subsequently 'scenes of action' can be constructed, each delineated by a set of actors, arguments, actions, and those decisions most determining for the cases under study. These scenes of action were identified by providing answers to the following questions: Why and when did the issue appear? By whom was it set on the agenda? Who were the other actors who expressed an opinion on this issue? What were the consequences on the decision-making process?

The analysis has produced elements for reflection about the new order in the field of decision-making in Europe, the role of the European initiative as well as about the way in which European policy is constructed.

Six Main Issues

There are six main issues in the contemporary landscape of European (Common) Transport Policy at the level of implementation of major infrastructure projects:

- the notion and problem of the 'missing-link';
- the role of the 'frontier' or of borderline zones;
- the territorialisation of the decision-making process and in relation to this the role of regional authorities and the question of risk sharing and responsibility;
- the issue of pricing as a strategic notion;
- the problem of financing; and
- the role of environmental appraisal.

The 'Missing-Links' in the Trans-European Network (TEN)

The adoption of the Christophersen list (Group of Personal Representatives of the Heads of State or Government, 1995) placed the TEN on the concrete political agenda. Thus the 'missing-link' emerged as a key concept or solution to the problem of integration and the constitution of a European space.

The key 'missing-links' or priority projects were selected according to the criterion of 'added value to the implementation of trans-European networks' (ibid.). This criterion of 'added value' was operationalised as characterising those international projects involving at least two different member states. The final list of priority projects was the result of a negotiation process among the Members States of the European Union. The final selection was assisted by adding another criterion, namely that of the 'maturity' of the proposed projects.

There are two important points to make for the present discussion: the first concerns the trans-boundary character of the 'missing links'. This reflects a specific understanding of 'European added value' and of subsidiarity by the Commission and the Member States, namely, that 'European' is the level of interface or the connecting tissue between nation-states.

The second concerns the value attached to these connections: the 'conquering' of these missing links is assumed to promote integration, physically – with respect to the inter-connection of national networks – but also politically: the construction of these links requires co-operation between nation-states; in turn this can contribute to the overcoming (or bypassing) of national differences in transport policy, thus the promotion of the Common Transport Policy.

In other words, the 'missing-link' concept and the TEN represented for their promoters a 'best-practice' model for CTP. In practice this model did not work in as straight-forward a manner as was expected.

The main barrier concerned the conflicting national interests of the traversed regions. The truly relevant question in terms of implementation has therefore not been the level of 'maturity' of the link as such, but rather its level of maturity in each country. In turn, this is a reflection of the degree of competitive advantage as perceived by national stakeholders, including the state. In other words, the objective of integration, as reflected in the construction of the 'missing links', must itself be confronted with – and hopefully integrated into – the comprehensive visions of transport networks at the national level and the way these prescribe specific (other) projects or improvements.

It should come as no surprise that the Øresund Fixed Link has been among the few successful TEN priority projects. It could eventually command support from both the Danish and Swedish governments as well as by the majority of the Danish and Swedish stakeholders and citizens as a project which would accrue benefits to both sides. Under these conditions, financing was not a major barrier despite the fact that higher priority was attached to other national projects.

The story of the Barcelona–Montpellier link and its connection with the French high-speed railway network has not been as successful. In this case, the Catalonian high stakes were faced with a rather cool French position at a time of a more general re-orientation of the French national transport policy away from a (strict) focus on the high-speed TGV railway concept.

Important to note in both cases is the low relevance of technical assessment studies as deciding factors. This is not to say that such studies were not prepared (indeed many were carried out) or were of little importance. Rather they did not substitute for a political decision which ultimately derived from the consideration of a wider set of factors than the criteria of efficiency of the transport system or operations move alone.

Besides, the TEN projects became conducive to international decision-making processes setting the problem of their implementation at a new level of co-ordination of action. The typical way of proceeding is based on the signing of international agreements. The latter are by themselves insufficient to render the projects operational. Even if comprising a legal compulsory stage, they are not binding, for instance, with regards the setting of a time framework. Rather, they tend to be mostly of a symbolic legitimating character, representing the acknowledgement by national governments of the demonstration of involvement by other actors. They also mark the beginning of supplementary action for promoting the projects in question.

The setting up of specific structures or *ad hoc* organisations as solutions to the co-ordination problem represents a new trend. In all cases where such structures were identified they were set up explicitly for supporting the decision-making process. Such organisations are of different types, depending on the subject matter they have to cope with, the level at which they operate, the issues they bear, or the functions they fulfil. They are typically organised in relation to the international part of the cross-border project.

These structures can be broken down into two categories, each corresponding to a different level of co-ordination, namely: structures for promotion and structures for operational studies.

Structures for promotion are a form of lobbying, whereby in this context they have also become a new way of defining the infrastructure problem, and a means for integrating the interests related to the European dimension and the national interests, i.e. the interests of various stakeholders. Of particular significance in this framework is the action of *'political entrepreneurs'*. Political entrepreneurs represent persons, groups or institutions that become central to the co-ordination process. We return to this theme latter in this chapter.

Structures for operational studies usually come in the form of a European Economic Interest Group (EEIG). These are typically established by the operators involved in the projects in order to jointly study different financial and technical scenarios. The choice of this specific structure is significant because an EEIG can be considered as a step towards the establishment of a public/private partnership. In other words, such an entity represents also the means to demonstrate the willingness to answer to European criteria regarding the form of financing. It also represents a way to join several objectives and interests that were traditionally separated, this time at the operational level.

In some cases there is not alone a plurality of stakeholders, there is also a plurality of decision structures. This raises yet another problem at the level of the co-ordination of action, namely, that of the co-ordination of the different structures. In the Lyon-Turin case at least four structures were set up around the project: an EEIG, an inter-governmental conference, a public interest group and a support committee of international industrialists. The multiplicity of decision structures is no guarantee for success: in the Lyon-Turin case, none of the four entities was successful in integrating the various problems relating to the project; and none could play the role of co-ordination between the different registers of action.

The European Frontier: Transport Networks in Borderline Zones

In several cases the implementation of TEN projects highlights an inter-regional European dimension that emerges as significant through the decision-making processes. This dimension refers to the role taken up by the 'frontiers' that the projects are expected to traverse. The case studies show that there are two distinct ways of considering this specific European resource: either as an obstacle or as delineating a specific zone of opportunity (cf. Burgarella-Mattei and Fustier, 1996).

On the one hand, the frontier can be considered as an obstacle and as such the target of structural cohesion policies seeking to overcome the perceived disparity in terms of regional economic development or accessibility: the Greek inter-island system of transport is typical for this category. The project which seeks to establish a helicopter network among Greek islands was inserted in the INTERREG programme which follows the procedures of the Regional Structural (and Cohesion) Funds.

At the other end of the scale the emergence on the scene of a major transport infrastructure project often provides the opportunity for the implementation of common actions with the objective of promoting the parallel development of cross-border regions. In the Eastern TGV case, Alsace proceeded to re-organise its regional transport services according to the neighbouring German and Swiss system in order to allow for trains to serve the combined cities' network of the region thus enabling cross-border services. In turn, this allowed the local authorities of the area to advance the argument that the Eastern TGV was the last block for completing an inter-regional network.

The Territorialisation of the Decision-Making Process

As transport infrastructure projects have to be integrated into specific spatial areas, the local authorities in charge of those territories come to play a special role linked to these. The process of spatial integration of an infrastructure project at regional or local level which we term territorialisation (cf. Offner and Pumain, 1996; Duran and Thoenig, 1996) comprises several dimensions.

Different geographical scales meet at the project level: the European one, the national one, and the regional one. These three geographical scales refer to three different systems of transport services the arrival of a new project sets the question of the integration or combination of these three systems.

Regional and local authorities often wish to use transport as a means to construct a new legitimacy for themselves as public actors. In the field of policy formulation, all the legal or institutional frameworks ruling the procedures related to the implementation of an infrastructure project foresee the organisation of a consultation with local representatives. Regional and local authorities see this as an opportunity to take a more direct part in the decision-making process thus strengthening the decentralisation trend. Seen from this perspective territorialisation occurs through a 'bottom-up' process.

However, there is also a 'top-down' dimension to the process of territorialisation. This relates to the wish of the state to bind several public actors in the implementation process through the differential allocation of competencies which, at the same time, implies a sharing of responsibility and of risk, in particular financial risk.

The bottom-up process of territorialisation One direct consequence of the intervention of local authorities in the decision-making process relates to the definition of the project itself as exemplifying integration of regional or local transport strategies with the national and European ones.

Important for understanding this bottom-up process of territorialisation is the close examination of the different systems of actors and of the underlying political relationships. It is important to question who are the territorial public interlocutors to the central governments and how they take their respective place in the decision-making process. Depending on the specific context, territorial public actors could be multiple (including communities, cities, regions, departments, etc.); they could be organised hierarchically or not; or, they could have different relative weights in the decision-making process.

A classical decision-making process characterises the Skaramanga interchange case. Here the central administration played the main role with regards the definition of the works to be constructed. The weight of the central administration was accentuated by the fact that the main territory to be serviced by the project, namely Athens, is also the capital of Greece. The main territorial question there was where to locate the road node.

Different was the situation in the case of the Øresund Fixed Link. A rail-only solution was originally advocated by the local authorities and stakeholders in Copenhagen. Under the pressure of their Swedish counterparts this Danish local coalition had to accept a combined rail/road solution. What they could nevertheless successfully bargain was the implementation of a user-paid link. This was perceived as an environment-friendly solution and secured public acceptance.

In the case of the Brenner corridor, we can observe the 'bottom-up' territorialisation process set against the federal framework of Austria at two levels: first, with respect to the regional and national dimensions, and second, with respect to the local and regional dimensions. The Tyrolean government used the issue of transit traffic through the environmentally sensitive Alpine region to claim 'emancipation' from the central government in Vienna. This same issue provided the vehicle of organised opposition of local communities against both the regional and national governments. The result has been a 'greening' of Austrian transport policy at all levels and the articulation of an explicit commitment towards restricting or controlling road traffic.

In the case of the PBKAL TGV to Belgium, the recognition of the regional level, supported through the ongoing federalisation process in Belgium, resulted in a serious questioning of the high-speed railway concept as practised in France. The PBKAL project was expected to serve the Belgian territory in a balanced manner. This meant providing direct access to the link to both Anvers and Liège. Given the size of Belgium, this would in parallel imply a shift in TGV policy away from the principle of servicing big cities separated by long or medium distances. A similar situation arose with the Eastern TGV project where local authorities were 'compensated' for their financial contribution by adjusting the project to allow it to connect directly to all the main Eastern city centres.

The main promoter for the Barcelona-Montpellier TGV project was the autonomous region of Catalunya. The Generalitat of Catalunya undertook all possible studies to demonstrate to the Spanish government that this was a new and necessary infrastructure for the region. The project was finally proposed as a mixed link (freight and passengers), a solution that integrates different public territorial interests: notably the modernisation of the railways and the development of the Barcelona seaports.

The Lyon-Turin TGV case presents other territorialisation characteristics. The local authorities have again been the main promoters, only their strategy in terms of co-ordination has been one of maximising benefits for all. What has emerged as a result is a grand global project which comprises a network more than a link and which seeks to integrate different elements across the territory of the actual railway extension line. The resulting project is composed of different sub-projects and involves both freight and passenger transport services.

The top-down process of territorialisation Constitutionally the responsibility for the final decision to construct a big infrastructure transport project lies with the central government. This entails a high political risk due to the financial constraints involved and the increase in the number of stakeholders. The general trend is for central governments to share these risks, notably with local authorities.

At the operational level this implies either or both of two things: first, the sharing of financial risk; second the re-thinking of the division of competencies in the field of transport policy. How these two issues are decided upon often determines the profile and scope of the decentralisation process. It is not uncommon to observe that the central government is more keen on the subject of co-financing and less so on that of competency sharing; whereas the local or regional authorities are more keen on having a say in the decision process but less interested in committing funds. The Eastern TGV project is one case in point.

At the political level, this top-down territorialisation process often implies co-operation across political parties insofar as the leadership at the national level and at the regional or local levels may not coincide. This can, but need not, complicate the decision-making process as it introduces political considerations which have little to do with the contents of the infrastructure policy under consideration.

Pricing as a Strategic Issue

At the level of the Common Transport Policy, the objectives of pricing measures are set in the framework of market regulation – the objective being to cover both internal and external costs. As usual, such measures reflect other objectives as well. Two of these subsidiary objectives are of relevance here, especially because they are contradictory if applied to the same project: one objective of implementing a pricing measure can be to regulate or even to restrict road traffic for the benefit of environmental protection; a second objective can be to make the infrastructure pay for itself. In the latter case it is conceivable that the tolls are calculated on the basis of maximising income, which, however, can also imply an increase in traffic.

The Øresund Fixed Link and the case of transit traffic across the Brenner axis exemplify the problems involved in this interplay of objectives of pricing policies.

The Øresund Fixed Link involves two countries which pioneered the idea of 'sustainable development' in the field of transport. This being the case, the original proposal to construct a rail-only link seemed the most suitable solution. By the early nineties the environmental protection issue came increasingly to be defined in technical terms and as not necessarily in opposition to economic objectives. In this context, it was then also possible to promote the mixed road/rail infrastructure solution for the link. The introduction subsequently of the user-paid principle for the road part of the project seemed initially to satisfy the demand to effect measures for restricting road traffic but also for effecting a cross-subsidising system between road and rail. On this basis it was possible to proceed with the construction of the link.

But the pricing level still remains to be fixed and the debate has re-opened. Clearly what pricing level is finally set will affect either the environmental implications of the project (restricting road traffic) or its socio-economic implications: will enough income be generated to pay for the infrastructure (whilst restricting road traffic) and if not, will this necessitate other taxation measures? Or should instead the toll be set low in order to ensure profitability (in which case traffic can be expected to increase)?

The Brenner corridor case is similar to the Øresund Fixed Link in a number of ways. The framework is set by the transit agreement between Austria and the European Union. The eco-point system which underlies this agreement was elaborated by the Austrian government in response to the strong citizen protest against transit traffic and its negative environmental impacts. Even though it is not clear whether and for how long this system will remain in operation, and if so under what conditions, its present existence does underline the significance assigned to environmental issues in Austria, in general and specifically concerning the Alpine region.

In this context, road pricing – recently introduced in the form of a motorway vignette as a general measure, but already in existence for the A4 Brenner motorway since the beginning of the seventies – is considered a measure for effecting the user-pay principle for infrastructure as well as a measure for restricting road traffic in sensitive regions. In the case of the Brenner corridor the pricing level is, therefore, under debate.

An additional element introduced by the case of the Brenner corridor concerns the earmarking of financial resources. Still pending is the decision on the building of the base tunnel which relates to the rail key-link. Despite wide acceptance, the project did not take off ground because of the lack of financial resources. The idea has subsequently arisen to connect the financing of this project to the charges collected on the A4 Brenner motorway (or from road pricing more generally). The fact that the same tolls across the A4 Brenner motorway were during the seventies earmarked to construct other motorways in sensitive regions creates a precedent. What is new is that if this idea were to materialise it would concern a case for the cross-subsidising between road and rail.

Financing: Which Partnerships?

Obviously, financing is a very common problem for all major infrastructure projects and, as a matter of fact, for all the TEN projects. The European Union has proposed the consideration of public-private partnerships as a solution (High-Level Group on PPP financing, 1997). In practice public-private partnerships are difficult to implement: the costs for major transport infrastructure projects are high and so are the risks.

Financing represents probably the biggest problem for the TGV projects. As already discussed, a new source of financing are the local authorities. In that the *Eastern TGV* appears to have set an example to be followed. However, since the regional budgets are restricted and partly dependent on state budgets, other partners are sought. And these will also be in the form of public financiers. Hence the partnership regarding the missing links is extended to include states, railways companies, local authorities and the European union. This specific 'public-public' partnership framework is quite new.

Another way to approach the financing problem has been through phasing the project (as in Lyon-Turin case) or through splitting it into independent, albeit inter-related elements (as in the Barcelona-Montpellier case). Phasing or splitting is also used to restrict the 'international' part of the project which in turn is financed on a public-private basis.

In most cases, the question of financing the project is closely related to its operation. It is in this connection that the potential relation to pricing with the pitfalls discussed above emerges.

The Role of Environmental Appraisal

Environmental appraisal is today a part of all decision processes concerning transport infrastructures. In the majority of cases, the concrete issue of such an appraisal is an impact study. But the positioning and significance of this differs from case to case, the differences deriving mainly from the differences in the national institutional frameworks. Interesting to observe is how the positioning of the environmental appraisal procedure in the decision process shapes both the strategies of the actors involved and the solutions they reach.

Environmental appraisal procedures are characterised by two dimensions. The first refers to a juridical aspect: a new infrastructure will cause damages and these ought to be compensated for. The second dimension refers to a democratic aspect, namely the access to and use of expertise by decision-makers. Increasingly this second dimension gains in importance in the implementation of major infrastructure projects and in transport policy more generally.

Two main conclusions can be drawn: The first, is that the environmental issue captures a cross-cutting agenda; even if it typically emerges first at the local level, it is not alone specific to this. Especially in national contexts where the notion of sustainability is strongly anchored in the political discourse and culture, the issue can often assume a strategic dimension with the involvement also of political parties. This is already the case with the Brenner and the Øresund Fixed Link cases; but it can indeed emerge into a strategic issue also in the case of the Barcelona-Montpellier and Lyon-Turin TGVs as well as the Greek inter-island system of transport.

The second major conclusion is that the environmental agenda raises the question of democratic participation in the decision-making process. The decision-making process characteristic of major infrastructure projects allows for the intervention of individuals (experts, political entrepreneurs) or specific organisations (*ad hoc* structures, citizens' associations). This produces a re-structuring of the issues in relation to more general public policies and their linked systems of actors. The traditional mode for democratic control on public action, i.e. voting, is losing in significance as new ways of intervention and registers of actions appear. This, in turn, raises questions regarding the format of direct public debates or public inquiries, both concerning who should participate and its contents.

A New Role for Co-ordination: TEN as Political Entrepreneurships

The need for co-ordination has emerged as a major issue in the implementation of major transport infrastructure projects. This is not alone the result of the increase of the number of stakeholders: the loosening of the boundaries of the decision process to include more actors has meant that today more and different interests have the chance to be articulated and heard. These are not necessarily consistent or congruent.

Conflicts of interest are no longer uncommon in the field of transport. They typically become evident with each major transport infrastructure project, but they also characterise transport policy at the level of the formulation of objectives. The resolution of conflicts of interest often requires mediation between actors and, necessarily, between issues and problems.

Two case studies illustrated well this new role of '*metteur en oeuvre*', new insofar as it was not led by states alone. In the case of the Øresund Fixed Link, the activities of Pehr Gyllenhammer, then a manager with Volvo and a member of the Round Table of Industrialists proved vital in integrating the international economic interests and the local concerns. In the case of the Lyon-Turin axis, Louis Besson, a representative of the Rhône-Alpes region, was successful in integrating a regional long-term development aspect into the international and national parts of the project with the support of the regional council.

A project can claim legitimacy if in the course of the decision-making process it manages to integrate the interests of the various stakeholders in a way which is acceptable to all (which need not imply a win-win solution for all). The arrival at this position necessitates co-ordination and mediation which might not be possible alone through state intervention.

The emergence of new territorial levels of competencies has led to changes in intergovernmental relations, institutionally as well as politically. The notion of 'political entrepreneurship' from the public policy analysis literature is the best term to describe this new mediation role. This concept allows to identify actors whose specificity lies in their political will to support and to implement a measure, on the one hand, and in their ability to induce collective mobilisation and to integrate the concerns of other actors, on the other. The need for such an actor does not necessarily imply a decline of national government. Indeed Jouve and Lefèvre (1999) put forward the hypothesis that the durability of a local mobilisation as well as its legitimacy depend on the national level of government.

Political entrepreneurship is therefore integrated in a system of interdependencies and of interactions between local and national scenes of action. As far as the TEN are concerned, states get the power to launch or to stop a major project (for instance, they have the control of the legal procedures of implementation); they sign the intergovernmental agreements; they negotiate the European status of 'missing-link'; they are the main financier both of the studies and of the infrastructure itself. The actions of the political entrepreneurs are dependant on this system of interactions, itself determined by the institutional and political contexts.

In the Øresund Fixed Link case, Pehr Gyllenhammer mobilised political parties and parliaments (in Sweden and Denmark) and relied on these same actors for support as well as for defining a *new* and sustainable missing-link that combined rail and road infrastructure. In the Lyon-Turin case, Louis Besson effected local mobilisation and managed to integrate this within the regional council which is the institutional interlocutor of the French state for the implementation of major projects. Owing to his several mandates, he could also use his own political resources at the national level of government. The complexity of the end-project combining high speed rail for passengers with the rail freightway concept was the result of this multi-faceted process of accommodation of various interests.

The main objective of the activities of the political entrepreneurs is to establish a rationale for the project under consideration and to grant it legitimacy. In order to qualify and characterise these political entrepreneurships, it is important to map their own representation of the collective interests and the way they manage to mobilise around these. The implementation of the TEN corresponds to a territorial public action. This in turn alters the space under consideration: in the Øresund Fixed Link of the Malmö-Copenhagen and the Scandinavian areas; in the Lyon-Turin case of the Alpine regions.

The Øresund Fixed Link: A Sustainable Missing-Link

The idea to connect Sweden to Denmark through a fixed link emerged on the agenda as early as the fifties. The 'isolation' of Sweden vis-à-vis Denmark but also the European continent was used as a symbolic resource to argue in favour of a fixed link across the channel of the distance of 20 km. The Scandinavians had to wait for 40 years, i.e. till 1994, to see the first brick of the work.

The first major step forward was achieved in the mid-eighties when the Danish parliament voted for the construction of a fixed link across the Great Belt. Even though the latter link connected the Danish islands Funen and Sealand and as such was less concerned with the international aspect of Denmark's inaccessibility, it did set a precedence regarding the technical possibilities, which influenced later decisions regarding the Øresund (Ronnest, Ohm and Leleur, 1997).

Two advocacy coalitions shaped the system of action of the Øresund fixed link: the first compounded those Danish actors in favour of the project; the second was international in character and brought together economic interests. Both coalitions developed under the defensive and often hostile surveillance of the public opinion and of a third coalition gathering local associations opposed to the project. Originally these three coalitions mobilised separately and showed little interest in negotiation.

Effecting communication between them was pivotal to the decision to go ahead with the construction of the link.

For both advocacy coalitions the development of transport infrastructure was seen as a means for the development of the urban pole Copenhagen-Malmö. It constituted a way to ensure the economic growth, the competitiveness of activities and the creation of new jobs. Infrastructure would then contribute to the collective interest. But the objectives ascribed to the project differed (regional integration vs. European integration) and the concrete technical solutions were likewise different (rail only and rail/road combined).

The Danish coalition and the economic and social problem of Copenhagen The Danish coalition was formed around the Social Democratic party with players from Copenhagen and its county. These actors recommended a rail-only solution. This coalition emerged following local protests in 1989 against the closure of a naval base which led to the loss of numerous jobs. The Prime minister acknowledged the legitimacy of the problem for the future of Copenhagen and set up a working group – Initiativgruppen – composed of local political players, among whom the mayor of the County and the Mayor of the City of Copenhagen. The working group came out in favour of the Øresund Fixed Link by setting the problem in economic and social terms, i.e. in terms of the conditions for employment and economic growth. The link, it was argued, would contribute to a widened urban pole by 're-uniting' Copenhagen and Malmö (the 'Growth Centre Theory').

The international coalition and the economic problem of the Nordic industrialists The second coalition was international and emerged through an initiative of the Nordic industrialists. The story of this coalition begins with the setting up, in 1983, of the famous Round Table of Industrialists under the joint initiative of the Volvo manager (Pehr Gyllenhammer), the Philipps manager (Wiesse Dekker) and the president of the European Commission (Jacques Delors). The aim of the Round Table was to come up with proposals for improving the competitiveness of the European industry – the construction of 'missing-links' was one major suggestion.[4] The Nordic countries were the first to benefit from this mobilisation as the Volvo manager was particularly active in Scandinavia. The Round Table opened an office in Copenhagen in 1986: the Scandinavian Link Consortium was born and the Øresund fixed link got a European range. Its objective became to connect Scandinavia to the rest of Europe and to do this in the interest of the industrialists, thus the wish to improve the freight transport connections including those on the road (given the growth of road traffic).

The Scandinavian Link Consortium was very successful in lobbying both towards national governments and European institutions. Its success was due, next to the good organisation, to its ability to phrase the problem and the solution comprehensively. The consortium formulated the political problem to be solved: the promotion of economic development and growth; and the solution to be implemented: a fixed link leading to the improvement of communications. More importantly, it managed to demonstrate the concrete legitimacy of the project by emphasising expertise and through dissemination activities. The 'package' was convincing: both the Danish and Swedish Prime Ministers jointly expressed their common interest in the action and the workings of the group.

Parliaments and political parties played an important role. This was the result of the institutional and political context in which this system of action was integrated. Insofar as the solution finally adopted was the one recommended by the Scandinavian Link Consortium, this entity could be considered as the actor who succeeded to integrate all other actors and their representations of collective interest.

Significant in this connection was the success of the Scandinavian Link consortium in convincing the Swedish Social Democratic party to support the combined rail/road solution rather than the rail-only solution which other members of the Danish advocacy coalition favoured, supported by the public opinion of both countries. Pehr Gyllenhammer seems to have played a major role in this connection. He succeeded to first convince the mayors of Copenhagen and its County and they in turn were successful in convincing other colleagues, members of Parliament. At the time, the Social Democratic Party was the governing party in Sweden but the leading opposition party in the Danish Parliament. The Liberals and the Conservatives were therefore governing in Denmark and they obtained the agreement of the Social Democrats to vote the Øresund fixed link (in its rail/road configuration).

The integrative solution: a sustainable missing-link The final solution combined rail and road infrastructures and foresaw the toll system for the road link. This solution could be qualified as integrative insofar as it allowed the different actors to declare that their viewpoint was taken into account.

The Øresund fixed link was elaborated by actors from those countries most closely associated with the notion of 'sustainable development', namely Denmark and Sweden. In the Nordic countries, more than in other countries, political actors have sought to accommodate the heightened environmental consciousness by presenting themselves as stakeholders of the sustainability idea and by 'dressing-up' their projects in an ecological dress. Environmental protection was not conceived as contradictory to the objective of economic growth.[5]

The fact that the system of actors included political actors – members of Parliament, Prime ministers and party members – contributed to setting the transport problem to be solved as answering to both objectives, environmental protection *and* economic growth. The combined solution rail/road with toll was thought the best technical answer to this. The system of action considered public acceptance as an important condition for going ahead but assumed this as conditional on effecting a balance of environmental and economic goals. The toll, or road pricing, would be introduced as a means to control road traffic (thus meeting the objectives of environmental policy) but also because it could allow the cross-subsidising between the road and rail parts of the link. This would in turn have the additional benefit of avoiding introducing other taxation measures for financing the project.[6] The Øresund fixed link appeared for its protagonists as a solution which integrated the problems of economic growth at European, national and local levels and that of sustainable development – hence, a sustainable missing-link.

The Lyon-Turin Case: A Missing-Link for the Alps Crossing

The Lyon-Turin project provided likewise the opportunity for political entrepreneurship. Its conditions of action and the fields where it occurred differed from those of the Øresund fixed link.

The story of the Lyon-Turin project is far from being over. The complex decision-making process that characterises this project unveiled in the course of the last decade and constituted a decisive factor in its progress. The Lyon-Turin case presents a new way to implement major infrastructure projects which not only integrates actors and their interests but also the problems to be solved by the project (Bernat, Fourniau and Rui, 1997). At the heart of this conflicting process, we find a form of political entrepreneurship with a strong territorial dimension. This resulted in part through the setting of the political problem around the question of the Alps crossing; and, in part, in connection with the person of Louis

Besson, a Savoyard politician[7] and member of the regional council of Rhône-Alpes.

The problem of the Alps crossing: from high speed rail to rail freightway
The problem and at the same time challenge constituted by the Alps crossing is an all-time one. In 1989 the SNCF proposed a high speed line for passenger transport through Chambéry. The regional consultation process foreseen by the procedures established by the ministry of Public Works made obvious soon thereafter a conflict of interests. Each local representative to the regional council sought to accommodate for themselves the TGV project by reference to its expected positive impacts on economic growth associated with the amelioration of communications.[8] Grenoble ended up in competition with Chambery on the precise routing of the East-West connection.

Two documents were used by the regional council for elaborating a first position. The first was an expert study commissioned by the council itself. This was a technical and economic expertise and was carried out by a local research university laboratory, the LET.[9] It confirmed the conclusions reached by the SNCF. The second document was a proposal put forward by Louis Besson, the then deputy-mayor of Chambéry. Besson re-defined the high-speed rail link into a wider transport issue concerning services and the Alps corridor as a whole. He did this by introducing into the picture the North-South axis from Geneva to Grenoble through Chambéry. This plan foresaw for Chambéry a position at the cross-roads between east and west as well as North and South. The rhetoric of the 'cross-roads' is often used by local political actors to justify their support for transport projects. The regional council adopted this proposal into its master plan approved on 14 May, 1991.

Several local representatives mobilised in favour of the project and this helped convince the French and European decision-makers that the project ought to become part of not solely a regional master plan, but also of the French and European master plans (in the latter case the TEN). This was however a beginning more than an end, especially in the context of the major conflicts surrounding the Mediterranean TGV project which had, in the meantime, led to a serious questioning of the TGV concept as such. Opposition thus also emerged against the Lyon-Turin project as a TGV project inscribed in the master plan.[10] By 1993 the opponents had joined forces under the umbrella of the *Observatoire face au TGV*.

Fortunately Besson's proposal considered both passenger and freight transport. It was this combination that could guarantee that the project remained on the agenda despite the growing opposition against the TGV. By focusing on transport services, the objective of the new project-in-the-making was not alone to service the Alpine winter sports stations but also to deal with the great volume of road freight transit crossing the area. To back up this vision, Louis Besson – by the early nineties also Minister of Public Works[11] – used the conclusions of an expert appointed by his administration which were published in the middle of 1991 and which foresaw the saturation of the road tunnels (Mont-Blanc and Fréjus) by the year 2010.[12]

At this stage of the decision-making process, the parallel consideration of freight services had two targets: it provided arguments in favour of the project vis-à-vis its opponents; and, it legitimised keeping the project on the national agenda.

The integration of the local opposition comprised several levels of action. Firstly, the prefect Paul Bernard[13] launched a local consultation process already in mid-1992 significantly earlier than foreseen by the official procedure (in the autumn of that year). This first attempt to bring the opponents together was a failure. The repeat, one year later in May 1993, was more successful and was made possible through the participation of the 'Observatoire face au TGV' at the meeting. Insofar as Bernard had connections with all relevant actors of the Lyon-Turin project, he was perceived as a legitimate integrating figure and not only as a spokesman of the state viewpoint. A second activity line was organised by Joseph Marty, regional director of a local department of the Ministry of Public Works,[14] who took up his post in 1992 and who was a determining factor to legitimise the freight problem through the Alps corridor as one demanding public action.

In order to convince the national decision-making level that the project should aim to solve both the passengers and the freight transport problem, the idea of two separate lines was put forward. Thus the argument of the SNCF and of the DTT[15] that TGV and freight trains should not be mixed (at least partly) was taken into account. Thereafter, the regional council organised a meeting to promote this idea. Among the invitees was Alain Poinssot, the then freight director of the SNCF who confirmed that the railways company was considering the proposals. An inter-ministerial commission was subsequently set up to elaborate the concept. With this form of institutionalisation, the twin passenger / freight project was firmly on the agenda.

A complex integrative solution: PPP and phasing The resolution of conflicts through the adoption of a solution to satisfy all actors' preferences led to the Lyon-Turin project becoming more complex. The problem that remained was that of costs and financing.[16] The regional council continued the political entrepreneurship by involving itself directly in ad hoc structures set up to resolve the financial problem. This 'territorialised' so-to-speak the financial problem.

In 1989, Philippe Essig[17] had helped form a partnership between the French state and the local communities for the financing of the Eastern TGV (Ollivier-Trigalo, 1997). In the middle of the nineties, the Rhône-Alpes Region and the local actors involved in the Lyon-Turin project searched for means to broaden the partnership by getting the private sector (the highways companies and the companies in charge of the tunnels) interested in the project. A European Economic Interest Group (EEIG) was formed for the international section of the project, namely the tunnel project. The first activity of the EEIG was to deliver financial and technical feasibility scenarios. This involved, on the one hand, the search for public/private partnerships; and, on the other, the consideration of the financing problem in conjunction with phasing and/or pricing measures.[18]

The promoters of the project proposed the adoption of the principle of phasing by elaborating realistic budgets for each segment of the project.[19] In addition to representing a technical procedure, this allowed once again to integrate actors, preferences and problems: the European and national interests with those of the tunnel operators; as well as the interests of the local communities in favour of the project and those of the opponents insofar as investment targeting the improvement of the existing infrastructures and the construction of new lines would be spread over time.

A territorial entrepreneurship to lead plurality In the Lyon-Turin case the political entrepreneurship was two-pronged and comprised an individual – Louis Besson – and an institution – the regional council of Rhône-Alpes. The institution was used by Besson to manage his entrepeneurship as well as for strengthening the territorial dimension of the enterprise.

Louis Besson was a political entrepreneur insofar as he played a catalysing role, achieving the acknowledgement of the Lyon-Turin project as a solution to a political problem by both the state and the local actors. He had two main resources to back his actions: his local political career – he was a well-installed and known territorial representative; and his governmental posts.

Louis Besson is a Savoyard politician. His first mandate as mayor of his native city dated back in 1965. In Savoie, he exercised (and exercises) mandates at every territorial level.[20] Incontestably, his political career granted him weight in discussions and negotiations with local representatives and gave him mobilising power. He could furthermore back his position with reference to expert studies to which he had access or which he commissioned.[21] As Minister of Public Works he received the Legrand report (July 1991) that diagnosed the road tunnels saturation, which supported the necessity to consider the freight problem. In 1992, he was himself appointed as an expert by his successor Jean-Louis Bianco to work on the question of the Alps crossing.[22] In this position he advocated his position vis-à-vis the state and the regional council which was designated by the former as its legitimate interlocutor. But his use of the council was not solely according to the rules. The regional council provided the institutional space for integrating local interests and problems. In that it itself became the initiator of studies and thereafter the organiser of meetings as described in the previous section.

The most recent activity of the regional council was the commissioning in 1997 of a new counter-expertise to the studies undertaken by the SNCF. This activity was undertaken in the framework of inquiry established by Alain Cabanes, a member of the regional council from group *Génération Écologie*, who in 1994 delivered a report[23] to the regional assembly on the conflicts surrounding major infrastructure projects in the region (TGV, A51, A89, notably). For the author of this report, there were two major problems with the activities of the regional council: first, it had failed to ensure the consistency of transports in Rhône-Alpes, as shown by the lack of co-ordination among the contractors of the various projects; second it had failed to adequately communicate the aims of the projects to the population. Both underlying reasons, Cabanes argued, were responsible for the recurrent conflicts.

The proposal of Cabanes on how to overcome these problems was an interesting one, not least for its implications for democratic decision-making. Basically, he argued that it would be important for the regional council to take up the role of co-ordination by elaborating a regional strategy in the field of transport policy. This would necessitate it becoming independent as well as independently commissioning expert or feasibility studies. The commissioning of a counter-expertise by the regional council in 1997 is an indication that these proposals were taken seriously.

Today the project has to deal with the absence of a similar institutional relay for co-ordination and action at the national level. The territorial political entrepreneurship which gradually led to the development of independent institutional practices is up against the sectorial logic of the French state which still tends to think separately for passenger and freight transport. Only very recently (November 1998) was the Alps Mission set up by Minister Gayssot. The objective of the Alps Mission is to elaborate '*arguments and proposals relative to the viewpoints and the actions of the Ministry with regards the French transport policy in the Alps*'.[24]

Multiplicity of Protagonists and Plurality of Viewpoints

Despite the differences in political contexts and political cultures, in all cases studied the decision-making process is mainly elite-oriented. This could be explained by the fact that major infrastructure projects remain in the State's hands when involving an international or European dimension. The State level is also needed by reason of the complex character of co-ordination and the stakes involved. Therefore, the weight of the administration in the decision-making processes remains significant, whatever the procedures relating to direct public participation might be. This also determines the character of the procedures, namely linear. What the different political systems of actors and cultures determine is when the public is consulted, or whether the national parliaments are involved. However, even where national parliaments are called to vote on a project – as in the Netherlands or Denmark – this does not necessarily imply the emergence of a public debate. All case studies, therefore, demonstrate a quite similar vision of representative democracy which obviously remains the dominant political model.

In the course of the last years however, a general confidence crisis regarding this political model of democracy has been observed. This is evidenced, for instance, by public opinion polls but also wildly fluctuating electoral results. This is occurring at a time when central governments have implemented a general political framework in order to share responsibilities with local authorities: all European States have run reforms regarding the decentralisation of responsibilities or a federalisation process. Therefore, the issue of representation and indirect public participation is shifted onto the local level. Local electoral results show a growing concern with environmental issues but also of protest votes more generally. Mobilisation occurs at the lowest level, through citizens' movements. There are, in other words, indications of a general trend towards the wish for more direct participation, as it is widely felt that decisions are taken without prior consultation, or arbitrarily without comprehensive analysis. This, in turn, induces (or calls for) a more local and daily way to approach transport infrastructures projects.

Currently, the shaping of the decision-making process through problem setting in the case of major infrastructure projects allows for the intervention of individuals (experts, political entrepreneurs) or specific organisations (*ad hoc* structures, citizens' associations). This produces a re-structuring of the issues in relation to more general public policies and their linked systems of actors. The traditional democratic control on public action – the election mode of arbitration: the vote – is losing in significance as new ways of intervention and registers of actions appear. This raises questions regarding the format of direct public debates or public enquiries, both with regard to who should participate and its contents whilst the multiplicity of protagonists characterises the decision-making process, the plurality of the viewpoints remains to be orchestrated.

Notes

1 The concept appeared for the first time within a resolution adopted by the European Council of Ministers in December 1989 in order to elaborate a long term programme with regards Trans-European Networks. The Maastricht Treaty (1993) confirmed the concept within its title XII. The TEN concerned the transports of data, energy, high speed rail and airports.

2 All the case studies were included in TENASSESS, Deliverable R(3), Technical Annex: Case Studies, 1997.

3 The comparison constituted the TENASSESS, Deliverable R(3), Main report: Comparative Report Case Studies. The Implementation of European Transport Projects, 1997.

4 The Round Table of Industrialists was the author of a report published in 1984, the title of which was precisely this metaphor. It experienced a big success in Europe and continues to be used as a political symbolic resource. Two years later, a new report was produced, 'the missing networks'. The European Commission, under the Delors presidency, published later in 1993 a White book 'Growth, Competitiveness, Employment' that established the role of major transport infrastructures for the integration and the development of the European space.

5 This was the reproach against the first French ecologists and still the one used against the local associations that express any opposition against a major project in France (Fourniau, Ollivier-Trigalo and Rui, 1999, Rui in this volume).

6 After the construction, the level of the toll was a new source of conflict: to control the road traffic and to finance the infrastructure by itself appeared concretely as incompatible.

7 Deputy-Mayor of Chambéry. Since 1997, he is Secretary of state in charge of Housing (Jospin government).

8 This was a similar line of argumentation to the Round Table of Industrialists (see above).

9 Laboratoire d'Économie des Transports (Lyon).

10 At the time when the master plan was elaborated, the SNCF and the French administration (DTT - Direction des Transports Terrestres) favoured only high speed lines in their investment policy.

11 Firstly, Louis Besson was ministerial delegate in charge of Housing (1989-1990), then, minister of Public Works (1990-1991).

12 Legrand report, July 1991.

13 In office from 1991 to April 1997.

14 'Directeur Régional de l'Équipement': Regional Director of a local department of the ministry of Public Works. This department is dedicated to the technical help of the prefect during the procedures related to transport projects.

15 Direction des Transports Terrestres: a department of the French central administration (Ministry of Public Works) in charge of the SNCF supervision.

16 The base tunnel alone - key element of the project - was assessed at average 40 billion FF. (1997).

17 A former president of the SNCF who, later, was several times appointed as an expert of the ministry of Public Works.

18 The call for public/private partnerships means that the tunnels should be operated by the way of a concession.

19 7 billion FF. phases of works were studied. There is to notice that in the case of the Aquitaine TGV project, similar average phases were proposed by the preliminary studies (Ollivier-Trigalo, 1998). This case study was included in TENASSESS, Deliverable R(6b), Case Studies & Amendments to the Barrier Model, 1999.

20 Mayor of Barby (1965-89), member (since 1970) then president (1976-82) of the general council of Savoie, deputy of Savoie (since 1973, socialist and left-radical group), member of the regional council Rhône-Alpes (1974-86), mayor of Chambéry (since 1989). Source: 'Who's Who in France' (1995-1996).

21 Louis Besson was ministerial delegate to the Minister of Public Works, Housing, Transports and Sea, in charge of Housing (1989-90), then Minister of Public Works, Housing, Transports and Sea (1990-91). In 1997, he became the state secretary in charge of Housing.

22 Louis Besson delivered his conclusions to another Minister, Bernard Bosson, in 1993. The latter, Mayor of Annecy in Haute-Savoie (which belongs to Rhône-Alpes

too), welcomed and opened a conference set up by the French Alps mission and the INRETS on the theme of the Alps crossing on the 9 and 10 September 1999.

23 Alain Cabanes, *Transports régionaux. Qualité et pluralité d'expertise*, Conseil régional Rhône-Alpes, 18 July 1994.

24 Noël Lebel, chief of the Alps Mission, Presentation note, 8 December 1999. Following the fire that happened in the Mont-Blanc tunnel in 1999, Jean-Claude Gayssot had also presented a memorandum transports through the Alps to the European council of transports on the 6 October 1999.

References

Bernat, V., Fourniau, J. M. and Rui, S. (1997), *La liaison ferroviaire Transalpine Lyon-Turin: complexifier pour mieux réaliser*, INRETS, Arcueil.

Burgarella-Mattei, M-N. and Fustier, B. (1996), 'Frontières et isolement, le cas des petites économies insulaires', *Sciences de la société,* No. 37, Presses Universitaires du Mirail, Toulouse, pp. 49-61.

Cabanes, A. (1994) *Transports régionaux. qualité et pluralité d'expertise*, Conseil régional Rhône-Alpes.

Crozier, M and Friedberg, E. (1977), *L'acteur et le système*, Éditions du Seuil, Paris.

Duran, P. and Thoenig, J-Cl. (1996), 'L'État et la gestion publique territoriale', *Revue française de science politique*, vol. 46/4, pp. 580-623.

Fourniau, J.M., Ollivier-Trigalo, M. and Rui, S. (1999), Recherche PREDIT 'Évaluer, débattre ou négocier l'utilité publique? Conflits d'aménagement et pratiques de conduite de projet', Volet 1, *Analyser l'expérience de la mise en discussion publique des projets. Ateliers de bilan du débat public*, 2 volumes, 'Première partie. Débat public, rôles et identités, pratiques politiques', 'Deuxième partie. Protagonistes du débat et expériences démocratiques', Rapport intermédiaire, Séminaire Expérience Démocratique-INRETS-DTT, Arcueil.

Friedberg, E. (1993), *Le pouvoir et la règle, dynamiques de l'action organisée*, Seuil, Paris.

High-Level Group on Public-Private Partnership Financing of TEN Projects (1997), *Final Report*, VII/321/97, European Commission-DGVII, Brussels.

Jouve, B. and Lefèvre, C. (1999), 'Pouvoirs urbains: entreprises politiques, territoires et institutions en Europe', in Jouve, B. Lefèvre, C. (eds.), *Villes, Métropoles. Les nouveaux territoires du politique*', Anthropos, Collection Villes, Paris, pp. 9-44.

Offner, J-M. and Pumain, D. (eds.) (1996), 'Réseaux et territoires— Significations croisées', Éditions de l'Aube, Coll. Territoire, La Tour d'Aigues, p. 281.

Ollivier-Trigalo, M. (1997) *The Eastern TGV Project: The End of an Epoch. Public Policy Analysis*, INRETS, Arcueil.

Ollivier-Trigalo, M. (1998), *The Aquitaine TGV Project: How a Priority Became a Problem. The Missing Co-ordination., Policy Assessment of Transeuropean Networks and Common Transport Policy*, Project TENASSESS (DG VII), Contract ST-96-AM.601, Work Package 8, INRETS, Arcueil.

Padioleau, J-G. (1998), *Prospective de l'aménagement du territoire: refondations liminaires de l'action publique conventionnelle*, Université de Paris-Dauphine, GEMAS/MSH, Paris.

Padioleau, J-G. (1982), *L'état au concret*, PUF., Coll. sociologies, Paris.

Ronnest, A.K, Ohm, A. and Leleur, S. (1997), *The Oresund Fixed Link. The Conflicts and the Players, Policy Assessment of Transeuropean Networks and Common Transport Policy*, Project TENASSESS (DG VII), Contract ST-96-AM.601, WP7, IVTB & COWI, Copenhagen.

TENASSESS, Deliverable R(3) (1997), *Main Report: Comparative Report Case Studies: The Implementation of European Transport Projects*, ICCR & INRETS, Vienna/Paris.

TENASSESS, Deliverable R(3) (1997), *Technical Annex: Case Studies*, ICCR & INRETS, Vienna/Paris.

TENASSESS, Deliverable R(6b) (1999), *Case Studies & Amendments to the Barrier Model*, ICCR & PLANCO, Vienna/Essen.

Thoenig, J-Cl. (1985), 'L'analyse des politiques publiques', in Grawitz, M. and Leca, J. (eds.), *Traité de Science Politique*, Tome 4, PUF., Paris, pp. 1-60.

3 Assessing Transport Investment Projects: A Policy Assessment Model

MARK BROWN, SIMON MILNER AND EMILY BULMAN

Introduction

This chapter describes the implementation of a model designed to provide a preliminary assessment of transport investment projects. The model developed is called the 'policy assessment model' or PAM. It is an example of an operationalised goals achievement matrix (GAM).

The model has been developed to meet two specific requirements:

- that it should be suitable for assessing the potential performance of the Trans-European Network investments for transport (TEN-T);
- that the investments' performance should be related to targets and issues contained within the Common Transport Policy (CTP).

The model thus marries the two major initiatives of the European Union in the field of transport, namely:

- the clear articulation and development of the Common Transport Policy, as first expressed in the European Commission White Paper (EC, 1992), and subsequently progressed in Action Plans (EC, 1998); and
- the realisation of a Trans-European Network for transport, including prospects of pan-European networks across the enlarging European Union (TINA, 1999).

The model is firmly grounded in the realities of planning of the TEN-T. This inevitably means tackling the different spatial implications of TEN-T schemes. The TEN-T have regional and national impacts, as well as impacts for the European Union as a whole. The impacts are of varying significance to the range of stakeholders involved in progressing plans, depending on their spheres of interest and influence.

Further, the impacts themselves are interpreted in different ways: valuation and evaluation techniques, as well as the decision making procedures, differ across Member States and regional bodies.[1]

The model tackles this heterogeneity through explicitly representing the different stakeholders. It forecasts their view of transport initiatives through relating impacts in their spatial domain to their policies.

Review of Rational Decision Making

The Decision Model

Hill (1968) defines rational planning as 'A process for determining appropriate future action by utilising scarce resources in such a way as to maximise the expected attainment of a set of given ends'. This definition provides the systemic framework for project appraisal, in which alternative courses of action are evaluated to identify which best achieve a set of given objectives.

The implication of this framework is that the objectives form the evaluation criteria, the benchmarks, against which the performance of each option is measured. Objectives form a statement of need; evaluation measures the extent to which needs are likely to be fulfilled by each option. Hence objectives and evaluation form two sides of the same coin (Brown *et al.*, 1991).

This decision model reflects a standard systems approach to planning. The model is designed to ensure that projects remain focused upon their objectives, and that their success or failure is measured and expressed in terms of the particular needs driving the projects.

Figure 3.1 The Classic Decision Model

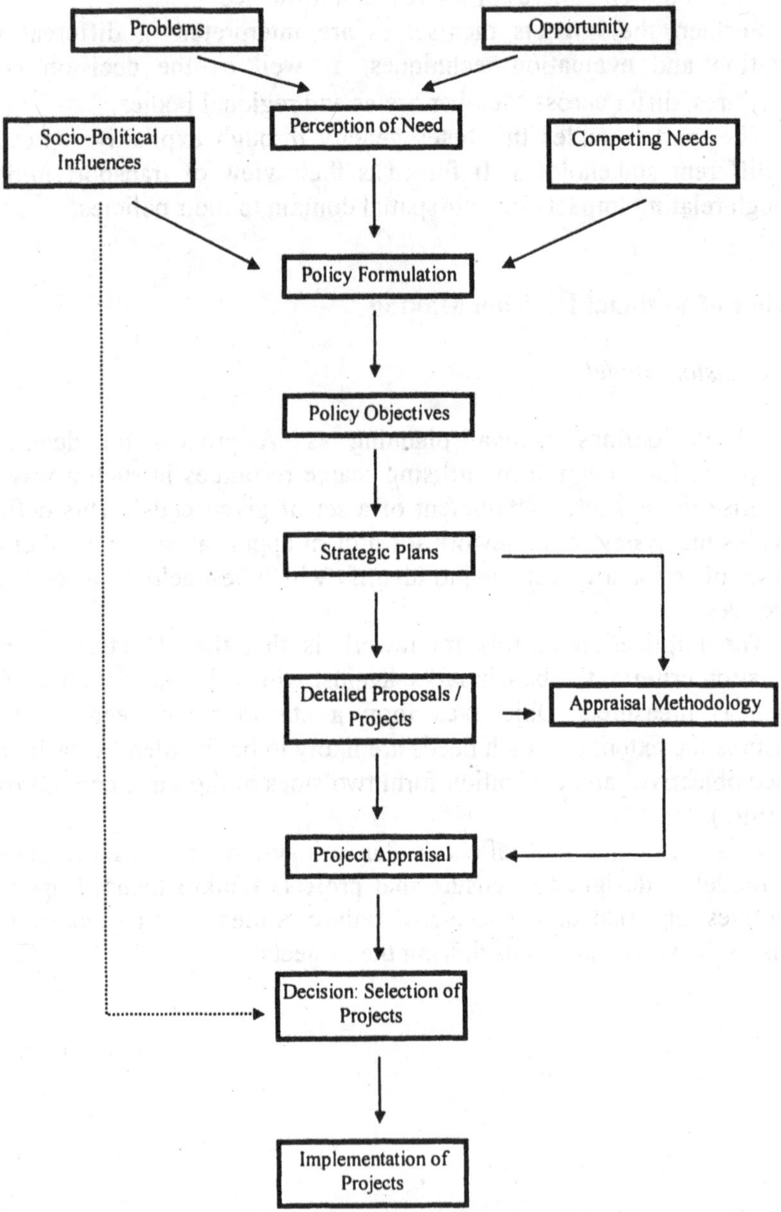

From Hill (1968) figure 3.1 illustrates the classic decision model. Key aspects of this are:

- policies are formulated in response to perceived needs, based on specific problems (congestion, safety, etc.) or potential opportunities (regional development, reduced travel costs, etc.);
- policy objectives articulate the desired end-state; that is, the change that must be secured to fulfil the policy and exploit the opportunity or solve the specific problem. Objectives are of greatest value when they contain explicit targets and thresholds which specify success and failure;
- strategic plans take the broad policy objectives and produce a set of refined project objectives; they also provide an overview of the measures required to achieve the objectives;
- detailed proposals represent the options for action (new highway alignments; high speed rail proposals; etc.);
- an appraisal method links the alternative options with the policy objectives; that is, it identifies the extent to which options meet the objectives. The instrumental elements here are the measures of performance which form the central feature of an appraisal methodology;
- project appraisal applies the measures of performance to the alternatives and concludes on the extent to which each option meets the declared objectives;
- following selection of the preferred project the implementation commences.

This classic decision model recognises the role of socio-political influences in the process of project appraisal and selection. Such influences are often driven by competing and conflicting needs of other sectors of the economy (social welfare; regional development; finance; etc.). Indeed, it is quite possible and sometimes common, for socio-political considerations to over-ride the results of a technical appraisal (the decision to route TGV nord via Lille (Rudeau, 1987) for example). The fundamental role of the classic decision model is to make explicit the basis for selecting one particular project ahead of another and to demonstrate precisely where socio-political influences have over-ridden an analytical appraisal.

The possible influence of socio-political factors in decision-making does not weaken the classic decision model; rather, it reinforces the need for it. The model makes explicit either how the selection of a project fulfils stated objectives; or where such a decision deviates from objectivity and submits to socio-political influences. In either case, the quality and integrity of decision-making is improved.

The principal focus of the classic decision model is the appraisal method. This engineers the explicit linkage between objectives and project outputs. Central to the appraisal method are the measures of performance. These broad issues are fundamental to a practical policy assessment method.

Alternative Appraisal Methods

To reiterate, the model to be used is required to have the following specifications:

- that it should be suitable for assessing the potential performance of the Trans-European Network investments for transport (TEN-T);
- that the investments' performance should be related to targets and issues contained within the Common Transport Policy (CTP).

These requirements have been translated into the following design features:

- *policy orientated* – the value system within the method must reflect the various policies to be incorporated within the appraisal;
- *project focused* – the method must address the desirability of major European transport projects;
- *comprehensive* – the method must be capable of addressing a large variety of issues and project impacts across several transport sectors;
- *performance focused* – policy objectives, the aspirations of policy making bodies, must form the central criteria by which the performance of projects is assessed;
- *practical* – the method is intended to be applied, ultimately, to a wide variety of transport projects across the EU; it must therefore be practical and impose realistic modest data needs on those using it.

Three techniques were considered as possible alternatives to meet these specifications. They differ in complexity and the extent to which non-quantifiable, subjective, judgements enter into their workings. They are respectively, cost-benefit analysis, the planning balance sheet and the goals achievement matrix.

Cost-benefit analysis Cost-Benefit Analysis (CBA) is a direct application of welfare economic theory. It follows the Kaldor / Hicks compensation principle (discussed in Pearce and Nash 1981, for example), that something is deemed socially beneficial if the gainers secure sufficient gains by way of benefits such that they can compensate losers and still have net gain. In other words, the social benefits exceed the social costs. In the schemes undergoing cost benefit analysis the process of compensation, in the main, does not take place.

The value system within which CBA operates has the aim of maximising the sum of social welfare across society, without placing any direct requirement on its distribution. All impacts are expressed in utilitarian (social welfare) terms, with valuation of the impacts defined as either the resource cost (e.g. fuel, capital items) or as willingness to pay to secure a benefit (e.g. time saving).

The application of CBA is several decades old. Its theory, practice, strengths and weaknesses are well documented. They are not repeated here other than in summary. A number of publications can be referred to for further detail, including Pearce and Nash (1981) and Ng (1983). The method is widely used in project appraisal in the transport field and elsewhere. CBA as a basis for decision making is accepted by most governments, development institutions and funding bodies.

Nevertheless, a CBA based method is not considered to be well suited to the assessment model specifications. For:

- the requirement of CBA to express impacts in monetary terms means that inclusion of certain impacts becomes problematic: consensus cannot be reached as to their value. These may include environmental, social and regional development impacts;
- CBA does not provide the explicit links between diverse policy objectives and project impacts.

Planning balance sheet/multi-criteria analysis The Planning Balance Sheet (PBS), first proposed by Lichfield (1964), greatly extends traditional CBA by incorporating all the impacts implicit in alternative courses of action. The PBS overcomes one shortcoming of CBA in that it does not require the monetary valuation, or even the quantification, of impacts. Therefore it allows the comprehensive inclusion of all relevant effects of a project within the appraisal.

The object of the PBS is to present a clear indication of (i) each impact; and (ii) the groups upon which impacts fall within a set of project accounts – the balance sheet. Impacts, costs and benefits, are presented in monetary terms where possible, quantified in other units, or presented descriptively.

The tradition of PBS emphasises the role of planning judgement in weighing impacts, reflecting a single value system. This can often be an over simplification which may negate the breadth of appraisal that the PBS is seeking to achieve. Thus, whilst PBS may be appropriate where there is a general consensus on values, goods or objectives, it has difficulty resolving resource allocation problems where there may be conflict within the planning or policy system.

The PBS method may be suitable for those project appraisals where a simple and consistent value system can be assumed. It is not considered suitable to address the complex policy issues inherent in major European transport projects. A more objective and democratic method is outlined below.

Multi criteria analysis (MCA) is similar to the PBS, though the emphasis on the distribution of impacts may not be so marked. MCA is an extension of CBA where all relevant impacts are incorporated and are not necessarily expressed in monetary terms. The weights used to compare different impacts may or may not be based on willingness-to-pay principles, and are subject to the same difficulties as the PBS when there is lack of consensus as to their worth.

The goals achievement matrix Cost benefit analysis and multi-criteria analysis appraises projects by evaluating impacts. The goals achievement matrix (GAM), in contrast, specifically relates impacts to achievement of goals or solving of problems. It interprets objectives into a form that allows progress towards, or away from, them to be measured (McLoughlin, 1969).

The goals achievement matrix is not as prevalent and established as cost benefit analysis in scheme appraisal, but there is evidence that its use is becoming more widespread. It has long been popular in local decision making, where assessing the ability of alternative measures to solve locally identified problems is a convenient and practical form of appraisal. Nationally, a form of the GAM is now the official method for appraising UK transport investments (DETR, 1998; MVA, 2000).

There are signs that organisations' policies become more clearly articulated, as typified by the Common Transport Policy (EC, 1992). Quantitative targets embedded within these policy statements are becoming more prevalent. These factors are making implementation of GAM approaches ever more practical and the explanatory power of their results increase.

Figure 3.2 illustrates the basic role of appraisal, in general, and of the GAM, in particular, in this process. It provides a clear link between projects and policy objectives, the focal point of which are the performance measures contained within the GAM.

In order to assess the full potential impact and benefits of the GAM to transport planning in general, it is necessary to review a number of key characteristics of GAMs and a number of guidelines in their design and applications. These are outlined below.

Value system GAMs reflect a value system based upon the policy environment, i.e. the policies dictate the values governing the appraisal. At a simple level, a 'good' project fulfils the policy objectives of the particular socio-political environment. Less emphasis is placed on direct economic or financial indicators. The French TGV network provides a good example of these processes in action: expensive projects that have been pursued for a much wider range of political objectives than the provision of an economically efficient rail network (Rudeau, 1987).

Given the importance of policy objectives in the classic approach to transport planning, as practised throughout most of Europe, the logic and rationale behind a GAM is clear.

Units of measurement In the typical policy assessment model there is no need to place a monetary value on project impacts. The method leaves the 'valuation' to the decision-maker to express directly or through policy documents which are interpreted.

In practice project impacts may be measured in various units including monetary terms. For example, a policy aimed at 'reducing the cost of transport to the user' requires the policy maker to know by how much a certain project may actually reduce costs – these costs will include valued time savings and vehicle operating costs.

Whilst the decision-maker then has to place a weight on the importance of this policy within all other policies, it does not represent a double valuation. The separation of 'citizens' valuations of say travel time savings from the importance that society (through the political decision making process) places upon time savings relative to other project impacts is an important distinction. The CBA valuation of individual impact areas is always done in isolation from other impacts – research into time valuation or accident valuations, for example, rarely presents the information in a context of a much wider range of scenarios and project impacts.

The GAM on the other hand, allows these trade-offs and inter-relationships to be explicitly examined – as all the information is in front of the decision-maker at the same point in time, and not aggregated into one overall 'bottom-line' number.

Figure 3.2 The Role of the Policy Assessment Model

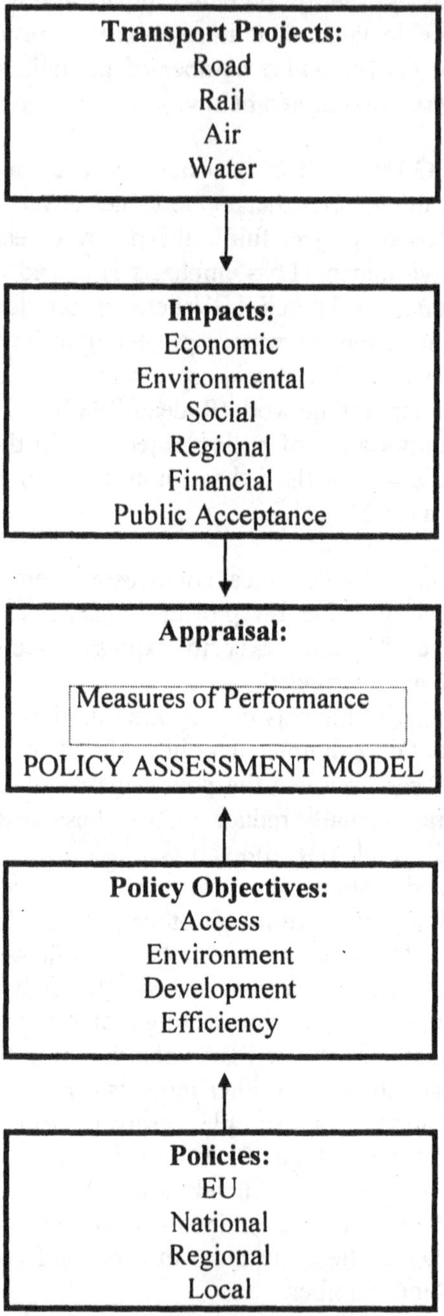

Flexibility In view of the relationship between GAMs and policies and given the transient nature of many policies, there is a clear need for flexibility in the design of GAMs. GAMs must be capable of reflecting policy changes, or different emphases within the policy environment. This gives the GAM a distinct air of realism – an assessment method that reflects the transient nature of the world must be closer to reality than a static and inflexible process.

Allied to this flexibility, a GAM should be capable of handling temporal policy evolution. A well designed GAM should be capable of handling policy changes and changing emphasis on existing policies as time progresses.

Versatility An advantage, and key requirement, of GAMs is that they are able to measure and trade-off impact in a wide variety of policy environments (finance, quality of life, regional development, traffic, etc.). The GAM must be capable of summarising a mix of impacts from across different sectors and allow practitioners to trade-off benefits and costs across sectors. This places a distinct need for some form of multi-criteria algorithm within the GAM.

Transparency A merit of a GAM is that it compels decision-makers to be transparent about the rationale underlying their actions. If a GAM is used to inform a decision-making process, it makes clear the extent to which the decision supports or conflicts with policy and the extent to which weights have been applied to particular groups of impacts (e.g.: environmental impacts).

Preferred Appraisal Tool

Table 3.1 provides a simplified summary of how the three appraisal tools reviewed relate to the identified criteria. The following characteristics are evident:

- the goals achievement matrix is *policy orientated* – in contrast to the other approaches, its value system is based on the policies;
- all three are project focused – they are established methods which appear to be capable of application in the context of the TEN, though are not fully tested. The CBA is clearly most widely used;
- comprehensive – only the GAM and MCA are naturally able to tackle a wide range of impacts. Efforts can be made to widen the scope of CBA, but the requirement to express impacts in monetary terms places very real constraints on this;

- performance focused – only the GAM uses the aspirations of policy making bodies as the central criteria by which the performance of projects is assessed;
- practical – CBA has been shown to be practical through its wide usage and acceptance. Application of the GAM and MCA to projects of the complexity inherent in the TEN-T schemes is not as widespread.

Table 3.1 Suitability of Methods to Meet Requirements for Appraisal

	CBA	MCA	GAM
Policy orientated	X	?	√
Project focused	√	√	√
Comprehensive	X	√	√
Performance focused	X	X	√
Practical	√	?	?

The table suggests that the GAM is most suited to the requirement for the appraisal model, provided that certain concerns about its practicality can be dealt with adequately.

Role of Appraisal Tools in Transport Planning

Before describing how such a goals achievement matrix can be implemented, it is useful to bear in mind the appraisal and wider transport planning context within which it sits. This includes aspects of best practice which are equally relevant to other appraisal tools.

Figure 3.3 shows the policy assessment model in the context of transport planning. Note that it corresponds closely to the classic decision model of figure 3.1. This systematic approach to transport planning reflects the classical, policy-led approach, outlined in various EC transport planning documents (EC, 1993). The development of such a tool corresponds closely with the general, objective, approach to policy-making and transport planning.

Some general points concerning appraisal methods that emanate from the diagram are:

- testing a sufficient range of project configurations is essential. The appraisal model is only able to assess the performance of the project configurations being tested. It is the responsibility of the user to ensure that superior alternatives are not overlooked;
- many assumptions must be made in order for the models to function. Testing the sensitivity of the results to the assumptions is the means by which these assumptions can be scrutinised to ensure that they are not producing a distorted picture.

The appraisal results should be interpreted with care, and not been seen as simply a bottom line figure. In the case of the GAM, the performance with respect to distinct goals, and priorities being put on those goals, all form important outputs to aid interpretation and decision making.

A GAM is not, by any means, the sole basis for decisions (Bruck *et al.*, 1996). This is equally true of cost benefit analysis, environmental assessment and other technical procedures. The aim is not to provide a mechanistic means for decision making, but to provide decision-makers with relevant, clearly presented information to allow soundly based decisions to be made. During the process of project development, it is likely to be desirable to use more than one appraisal method, which have different attributes to offer to aid decision making.

Figure 3.3 The Policy Assessment Model in Context with Transport Planning

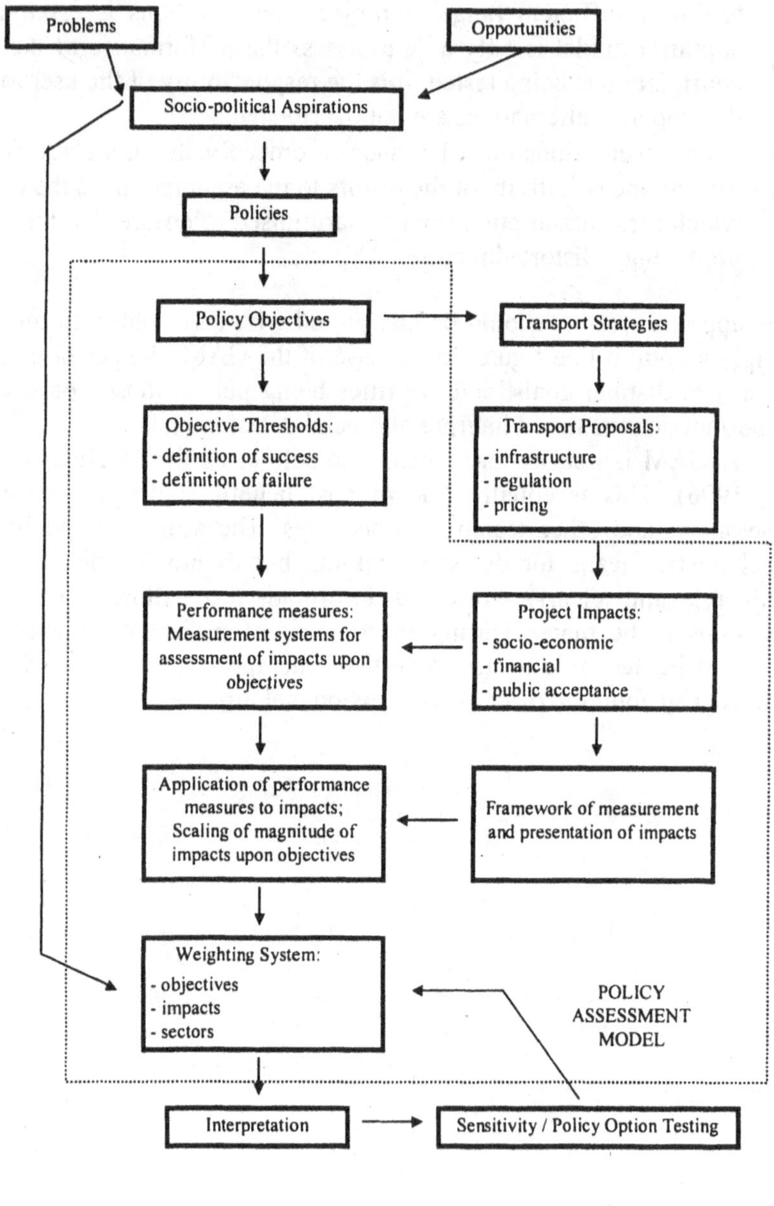

Study Methodology

The section that follows outlines in more detail how the theoretical aspects of a goals achievement matrix have been transformed into an operational policy assessment model.

Figure 3.4 provides a basic outline of the structure of the policy assessment model, along with its linkages to other parts of the policy appraisal process. Key features are as follows:

- the assumed starting point for both objectives and transport projects are the various national, regional and local policies. Projects should be designed to achieve particular policies;
- transport projects under consideration include infrastructure projects (new rail lines, highway improvements, waterways, etc.); pricing proposals (e.g. road pricing); and regulatory proposals (deregulation, liberalisation, border controls);
- a comprehensive range of impacts must be identified for the projects likely to be addressed by the methodology. These include economic, environmental, social, financial and regional development impacts. In addition the likely implications of projects for public opinion should be considered, as this can be a major determinant of whether a project progresses to implementation;
- impacts should be presented within a structured framework, a Group-impact Framework (GIF). This identifies:
- the category of impact (economic, environmental, social, etc.);
- the group upon which each impact falls (user, non-user, operator);
- the method for measurement and forecasting of each impact;
- where it is not possible to forecast a particular impact quantitatively, a qualitative index is developed;
- a generic set of policy areas has been identified to structure and rationalise the diverse range of policies which must be considered within appraisals. These cover broad policy issues, for example environment, pricing and safety;
- policy objectives of each relevant level in the policy hierarchy (local, regional, national, and EU) are examined through publicised documents and statements. Ideally, objectives will be stated explicitly within policy documents. Otherwise, the analysts must use judgement to define objectives;
- the project objectives are mapped to the generic policy areas. In some cases the generic policy areas may not adequately represent the project objectives, and it is necessary to consider certain objectives separately;

- for each policy area, a definition of success and failure must be produced. These definitions may relate to the objectives gleaned from policy documents, or may be more generic in nature. The definitions make explicit the point at which a project can be judged to have made a significant impact, either by supporting or constraining the objective;
- measures of performance provide an explicit linkage between project impacts and objectives. They measure the extent to which an objective is achieved as a result of implementing a new project. These may be quantitative measures (e.g. changes in levels of atmospheric pollution; changes in modal shares) or qualitative indices (levels of harmonisation);
- a cardinal, numeric scale provides a common means of scoring each performance measure. A scale of +5 to -5 is used in this study;
- the model shows performance of projects with respect to the policy areas. A more aggregate picture can also be useful and this is achieved through applying a system of weights to each of the policy areas reflecting their relative importance. The analyst can assign weights, and would seek to represent specific policy perspectives in this process. The task is necessarily subjective, heightening the need to conduct sensitivity tests on the weights used and make the weights assigned explicit and transparent when results are presented;
- it is also possible for the decision-maker themselves to quantify the importance they attach to different policies by assigning the weights directly;
- results are presented in a variety of ways, involving an array of scores against each policy area, at each level of the hierarchy; summed scores across all policy areas and hierarchical levels; and sensitivity tests involving the application of alternative weights. It is important that presentation and interpretation of results do not rest on single scores – there is no equivalent of net present value, from cost benefit analysis, or internal rate of return. It should also be noted that, as with other technical decision aides, the final choice is taken by the decision maker after consideration of all sources of information.

Figure 3.4 Structure of the Policy Assessment Model

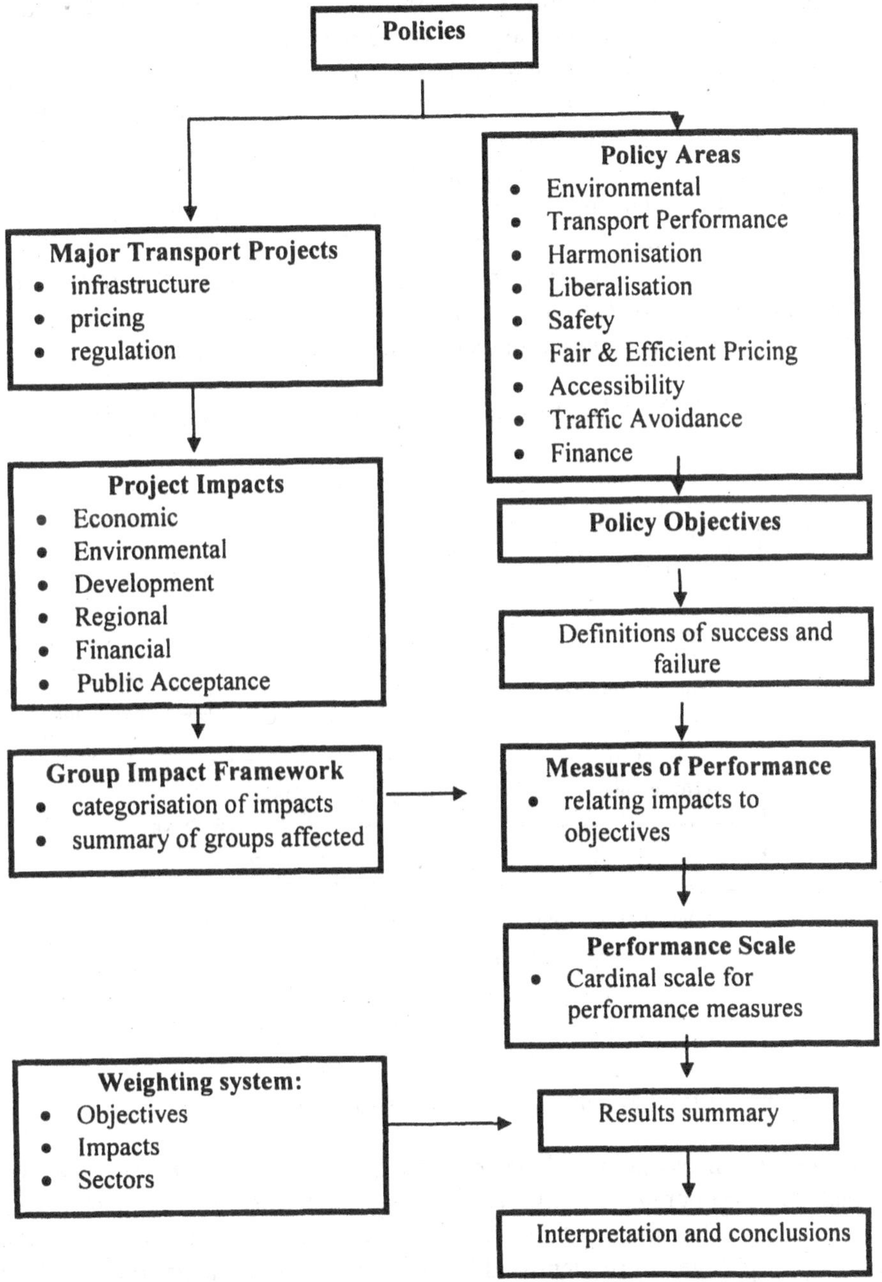

Figure 3.5 shows the process undertaken to develop the policy assessment model. The model has two starting points. From the 'top', looking down, are the policies and objectives to be borne in mind when planning transport investment. These are the policies of the stakeholders concerned. From the 'bottom', looking up, are the impacts of the transport projects themselves. The construction of policy measures of performance brings these two aspects together to create the policy assessment model in its design stage. The model is then refined through its application on a series of case studies.

Figure 3.5 usefully illustrates the data requirements of the PAM: From the 'top-down' information needed on the policies being considered. From the 'bottom-up' the forecast impacts of the project are required.

Figure 3.5 Method for Producing the Policy Assessment Model

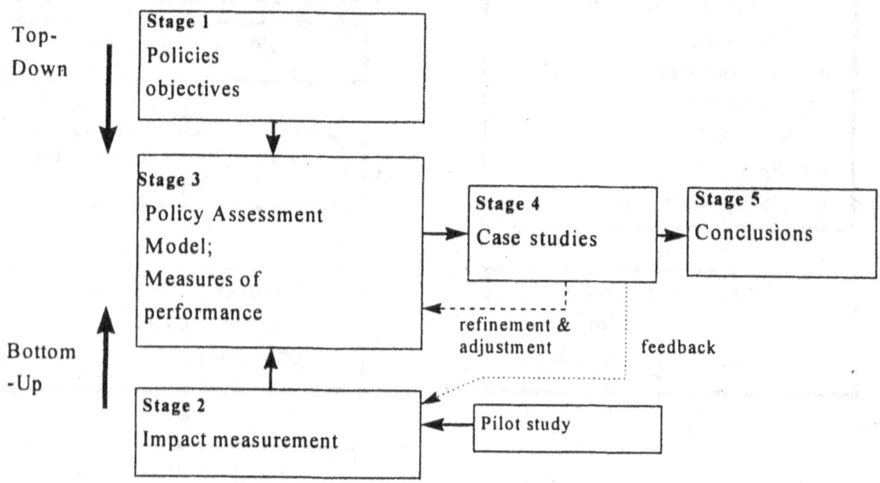

'Top-Down' Analysis: The Policy Structuring Process

To examine the scope of policies relevant to transport that the model would need to incorporate, an overview of policies for all EU states was undertaken. This included national, regional and local policies. A wide variety of policies were identified, expressed in a broad range of qualitative and quantitative ways. In order that these policies could be represented in a comparable manner, it was necessary to develop a standard format of classification.

Table 3.2 Initial Grouping of Policy Data into Aggregate Areas

POLICY AREA	OBJECTIVES
1. Environment	Δ environmental impacts
2. Fair and efficient prices	Δ quality of transport; increase safety Δ costs Δ environmental impacts Δ tonne kms/pax kms internalisation of externalities; increase mobility; increase system efficiency
3. Improve transport	Δ modal split Δ quality increase safety Δ costs Δ environmental impacts Δ competitiveness, Δ tonne kms/pax kms Δ capacity; improve efficiency Δ accessibility Δ interchange costs
4. Improve accessibility and regional development	Δ income co-ordination of transport & regional policy Δ land use Δ employment Δ tonne kms/pax kms
5. Harmonisation and common market (intermodality, interconnectivity, interoperability)	promote combined transport; reduce bottle necks; increase mobility Δ costs Δ quality Δ modal split Δ environmental impacts; improve efficiency
6. Avoid traffic	Δ environmental impacts Δ quality increase safety Δ costs Δ mobility Δ congestion
7. Deregulation, privatisation, liberalisation	Δ costs Δ labour Δ quality improve competitiveness; reduce public spending, lower tax burden; improve efficiency
8. Restrict transport	increase safety Δ environment Δ modal split Δ quality
9. Improve safety	Increase safety

Note: Δ = 'change in'

The first task in the analysis of the policy data structured the policies, as supplied, in accordance with their stated (verbalised) objectives. This exercise highlighted the fact that, in terms of objectives, many policies shared common goals and, more importantly, the policies could be grouped into nine broad categories into which they each would fit, thus permitting consistent treatment across administrative boundaries. This categorisation is reproduced in Table 3.2.

For each aggregate policy area, an overall aim exists. For example, the policies grouped under the 'Improve Transport' category all have the aim of improving transport quality or attributes in a certain manner and those under 'Fair and Efficient Pricing' heading all aim at influencing relative prices of transport modes.

It is to these aims, rather than the policy specific objectives, that measures of success and failure have been constructed. This important feature of the PAM makes it manageable for application on complex transport projects. If it was necessary to derive measures of performance for each objective for each policy perspective being considered, the model would quickly become unmanageable. That said, the generic policy areas can evolve over time also.

Much of the initial detailed analysis was undertaken using the transport policy material from Austria and Germany (ICCR, 1997) which was the most complete and quantified material available. Subsequent case studies helped to identify where the groups of aims thus developed were unable to sufficiently represent a stakeholder's transport policy. In these cases, it has been necessary to supplement the generic policy areas with specific project objectives. Fortunately, additional objectives are usually of high priority to the government or other policy perspective being considered, otherwise they would not need explicit representation in the PAM. They are therefore well articulated and measures of performance can be relatively easy to devise in these circumstances.

For example, a specific French 'regional accessibility' criterion was deemed necessary in order to reflect a very explicit French policy goal. Similarly, additional policy areas were required for the Portuguese case study to reflect some specific Portuguese developmental objectives.

In other instances, some of the original policy areas proved irrelevant to the policy debate – for example, traffic avoidance and traffic restraint policies do not feature at all in the policy debate that currently exists in Greece or Portugal.

'Bottom-Up' Analysis – The Group Impact Framework

A policy assessment method measures the impact of transport projects on policies. The previous section describes the research underpinning the identification and classification of policies. This section outlines how project impacts are treated.

The group impact framework (GIF) has been designed to manage the measurement and prediction of impacts. The GIF summarises the impacts of projects, the groups on which they fall (from here onwards, these are termed 'incidence groups') and, most importantly, the techniques required to quantify them. As such, it provides the means of deriving measures of performance for the PAM.

The policy assessment model has been designed to draw together existing methods for measuring impacts. This allows it greater flexibility to exploit the impacts assessed for a particular project, perhaps as part of a wider appraisal process. The model was used under these circumstances in Giorgi and Tandon (eds., 2000) where more sophisticated assessment was developed for certain impacts, and the results were adopted to measure the achievement of certain policy aims.

Impacts The GIF relates impacts of projects on the defined incidence groups. The framework distinguishes three major groupings of impacts:

- socio-economic impacts;
- public acceptance;
- finance.

The economic evaluation, through the socio-economic impacts, shows whether a project is feasible or not from the economic point of view. It is entirely possible that an economically sound project may not, however, be acceptable in a broader sense. Public and political acceptance (public opinion/pressure) or lack of financial viability can stop a project with good economic returns.

Incidence groups When considering possible impacts of projects it is important to consider which groups are involved. Different groups may be afflicted or involved in different ways, and there also might be grounds for conflict between groups.

In the GIF, all impacts are related to all relevant incidence groups and thus conflict between groups is explicitly internalised within the framework. The following incidence groups are distinguished:

- Users: the users of the new infrastructure.
- Operators: the potential service operators.
- Providers: the potential (non-governmental) providers of the new infrastructure.
- Non-users: persons that are not potential users of the new infrastructure, but are directly faced with the impacts of it.
- Government: granter of subsidies, possible provider of infrastructure.
- Society: payer of taxes, bearer of externalities.

It is helpful to group 'Government' and 'Society' together because democratically elected governments are elected to represent society, and the perspectives of the two groups often coincide.

Functional relationships Table 3.3 gives a schematic overview of the principal functional relations between impacts and incidence groups. Other relations can be added if thought to be relevant in particular contexts.

Table 3.3 Functional Relations Between Incidence Groups and Impacts

Impacts	**Incidence Groups**				
	Users	Service Operators	Infrastructure providers	Non-users	Society & Government
Socio economic impacts					
Investment costs	✗	✓	✓	✗	✗
Economic costs	✓	✗	✗	✗	✗
Safety	✓	✓	✗	✗	✗
Quality	✓	✗	✗	✗	✗
Employment	✗	✗	✗	✗	✓
Environment	✗	✗	✗	✓	✓
Regional development	✗	✗	✗	✗	✓
Social impact	✗	✗	✗	✗	✓
Public acceptance	✓	✗	✗	✓	✗
Financial viability	✓	✓	✓	✗	✓

Socio-economic impact Within the group impact framework, as can be seen in the first block in Table 3.3, the following socio-economic impacts are distinguished:

- investment/maintenance costs of infrastructure;
- economic costs;

- safety;
- quality;
- employment;
- environment;
- regional planning; and
- social impact.

Some of these impacts are said to be primarily efficiency impacts. The emphasis is placed on the size of the impact rather than its spatial or social distribution. Such impacts would feature in conventional cost benefit analysis, which is concerned with maximising social welfare, with indifference to its distribution. These impacts would include economic cost, safety and quality.

The regional planning and social impact are intended to be concerned with equity rather than efficiency: it is the distribution of the impacts that matters. Regional planning concerns economic issues, but not in absolute terms, which are covered elsewhere, but in purely distributive terms: how different sections of society and different regions will be affected. Social impacts, in the context of transport investment, is closely related to accessibility, but again the focus is on the distribution of change across different regions and social groups.

Employment and environment have efficiency and distributive implications.

The focus in considering each impact is the contribution of new project to transport related policies on a EU scale. This scale and the chosen general framework methodology lead to presenting minimum requirements for impact measurement. This makes the framework broadly applicable and data request minimal.

Public acceptance The acceptance impact is mainly related to non-user and user groups.

Acceptance cannot be measured directly. To get an idea of the actual acceptance situation the concept of 'acceptance' has to be operationalised. This has to be done, on the one hand, by comparing in which way product characteristics correspond with needs and interests of the specific target groups, on the other hand which image qualities are connected to the project and the ones who are responsible for it.

By means of information policy (studying literature, expert interviews) researchers carrying out measuring acceptance should examine which product characteristics (= technical data of the project) could cause problems, e.g., which characteristics meet with lack of acceptance. The results of these analyses will help to obtain a general view of the actual situation for the researcher and will be the basis on which questionnaires for interviews will be developed. Depending on:

- which target groups have been identified;
- which larger infrastructure projects are going to be built;
- where the larger infrastructure projects are going to be built.

Financial acceptance Three aspects of financial acceptance have been identified:

- an assessment of financial viability expressed conventionally as the financial net present value or internal rate of return;
- an analysis of the distribution of financial benefits, represented through reference to the groups within the GIF;
- an assessment of risk, addressed through a conventional financial risk assessment.

Measures of performance The objectives expressed in policy documents and impacts identified within the group impact framework are typically twinned in some way: each impact has an associated policy for some stakeholder group. The link is formalised in the model through the measures of performance. Given that the model is operationalised primarily through the generic policy areas, the challenge is then to identify impacts which can adequately measure achievement or failure with respect to the policy area.

The generic policy areas used are:

- Environment;
- Fair & Efficient Pricing;
- Improve Transport;
- Accessibility & Regional Development;
- Harmonisation & Common Market;
- Traffic Avoidance;
- Reduce 'price' of Transport;
- Restrict Road Transport;
- Improve Safety;
- Deregulation, Privatisation & Liberalisation;
- Financial Acceptability;
- Public Acceptability.

Note how closely these correspond to the impact groupings. The group impact framework distinguishes between socio-economic impacts, public acceptance and financial viability.

One impact that is not aligned with a policy objective is that of investment cost. The measures of performance are designed to measure the extent, in absolute terms, to which a policy is achieved within an appropriately defined study area. However, the magnitudes of all impacts and, therefore, measures of performance, are a function of the size of the investment cost. For any given project, there will be a maximum contribution towards policy aims that can be achieved, for given investment. If a larger project is planned, the impacts will be greater and consequently the potential contribution of the project to policy objectives is enhanced. The investment cost of a project is, therefore, presented as a separate item in the goals achievement matrix.

The measure of performance is a mapping from project impacts to a score between -5 and +5. A positive score represents some degree of success: some progress of achievement towards that policy has been made. A negative score represents the opposite.

In some contexts it may be possible to develop a goal achievement matrix drawing the definitions of success and failure directly from policy documents or other sources. Applying a GAM in a trans-European wide setting, this is unlikely to be a practical option. The scale of the task requires a more generic system, as already achieved by dealing with generic policy areas rather than directly with the objectives of each project stakeholder. Indeed the provision of clear and explicit measures of success and failure of a policy are only evident in a few instances.

Having identified the impacts to be measured, the basic function of the measure of performance must be defined. This involves the definition of the boundary point between success and failure, i.e. what constitutes a score of zero, but also the end points of the measure of performance to be assigned a score of +5 and -5. With these points defined, an explicit mathematical relationship is imposed that traces the path between failure and success. In most instances a linear relationship has been defined, but there is no reason, in principle, why other mathematical forms cannot be used.

When developing measures of performance, maximum and minimum scores are chosen to be appropriate to achievement of the policy from the perspectives of the country, or other interests, being represented. In some cases these cannot be derived, or there are too many policy perspectives being considered for detailed tailoring of the model in each case. Then the range of scores is set to reflect the range of performance that can result from different transport initiatives. Thus a score of 5 represents performance close to the maximum attainable by a transport project within the study area. A score of zero represents the 'do-minimum' option.

For example, in the case of the policy area 'Harmonisation and the Common Market' an indicator in relation to transport projects was selected to be the ratio between international and domestic traffic, of all modes. The benchmark drew on the Spanish and Portuguese experience of quick progress towards integration following their membership. At that time, the ratio of growth in international to domestic traffic was 140 per cent. This was used as a benchmark for the maximum score. The neutral score of zero related to the current experience across the EU, which averaged 104 per cent.

Another example is the policy area 'Fair and Efficient Pricing'. The benchmark score of +5 was given if transport modes were efficiently priced relative to each other, so that their price either equalled marginal cost, or the distortions were balanced across modes. Again, the score of zero consisted of maintenance of the status quo.

The full mathematical specification of and justification for the adoption of the measures of performance operationalised within the policy assessment model is detailed in Halcrow Fox (1998).

There is concern that the assessment is vulnerable to subjective judgement and hence distortion of the results. Indeed it is clear from the above description that measures of performance contain components of the analyst's discretion. It is argued that this is as true of other assessment methods.

For example in cost benefit analysis where social welfare components are interpreted in quantified terms. In CBA bias and subjectivity are minimised through application of best practice to surveys and other techniques designed to 'reveal' social value systems. Equivalently bias in the 'revelation' of policy objectives and measures of performance adopted in the PAM is minimised by a thorough understanding and appreciation of policy. This is made more difficult if policy is not well articulated, which is why the current trend towards clearer policy statements and targets offers real opportunities for wider usage of goals achievement methods.

Ultimately, and crucially, bias is subject to sanction. For, as with best practice in CBA where assumptions are made explicit, the objectives and benchmarks used in PAM are transparent and can readily be altered by the policy maker.

Weighting Systems

Weights are used in the PAM to combine the policy areas into overall scores. The weights are used to reflect the policy perspective being represented. Alternatively they could be selected for direct investigation by the decision maker themselves. They also enable the sensitivity of the results to be assessed with respect to changes in the perceived importance of different objectives.

Weights are used to multiply the scores (performance measures) allocated to each objective within the policy assessment model. They are, essentially, a measure of importance. The score (+5 to -5) indicates the extent to which a policy objective is furthered or constrained by a particular project, as estimated by the measure of performance. The weight indicates the importance of the policy area from the particular policy perspective under consideration. The product of these two factors indicates the value score for that particular performance measure. This value score is carried forward to the final interpretation stage.

The concept of 'different policy perspectives' can be considered in several ways:

- importance of one or more specific policy areas (environment, safety, etc.);
- importance of a particular Member State's policies (Germany, Finland, etc.);
- importance of policies at a particular level of the hierarchy (local, regional, national, EU).

Application of the weights is not complex, and can readily be applied by the decision-maker themselves. This allows the decision-maker not only to examine how a transport project performs with respect to different policy areas, but to investigate how favourable the project appears if different policies are traded against each other, using the values that the decision maker accords them.

The weights can also be applied by the analyst. The analyst would strive to interpret policy material and thus estimate the weights accorded to each policy area from certain policy perspectives. This process is useful as it allows the reaction of different stakeholders to be investigated, prior to their involvement, which may occur at a later stage of project planning.

Given that the process for applying weights is not complex, the model is ideally suited to sensitivity tests which alter the policy weights. Such manipulation would allow the analyst to investigate the sensitivity of assumptions to the overall performance of the project being forecast.

Table 3.4 Example Application of Weights; the Policy Assessment Model

Policy Area	Unweighted score	Weight for Policy Perspective A	Weighted score
Environment	3	5%	0.15
Fair & Efficient Pricing	0	0%	0
Improve Transport	3	0%	0
Accessibility & Regional Development	2	25%	0.5
Harmonisation & Common Market	4	10%	0.4
Traffic Avoidance	3	5%	0.15
Reduce 'price' of Transport	1	10%	0.1
Restrict Road Transport	4	5%	0.2
Improve Safety	2	10%	0.2
Deregulation, Privatisation & Liberalisation	-5	0%	0
Financial Acceptability	-5	20%	-1
Public acceptability	5	10%	0.05
Total	N/A	100%	0.75

It is suggested that the weights are expressed in percentage terms. An example is shown in Table 3.4. The table shows that the total weighted score is 0.75 out of a range of -5 to +5. The score is therefore very close to 0, and the project is not highly favoured or disfavoured from this policy perspective. If the perspective being considered was of primary importance, it would be appropriate to conduct a series of sensitivity tests on the weights used, to see if slight alteration of assumptions may lead to different conclusions. Also, in this case, the result is clearly very dependent on the financial feasibility of the study, which suggests the financial aspects would merit further examination.

Using percentage terms for weights has marginal advantages over applying absolute terms:

- the policy areas are not mutually independent. If two policy areas are similar and both deemed 'very important' there is a risk of double counting their significance. Assigning percentage terms overcomes this problem as attaching more importance to certain areas necessarily means attaching less importance to others;
- percentage weighting systems permits direct comparability between policy perspectives being represented by the weights, as they have the same possible range of scores.

Clearly, the application of weights to policies is a subjective activity. This should not be regarded as a weakness of the policy assessment model; rather, it represents a key strength. All appraisals carry an element of subjectivity, but in many cases this is not clear to the onlooker.

The benefit of the weighting system within the model is the transparency of the process. The method compels the user to be explicit about the size of weight, where it is applied and how it is interpreted. This makes for a totally open and honest approach to appraisal.

Whilst the weighting process as defined does not require an extensive set of pairwise comparisons, it is complex. Undertaking a Delphi analysis to understand policy conflicts within European decision-making is one way of defining weights.

Operationalising the Policy Assessment Model

Table 3.5 summarises what the application of the PAM would consist of in practice.

For each policy perspective, a weighting system must be devised. In some cases it may be necessary to add further policy objectives to the generic set already defined. This is the so-called 'top-down' information and analysis requirement.

As for all appraisal methods, each project option requires separate assessment of the forecast impacts. If the spatial area or incidence groups affected differ by the policy groups, then the group impact framework must reflect this, and the impacts be disaggregated accordingly. To allow results to be comparable, measures of performance and weights associated with the policy areas must not vary between project options. This is the so-called 'bottom up' information and analysis requirement.

Case Study: Rail Upgrade, Czech Republic

Introduction

Six case studies were undertaken as part of the testing and refinement of the policy assessment model. The projects are as follows:

- IC5 / IC25 motorway, Portugal;
- Igoumenitsa – Volos/Lamia motorway, Greece;
- TGV Nord High Speed Railway, France;
- Decin-Prague-Breclav Rail Corridor Upgrade, Czech Republic;
- Twente-Mittelland Kanal, Germany; and
- Amsterdam Ring Road, The Netherlands.

In this chapter we describe one of these case studies, that of the Decin-Prague-Breclav Rail Corridor Upgrade, Czech Republic. The corridor is part of the wider pan-European Corridor, as defined by Third Pan-European Transport Conference at Helsinki in 1997.

The case study concerned upgrading of the inter-city rail corridor between Berlin and Vienna, via Decin, Prague and Breclav. Though all of the upgrading works take place within the Czech Republic, the corridor is of major international importance in providing links between two EU Member States, Germany and Austria.

Table 3.5 Operationalising the Policy Assessment Model

Model Component	Work needed to apply the model
Policy areas	The policy areas are generic and are already defined.
Policy objectives	Examine transport policy *from each policy perspectives* being considered.
Group Impact Framework	The group impact framework structure is already defined.
Measures of performance	The generic structure is in place. The measures of performance can be tailored further, for example by reviewing targets, and definitions of impacts.
Impacts	These must be assessed in a format that can feed into the measures of performance for *each project option* being considered.
Weights	These should be derived by relating the policy areas to the policy being represented. A set of weights is needed for each of the *policy perspectives being considered*. If the generic policy areas are not sufficient to fully represent policy, further project objectives may be needed.
Sensitivity tests	The tests would consist of changing some of the weights. They would be tested across viable project options.
Results	These will be produced for each of the project options tested and for each of the policy perspectives. So x project options and y policy perspectives will produce x ·y sets of results.

The geographical context of this case study raises a number of important policy issues, which are intended to test the sensitivity and relevance of the policy assessment model. These include:

- domestic policy issues within the Czech Republic;
- Czech policies towards eventual membership of the EU;
- EU policies towards relations with central Europe; and
- German and Austrian policies towards domestic and international transport links.

This case study thus provides an opportunity to evaluate the ability of the policy assessment model to address a complex mix of domestic, international and non-EU policy issues.

In developing the case study, it has been necessary to collect policy information on the Czech Republic, which was added to the policy information already available for each of the Member States.

Much of the impact data for the case study has been taken from a preinvestment study for the European Commission and EBRD (Halcrow Transmark, 1995). The policy data was analysed in 1997. Both have subsequently been superseded, and the upgrade of certain sub sections of the railway line is already complete.

The following sections provide a description of the project and its background, summarise the policy issues surrounding the project, describe the application of the policy assessment model, and summarise the case study.

The project involves up-grading 453 km of existing infrastructure in order to allow faster running speeds, employing new, tilting rolling stock. The line forms the central segment of the proposed Central European Axis from Berlin to Vienna via Dresden and Prague.

Financial structuring. In 1994, the total investment cost of upgrading the central segment within the Czech Republic was estimated to be ECU 880 million of which around 20 per cent was for investment in new rolling stock. Funding was secured from central Government and a variety of external sources, including the European Investment bank (ECU 125M) and the European Bank for Reconstruction and Development (ECU 42.6M). Export-Import Bank and four other Japanese banks are providing an ECU 100M loan to the Czech national railway company, Ceske Drahy (CD). The EU's PHARE programme was to provide ECU 350M between 1995 and 2000 for the upgrading of Czech Infrastructure, including the Berlin–Prague–Vienna main line.

Upgrading approach The decision was made to upgrade the existing infrastructure for high speed running (160 kph), rather than to construct a new, high specification alignment. The onerous terrain of the corridor, as well as the economic circumstances of the Czech Republic, makes the construction of a brand new railway prohibitively expensive. Moreover, the upgrading of the traditional network allows benefits to freight traffic, which can also use the new infrastructure.

In order to obtain service speeds of 160 kph, it has been decided to replace much of the existing fixed equipment. The project entails track relaying, curve realignments, new signalling, telecommunications and train control, and the electrification of the remaining 18 per cent of the corridor for which trains are currently diesel-powered. However, crucially for the attainment of higher speeds, particularly where onerous terrain restricts expensive re-alignment, will be the provision of tilting passenger rolling stock.

National context The Czech Republic has a total population of 10.3 million. The Decin–Prague–Breclav corridor serves a total potential market of approximately 2 million inhabitants. As well as the capital, Prague, the region of Northern Bohemia is traversed, serving towns with a total population of 190,000. To the east of Prague, the corridor passes through Mid and East Bohemia, providing access to towns such as Pardubice, Hradec Kralove and Ceske Budejovice, with a total market catchment of 200,000 inhabitants. However, after Prague, the town of most significant size, served by the route is Brno.

The town of Brno is located in the region of South Moravia, in proximity to the Austrian border, and has a population of 370,000. With the provision of upgraded infrastructure, and new tilting trains, the journey time between Prague and Brno will be reduced from the current 3h06 to 2h14. Service frequencies will also be improved significantly.

Although the corridor upgrading will primarily provide benefits to passenger services, freight services will also benefit. The Czech government is keen to minimise the mode shift of freight traffic towards the roads as the country transforms towards a western market economy. Moreover, the rail-freight business in the Czech Republic is potentially highly profitable, due to the geographic location of the country with respect to central Europe.

European context For the complete Berlin–Prague–Vienna corridor, the section between Berlin and Dresden is being re-built to provide a service speed of 200 km/h. The aim is to cut Berlin–Prague journey times from 4h40 to 3h00 and Prague–Vienna from 4h50 to 3h30.

The study results The study results, in general, failed to provide the economic and financial support for the corridor segment's potential. The best financial internal rate of return was only -6 per cent (very poor). The best economic rate of return was little better at -5 per cent (Halcrow Transmark, 1995).

Whilst the upgraded railway was forecast to make an operating profit, the very high capital cost of the new tilting train technology was largely responsible for the poor results. This was compounded by the relatively low values of time in the Czech Republic, which constrained the benefits from time savings and the low fares, which similarly constrained the farebox revenues.

The study concluded that justification would be needed on wider grounds than economic and financial results alone. Such grounds would include wider economic development of the country; improved links with the EU; reduced levels of road traffic; and general improvements in operational efficiency of the rail system.

Policies and Objectives

The following sections outline the application of the policy assessment model to the appraisal of the Corridor I upgrading project.

Czech policies At the time of undertaking the study the Czech Republic was undergoing transition from a centrally planned to a market economy. It was widely regarded as one of the most successful transitional economies, both in terms of the level of economic growth being sustained, and its ability to avoid some of the social disbenefits that afflicted a number of neighbouring states.

Czech policies at the time of the rail study were typical of those of several transitional economies. They generally reflected a desire for swift change to market economy principles, whilst minimising the risk of major social upheavels. Thus market economics tended to dominate in those areas where social impacts could be minimised (deregulation of the bus and road haulage industries) whilst more protective policies were maintained in more vulnerable sectors (health and education). The rail sector fell between several types of policy issue. There was a strong awareness of the need to improve the level of cost recovery and the general level of service throughout the network. At the same time policies which increased levels of unemployment within the rail sector were not favoured.

One consequence of this general policy mix was that considerable emphasis was placed on investment projects. These have the general characteristics of stimulating construction activity (and therefore employment) in the short term, and stimulating improved cost recovery through market growth in the medium term.

The principal areas of relevant Czech policies are listed below. It should be stressed that these policies were current at the time of the study in 1994-5.

Environment The country was badly affected by a number of highly degrading industries for more than half a century. A high awareness of environmental issues exists, although there is acknowledgement of a potential trade-off with economic growth. No explicit policy objectives were identified, however, general policy statements have been interpreted to indicate that the aim is to conform to Rio Summit standards (reduction to 1990 emission levels in 2000).

Fair and efficient pricing No road pricing is envisaged in the short-term and a general aim appears to be to maintain affordable prices for all modes. In reality, the Czech government is likely to attempt to limit price increases to the rate of inflation.

No explicit pricing of externalities (e.g., environmental degredation) is envisaged.

A commitment does exist towards price reform and the gradual erosion of price distortions introduced during the Communist era. However, the government is conscious of the short-term social impacts of large price rises.

The general policy towards pricing is thus assumed to be that of price reform and economic deregulation throughout the economy, including public transport. However, the rate of such reforms is likely to be governed by the need to minimise the social costs of large price rises. A long-term aim of bus deregulation and rail privatisation exists, but there is no commitment to road pricing.

Improve transport No specific targets exist for passenger traffic with the long-term aim being to grow the market for all modes. To this end, major investment projects are planned for road, rail and air. The issue of traffic congestion and demand management has not really emerged onto the political agenda, with the lack of highway capacity being the principal concern.

With respect to freight, the main policy is to attract international through freight traffic to rail, ideally combined/container transport. As a minimum, there should be no loss of market share from rail to road. This is largely driven by a desire to reserve Czech highway capacity for Czech economic activities, not for transit vehicles.

Accessibility and regional development At a national level, there is a strong policy imperative to improve inter-regional transport links across the country and to facilitate a general improvement in accessibility.

At a regional level, the main policy is to promote industrial development in northern Moravia (Ostrava, etc.). No major regional issue affects this project other than slowing the decline in the traditional heavy industry heartland.

Harmonisation and common market This is a key area of policy, with the objective of gaining membership of the EU by early next century. To achieve this, the transport system of the Czech Republic must be integrated with those of neighbouring EU states, including, physical links, operating systems and service levels. All of this has implications for the rail project.

Total harmonisation of the Czech transport network includes:

- rail power supply/operations/through services/rolling stock;
- developed network of air routes; and
- integrated motorways with Germany/Austria/Hungary/Poland.

Priority is given to pan European corridors. Upgrading Corridor I is the focus of Czech regional transport policy.

Reduce the price of transport The relevant policy is that of encouraging no real increase in prices for all modes. Ideally, the price of transport should fall relative to GDP, at or below price inflation. This will achieve the aim of affordable transport for the population, and a declining proportion of disposable income spent on transport.

Reduce (road) transport There is no policy of effecting a passenger modal shift, nor of deterring private/road transport. The explicit aim of Government is to provide infrastructure to cater for the growing demand for transport by all modes; i.e.: to expand supply to meet growing demands for transport in order to assist short-term economic development. This also supports the 'European Harmonisation' objective. These above considerations also apply to the 'Traffic Avoidance' objective.

Improve safety The focus of safety policies and programmes is on improved design standards of highways and public transport technology. This also has implications for the Corridor I study, with its high-specification rolling stock.

Public acceptance No opposition to transport projects appears to exist. In fact, the opposite appears to be the case, with strong support for investment in the supply of transport capacity. A strong regional argument exists for investment in Northern Moravia, though this is peripheral to the study in question.

Financial acceptance The private sector needs a Government guarantee for any loan, which effectively necessitates Government taking the risk for the Corridor I project.

The Government desires to balance investment between road, rail and air, which provides some driving force for major rail projects to complement those on other modes.

There appears to be minimal attraction of an equity stake from any private party – i.e. only debt finance is likely. So the public contribution represents the equity share of the project.

A 20 per cent internal rate of return is needed for private investment (with government guarantee). A 10 per cent public/economic discount rate exists. The consequence of these disparate points is that the project has the outward appearance of a private finance initiative, but in reality, the vast majority of the financial risk is borne by the public sector. The key financial issues are thus unlikely to be dominant and are secondary to social and economic policy issues.

Policies of neighbouring states Corridor I provides a missing link between two major EU cities, Berlin and Vienna. It also offers a public transport mode in a region where car travel tends to dominate. The scheme directly affects a number of German and Austrian policies. These, in turn, can be translated into relevant policy areas within the policy assessment model.

General policy areas of concern in Austria are:

- restriction of long distance freight traffic;
- avoiding unnecessary traffic (so as to minimise environmental degredation);
- improving rail infrastructure;
- fair and efficient pricing in transport;
- co-ordination of transport investment.

Relevant policies within Germany include:

- elimination of capacity problems between Berlin and southern Germany;
- promotion of multi-modal transport chains;
- promotion of inter-urban rail;
- promotion of economic development through investment in transport, including links with other EU states.

Corridor I has major implications for three key policy areas, as defined within the Policy Assessment Model, in both Germany and Austria:

- harmonisation and the Common Market – by providing a fast and efficient link between south and east Germany and eastern Austria;
- accessibility and Regional Development – by facilitating access and development in two relatively isolated parts of the EU. The whole of former east Germany is recognised by the EU as lagging behind in development, as are parts of Burgenland in Austria; whilst parts of Niederosterreich are classified officially as 'vulnerable rural areas';
- reduce the Price of Transport – both Germany and Austria are keen to improve the competitive position of public transport by reducing the generalised cost of travel, thereby providing an alternative to the car.

It can be seen that 'Harmonisation and the Common Market' and 'Accessibility and Regional Development' are of common interest to the Czech Republic and to Germany/Austria. However, 'Reducing the Price of Transport' is a priority for Germany and Austria only. This emphasises the importance within the Policy assessment model of being able to weight and prioritise goals by country so as to reflect such diversity and differences.

Priority policies Issues of moderate/low importance to the Czech Republic are:

- the Environment – conforming to EU standards;
- reducing the Price of Transport;
- public Acceptability;
- financial Acceptability.

Unimportant issues with regard to the Czech Republic are:

- fair and efficient pricing;
- improved transport;
- restricting transport;
- improved safety.

Primary Czech objectives are:

- harmonisation and the Common Market;
- accessibility and Regional Development.

Key Austrian and German policy areas are:

- harmonisation and the Common Market;
- accessibility and Regional Development;
- reducing the Price of Transport.

These priorities will be reflected within the weighting system in the policy assessment model appraisal.

Project Appraisal

The Policy Assessment Model was run for a variety of national and EU policy scenarios, namely: Czech policies, EU policies and German/Austrian policies. It would also have been possible to explore regional policy perspectives. The tests involved both unweighted and weighted model runs, with weights being derived from policy documents. The principal results of the tests are summarised in Table 3.6. The scores are within a range of -5 to +5.

Table 3.6 Results of the Czech Case Study

	Scenarios			
Policies	**1 – Standard Weight (1.0)**	**2 – Czech policies version A: Positive Weighting: Accessibility and Regional Development & European Harmonisation**	**3 – Czech policies version B: as 2, with Low Weighting for Policies Favouring Traffic Restraint**	**4 – Weighting of Main German and Austrian Priorities**
Czech Republic	-0.04	+0.01	+0.5	
Germany and Austria	+0.11			+0.6
Combined National Policies (Weighted CR +0.6; D +0.2; OS +0.2)	+0.02	+0.05		+0.2 to +0.5

The absolute values of scores are of little relevance; however, their signs (positive or negative), together with their magnitude relative to each other are important.

The results indicate that, using a basic, unweighted test for the Czech Republic alone, the proposed project is not viable. The project has a net negative contribution to Czech policies (-0.4). However, when weights are introduced for key policies for which a preference has been declared (e.g., accessibility and regional development as well as European harmonisation) the appraisal records a small, net, positive score (+0.01).

Further analysis of the appraisal results indicated that the scheme scored badly against 'western' driven policy areas such as improving transport, restricting transport and fair and efficient pricing. However, these are not priority areas in the Czech Republic, as traffic congestion, environmental degradation (due to traffic) and the 'user-pays' concept are not currently valued.

Weighting such policy areas *down* further improved the appraisal score, to +0.5. Hence, once those policies which are valued are weighted up, and those which have little value are weighted down, the Corridor I project returns a reasonable positive score, indicating that it has a net contribution to achieving the main Czech transport-related policies.

When the appraisal was carried out for German and Austrian policies only (a combined test incorporating both states together was undertaken), a positive, net, score was returned for the unweighted test (+0.11). This reflected the positive contribution to improving accessibility, European Harmonisation, and policies aimed at restricting and improving transport (i.e., the 'western' policies).

A further test was carried out for Germany and Austria, in which weights were applied to topical national policies (i.e., improving accessibility, European Harmonisation, and policies aimed at restricting and improving transport). This resulted in a highly positive net score (+0.6).

The final row of Table 3.6 shows the results of a combined test involving Czech, German and Austrian policies. It can be seen that the appraisal score gradually increases as those prioritised policies are subject to weights within the Policy assessment model (as would be expected). The principal policies driving the net positive score were:

- harmonisation and Common Market (in all three States);
- accessibility and Regional Development (in all three States);
- improved and Restricted Transport and Reduced Price of Transport (Germany and Austria only).

Most other policies within the Czech Republic had little influence, whilst financial policies returned a strong negative score due to the poor rate of return.

The use of the policy assessment model in the Czech case study illustrates how a project with a poor economic and financial return can be justified in terms of supporting a broader range of policy goals. It also raises the importance of considering policies from outside the state in which the project is set in order to appreciate the full benefits and impacts.

In reality, the Czech Government sanctioned the Corridor I upgrading. It thus appears that considerations of broader policy issues, *de facto*, may have influenced the political decision to proceed with the project.

Summary

This case study illustrates a number of important points concerning uses and merits of the policy assessment model. These include:

- the importance of applying weights to key, prioritised policy areas;

- the value of considering policies across state frontiers and the effect of this on the result of an appraisal;
- potential conflicts between 'western European' policies set in the context of congested networks, concerning traffic management, and the policies of developing/transitional economies, which are growth focussed;
- the ability of the policy assessment model to focus on key policy issues.

In general, the unweighted analysis does not produce favourable (i.e., supportive) results. This largely corresponds with the poor results of the economic and financial analyses. Indeed, the low/negative unweighted scores within the Policy assessment model are driven by 'traditional' traffic volume and cost/benefit data.

The application of weights to two, key, Czech policy areas (accessibility and regional development as well as harmonisation and the common market) results in a net positive score and illustrates how the project could be justified in a highly focused, development-led policy context. Such focus is not uncommon in developing transitional economies, where planning decisions are heavily influenced by a desire for growth and integration with other trading partners. By contrast, more mature, stable economies tend to be increasingly concerned by the intricate trade-offs between development, transport efficiency and the negative impacts of transport investment.

Given that the Corridor I upgrading is being implemented, it appears that the implied weights identified by this case study are indeed of relevance in the Czech Republic. An opportunity exists to turn this methodology around and conclude that project appraisals in the Czech Republic should, as a matter of course, apply weights to the policy areas: accessibility and regional development and harmonisation and the common market. That is, use of this method in an ex-post context enables standard weights to be determined for particular projects in particular states.

The value of considering policies from other states is also illustrated by the case study. Consideration of the policy benefits to Germany and Austria significantly increases the value of the project. This raises a number of issues, including whether Germany and Austria should contribute financially to the project in return for these benefits. In the absence of such a contribution, they could be accused of exploiting a 'free rider' status.

Finally, perhaps the main conclusion to draw from the Czech case study is the value of this policy assessment model in focusing a project's appraisal on diverse, international policy issues, and away from simple economic and financial evaluations. Moreover, it demonstrates that different recommendations can emerge when such a broader perspective is adopted.

Discussion and Summary Findings

Overview

This section has described the construction of the PAM policy assessment model in the complex policy environment typified by TEN projects. The model focuses upon the key area of project impacts on policies and appears to be a powerful analytical tool for exploring factors underlying the project-policy relationship. Attributes include:

- flexibility – the PAM addresses a wide variety of policy areas and is amenable to changing policies and new policy emphases;
- versatility – the PAM can assess policies from a variety of sectors;
- transparency – all inputs, transformations, weights and outputs are open to inspection and audit;
- analytical power – the case studies demonstrate the wide variety of issues that the PAM can address, along with its potential for use as an analytical tool.

Role of PAM in Transport Planning

The PAM policy assessment model is a form of appraisal of transport projects with respect to different policies. It has been designed as a preliminary assessment tool, where it can screen a large number of projects. This screening process allows projects that clearly do not conform to a reasonably wide set of goals and objectives to be removed from the decision-process before the costs of detailed project studies (where cost benefit analysis and environmental impact assessment have their role) are incurred.

The model also has the potential to act as a monitoring tool within the overall appraisal process. The period from project inception to final design and feasibility can be very long winded. Given such long project lead times, it is entirely possible that policy objectives and preferences will evolve during the course of the project planning lifetime. In this context, the PAM approach can monitor projects – reassessment during the planning process can ensure that upon completion of full project evaluation and design, the scheme is still broadly in line with the aspirations of decision-making bodies.

The PAM is compatible with other forms of assessment, be they socio-economic, financial or environmental. It is not intended to replace other assessment tools, but rather, to support them and allow a more comprehensive evaluation of major projects with significant policy implications. Indeed the PAM could be viewed as one of a family of policy-related models, for example, alongside a model of barriers to implementation. Together, such a system of models could be used, not only as assessment tools, but as means of exploring the broader technical, social and political implications of major transport projects. This concept has been explored in the area of strategic assessment of transport programmes (cf. CODE-TEN Final Report, Giorgi and Tandon, eds. 2000).

Explanatory Power

The policy assessment model is adept at illustrating and exploring policy conflicts, between sectors, different levels in the policy hierarchy, etc. The case studies have demonstrated how practical policy conclusions can be drawn from the model's applications. They also illustrate how past assessments using other methods can be replicated or audited using the PAM.

The Policy assessment model clearly highlights conflict within the policy hierarchy. The standard deviation of the individual policy area scores, together with the graphical presentation of the results, gives a clear indication of the degree to which projects are in line with policy objectives or in conflict with them.

In terms of policy scores, road projects tend to have a high standard deviation and rail projects a low one. In general, rail projects tend to score positively across the entire range of policy areas whereas road projects tend to score very highly in some areas and poorly in others. This finding would tend to support the hypothesis that the current policy thrust in many European countries is towards rail and away from road projects.

The Czech case study highlights that the incorporation of the policy objectives of other countries who are affected by the project can have a deciding impact upon the project score. One of the most important issues here would appear to be: if the project benefits are felt abroad, can any of the project costs be recouped from the beneficiary state?

The weighting system allows users to reflect differing levels of importance afforded to various policy areas (environmental, social, economic, etc.); this enables various perspectives to be explored and their implications assessed in advance of the actual decision-making process.

Assigning weights is necessarily subjective in nature, which makes transparency of their presentation all the more important. The weights can readily be altered, and sensitivity tests of the weights can provide some of the richest outputs of the model to aid understanding of policy interactions and conflicts. A delphi panel could be used to explore suitable representation of policy by this means on a consensual basis.

Requirements for Operation

The development work carried out to date demonstrates how the PAM can be operationalised within a reasonable time and budget constraint. Data needs are not a major constraint, nor are programming requirements. Much of the background data required for operating the PAM is available from national and regional sources. The essential data requirement is that of a traffic forecasting model.

Conclusion

The planning environment underlying multinational transport projects can typically be guided by economic, financial and environmental assessment. Yet such assessments are not designed to reflect the diversity of policy issues at stake. As the project planning progresses, it can then become difficult to manage or alleviate the potential policy conflicts, both within and across institutions, that arise. A policy assessment model, as described here, specifically seeks to address the policy complexity inherent in such projects. Its qualities are becoming ever more relevant as the realisation of a pan-European transport network draws nearer.

Note

1 See Nellthorp *et al.* (1998) for a useful review.

References

Brown, M. B., Evans, R. C. (1991), 'The Evaluation of Traffic Management & Parking Schemes: Whither Now?', *Traffic Engineering and Control*, Vol. 32, No. 3.

Bruck *et al.* (1996), 'Evaluation of Alternative Transport Proposals', *Journal of the American Institute of Planners*, Vol. 23.

Danish Transport Council (1995) *Issues of Accountability - Lessons and Recommendations Regarding Appraisal of a Fixed Link Across Fehmarn Belt*, Report No. 95.03.

DETR (Department of the Environment Transport and the Regions) (1998), *Understanding the New Approach to Appraisal*, The Stationery Office.

European Commission (1992), *Transport White Paper*, COM (92) 494 Final, European Commission, Brussels.

European Commission (1993), *The Future Development of the Common Transport Policy - A global Approach to the Construction of a Community Framework for Sustainable Mobility*, Bulletin of the European Communities, Supplement 3/93, European Commission, Brussels.

European Commission (1998), *The Commission's Action Programme 1998-2004* for Transport & *The Common Transport Policy - Sustainable Mobility: Perspectives for the Future*, European Commission, Brussels.

Hill, M. (1968), 'A Goals Achievement Matrix for Evaluating Alternative Plans', *Journal of the American Institute of Planners*, Vol. 34, pp. 19 - 29.

Halcrow Fox (1998), *Final Report Assessment Methodology - Project Tenassess - Policy Assessment of Trans-European Networks and Common Transport Policy*, Funded by the European Commission under the Transport RTD Programme of the 4th Framework Programme.

Halcrow Transmark (1995), *Preinvestment Study of Decin - Praha - Breclave Rail Upgrade*, For European Bank of Reconstruction and Development (EBRD) and European Commission (Phare).

Litchfield, N. (1964), *Cost Benefit Analysis In Plan Evaluation, Town Planning*, Pergamon, Oxford.

McLoughlin, J. B. (1969), *Urban and Regional Planning: A Systems Approach*, Faber. London.

MVA Consultancy, Institute of Transport Studies, Environmental Resources Management, David Simmonds Consultancy, John Bates Services, Countryside Agency, English Heritage, English Nature (2000), '*Guidance on the Methodology for Multi-Modal Studies*', London.

Nellthorp, J., Mackie, P. and Bristow, A. (1998), 'Measurement and Valuation of the Impacts of Transport Initiatives', *EUNET Socio-economic and spatial impacts of transport. Deliverable D9*, Institute for Transport Studies, University of Leeds. Funded by the European Commission under the Transport RTD Programme of the 4th Framework Programme.

Ng, Y. K. (1983), *Welfare Economics: Introduction and Development of Basic Concepts*, Macmillan, London.

Pearce, D.W. and Nash, C.A. (1981), *The Social Appraisal of Projects - A Text in Cost Benefit Analysis*, Macmillan, London.

Rudeau, R. (1987), *Rapport de la Commission d'etude des traces du TGV Nord*, Paris.

SNCF (1996), 'La Construction de la ligne nouvelle du TGV Nord', *Rapport Annuel de la Cour de Comptes*, Paris.

TENASSESS Consortium (1997), *Country Profiles: National Transport Policies,* Project Report TENASSESS, [D(1)], Technical Annex, ICCR, Vienna.

TINA Secretariat (1999), *Transport Infrastructure Needs Assessment in Central and Eastern Europe*, Final Report. Phare Multi-Country Transport Programme. European Commission, Brussels.

Viegas, J. M. and Figueira, P. (1999), Strategic Assessment of Corridor Developments, TEN Improvements and Extensions to the CEEC/CIS CODE-TEN [D(5)], CESUR, Lisbon.

4 Sustainable Transport Policies: Scenarios for the Future

DAVID BANISTER AND DOMINIC STEAD

Introduction

Travel patterns in Europe are increasingly dependent on the car. Levels of mobility and car ownership have risen substantially over recent decades and that increase seems likely to continue. The number of private vehicles increased by over one third in the ten-year period between 1985 and 1995, and it is likely that this number may increase by a further 50 per cent by 2020, which would bring vehicle ownership levels to over 600 cars per 1,000 population (OECD/ECMT, 1995). Road capacity has not increased by a similar amount (around 10 per cent between 1985 and 1995), so congestion has increased, particularly in cities where little new infrastructure has been built. The growth in congestion is now officially estimated to cost about 2 per cent of Europe's Gross Domestic Product (EUROSTAT, 1997).

Space is at a premium in most European countries and population density is high. This has advantages as distances between cities are shorter, but it also means that urban sprawl and edge city phenomena are not attractive options. Much of the undeveloped land is safeguarded as open space, green belt or recreational areas that cannot be used for city expansion. The role of public transport has remained important in many European countries, although the car is the dominant mode of transport and its use is increasing. Air transport is increasing at a rapid rate across Europe.

In this chapter, we report on the recently completed POSSUM project[1] (EU DGVII Strategic Transport Research Programme), where a new approach to scenario-building has been developed. Firstly we suggest a number of reasons why scenarios provide useful tools for policy making. Secondly we report the main features of the scenario-building process that has been developed in the project. Thirdly we highlight some of the more interesting conclusions from the project.

The Role of Scenarios in Policy Development

The dynamic nature of policy objectives, priorities and advice requires a way of identifying policies and proposals that are robust and flexible enough to withstand change. Policy scenarios allow the role and effect of different policies and proposals to be studied across a range of possible futures. May (1982) identifies a number of potential benefits of policy scenarios to decision-making, including:

- *providing useful frameworks for decision-making* – scenarios allow decision-making issues to be explored using a range of alternative scenarios, reflecting different assumptions about the future;
- *identifying dangers and opportunities* – considering a range alternative futures increases the likelihood of identifying possible problems and opportunities in policy-making;
- *suggesting a variety of possible approaches* – the use of scenarios may generate a range of approaches to tackle issues or problems whereas the use of forecasts, often based on single theories or simple extrapolations, often leads to the pursuit of singular solutions;
- *helping to assess alternative policies and actions* – scenarios may, for example, be used to identify the usefulness of different policies under alternative future conditions; and
- *increasing creativity and choice in decision-making* – identifying possible future developments and avoiding the acceptance of current trends as inevitable opens up new possibilities for policy development.

It was within this context of creative thinking about desirable future visions, together with the necessary policy actions to move towards those visions, that the research reported here was framed. The objectives of the project were:

- to develop a set of alternative policy scenarios to assist in decision-making on the Common Transport Policy and the Trans-European-Networks development;

- to develop and test policy scenarios with help from expert groups to give a range of different futures, each of which will combine elements of economic growth, regional development and the environment;
- to identify criteria for sustainable mobility and to link them into policy scenarios through clearly stated objectives and targets, which will reflect the priorities of a sustainable transport policy;
- to design transport policy scenarios which present a range of future situations together with a set of consistent events which may link the current position to future positions according to clearly defined policy objectives;
- to establish policy packages and paths, illustrating how the targets can be achieved, what range of actions are available, and when decisions have to be taken;
- to test the scenarios, together with the criteria and sustainable mobility objectives with experts to establish whether the actions are feasible or desirable and what actions need to be taken to achieve the policy targets; and
- to assess the implications of the scenarios across the EU countries and in the wider Europe, in particular the CEEC, CIS and the Baltic States.

The time horizon of the project was from 1995 to the year 2020. Clearly, scenario analysis was central to the project and in the following section we outline the process developed (for full details see POSSUM, 1999 and Banister *et al.*, 2000).

Scenario Construction and Literature Review

A scenario is a tool that describes pictures of the future world within a specific framework and under specified assumptions. The scenario approach includes a description of two or more scenarios, designed to compare and examine alternative futures (CEC, 1994). According to Becker (1997), there are a number of distinct different traditions and approaches in scenario construction.[2]

The *American approach* is more appropriate when a cautious strategy is required (Becker, 1997, p.88). It is particularly strong when the main actor has limited powers, and if the actions of rivals are taken into account. A distinction is made between context and strategy. The scenarios first are presented as the context within which the system operates and policy making takes place. Various actors are then asked to choose between alternative strategies and to adapt these so that 'least regret' strategies can be selected by the user of the scenarios. In this sense, the process tries to minimise losses rather than to encourage innovative or radical solutions to problems.

In the *French approach*, a more utopian, mind stretching process is involved (Becker, 1997, p. 88). In this tradition, the central actor's role is given most prominence so that more space can be created in which to act imaginatively. The future is explored in terms of what it should be, rather than what it is likely to be (Godet, 1986). A comprehensive picture of the future is presented in terms of the current situation, a description of some future alternatives and a description of a number of events which may connect the present situation with future ones.

A particular version of the French approach has been adapted and used in Swedish research, so we also make the distinction of a third approach, although it is related to the French approach in many ways. The *Swedish approach* has certain clearly distinctive characteristics and it has been mainly used for policy analysis (see Löhnroth *et al.*, 1980; Johansson *et al.*, 1983 or Olson, 1994 for example). It is normative in its structure and based on desirable futures or choices (Robinson, 1990). It uses a backcasting approach (rather than forecasting) where an Image of the Future is constructed without taking account of current trends. A path is then constructed on how to move from where one is at present to this desirable future position. Experts are used to validate the process at various stages, so that feedback and modification of the scenarios can take place. The intention is not to provide a prescriptive view, but to illustrate possible future policy paths and indicate the nature and scale of actions (together with a timetable) necessary to achieve the scenario targets. The Swedish approach was the approach used in the POSSUM project, although the basic backcasting methodology was slightly modified (Figure 4.1).

Scenarios form the basis of an increasing number of policy-orientated research projects in Europe (see Rienstra, 1998 for example). Few of these projects, however, contain detailed information about the scenarios or the scenario-building process. In this respect, this project is different: it has developed a clear, detailed set of scenarios and a systematic scenario-building process. The process has been developed partly through the experience of other scenario-building projects (e.g. Khakee and Strömberg, 1993) and partly through an iterative, heuristic process.

Figure 4.1 The Scenario Building Process

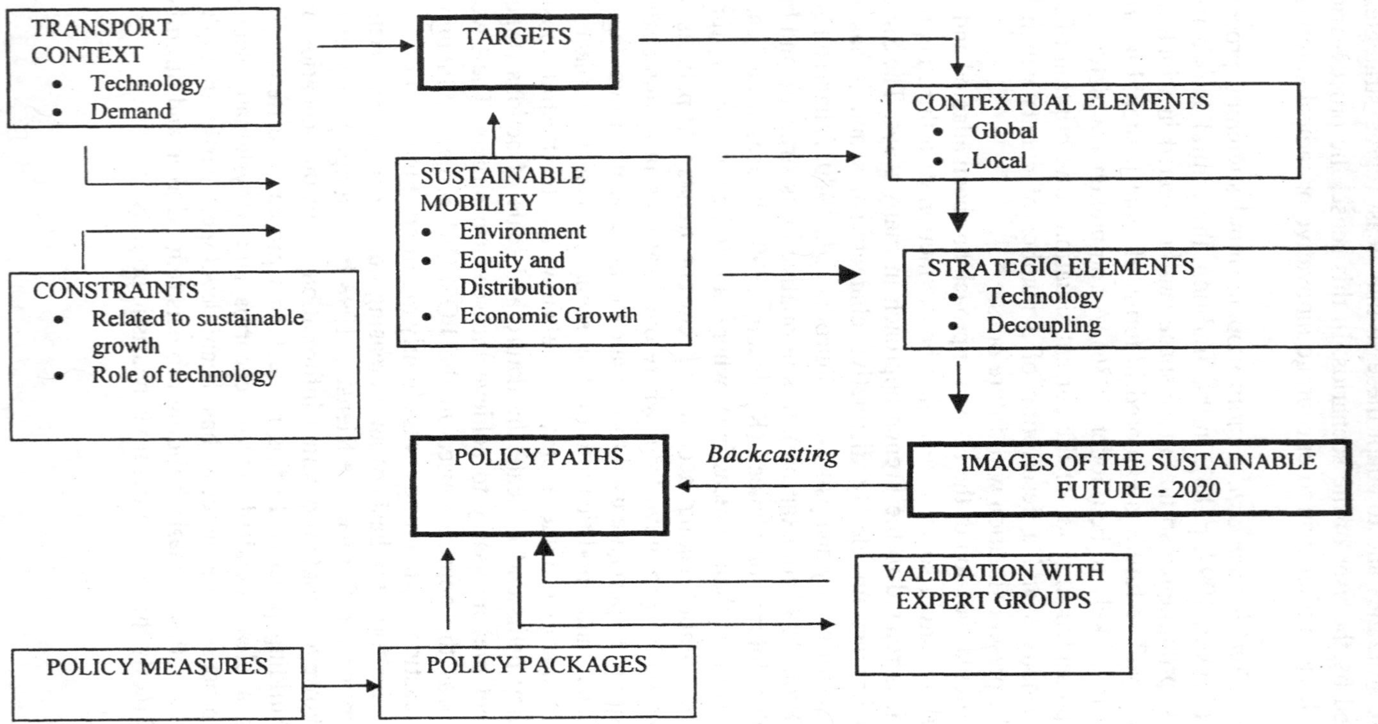

The Eight Stages in the Scenario Building Process

Eight main stages in the process can be distinguished and each of these stages are discussed below. Although some stages are reliant on one or more previous stages in the process, the link between each stage does not form a simple sequence. There are interactions and feedback loops between many of the main stages (Figure 4.1).

Identifying Key Issues

The first stage in the scenario-building process is the identification of key issues facing policy-makers at the moment, and emerging issues which could be important to policy-making in the future. Key issues can be identified through questionnaires, discussions with professionals and literature reviews. Examples of key issues for transport policy between now and 2020 include global warming, the growth in passenger and freight transport (particularly by road), increasing congestion and pollution (particularly in urban areas), and the growth in air traffic. At the same time as identifying key issues, the driving forces behind them (increasing car ownership and more leisure time for example) also need to be considered if effective policy actions to tackle them are to be identified.

Making Projections of Key Issues

Having identified the *key issues*, trends are extrapolated into the future to give some indication of future conditions in the absence of policy change. These extrapolations form the basis of the *Reference Case* against which other scenarios can be compared. Table 4.1 indicates the reference case for transport volume for the year 2020 based on recent transport statistics. The Reference Case is built upon fairly conservative assumptions that growth rates will decrease over time.

Table 4.1 Assumed Change in Transport Volume Between 1995 and 2020 in EU Member States, Norway, Switzerland and Turkey

	Mode	*Transport volume in 1995 (billion passenger-km / billion tonne-kilometres)*	*Actual change in transport volume 1970 - 1995*	*Assumed change in transport volume 1995 – 2020 (Reference Case)*
Passenger	Car	3590	125%	50%
	Aeroplane	400	250%	200%
	Bus	370	50%	30%
	Train	290	40%	20%
Freight	Lorry	1130	160%	100%
	Train	240	-5%	0%
	Inland Water	120	10%	10%
TOTAL		6140	107%	63%

Sources: ECMT (1997) and EUROSTAT (1997)

Generating Policy Targets

Policy targets specify desirable points in the future and form the basis for exploring the types of policies that might be used to reach these points. Policy targets need to be challenging but achievable, and in the context of this project relate to the achievement of *sustainable mobility* – defined as using substantially less (about 25 per cent) non renewable energy in 2020 in the transport sector than is used at present. Policy targets were generated on the basis of the *key issues* (see above) and existing (often shorter-term) policy targets which were made more challenging and extended to the year 2020. For example, there is currently a European carbon dioxide (CO_2) emissions target for 2010 (8 per cent reduction between 1990 and 2010). A demanding 25 per cent reduction in CO_2 emissions between 1995 and 2020 was set as a policy target. Each of the targets in the study was developed to relate to one or more of the main objectives of the Common Transport Policy (CTP). The targets were mainly quantitative, although this was primarily to indicate the orders of magnitude of change rather than absolute levels of change.

Policy Targets for Sustainable Mobility for 2020

Environmental Targets:

25% reduction of CO_2 emissions from 1995-2020.
80% reduction of NO_X emissions from 1995-2020.
No degradation of specially protected areas.
Minor (2%) increase of net infrastructure surface in Europe.

Regional Development Targets:

Improve relative accessibility of peripheral regions (both internal and external).
This general target includes cost and time, and allows for substitution of physical accessibility by telecommunications.

Economic Efficiency Targets:

Full cost coverage (including external costs) of transport under market or equivalent conditions.
Reduce public subsidies to all forms of transport to zero, except where clearly identified social equity objectives can be met.

Generating Images of the Future

Scenario-building requires a number of 'Images of the Future' to provide the basis for policy analysis under a range of alternative futures. Images of the Future specify a variety of assumptions about future conditions for policy-making. They contain assumptions about both 'Strategic' and 'Contextual' elements. Strategic elements are factors which policy decisions in the transport sector (and other related sectors) can directly influence (the rate of introduction of clean technology into vehicles for example). Contextual elements on the other hand are factors which have a direct effect on policy-making but are taken as given in the scenarios (for example, the level of cooperation between different levels of decision-making). A number of possible Images of the Future were identified by combining different strategic and contextual elements. From these, three quite distinctive ones were chosen for the context within which to examine policy options (Table 4.2). The main strategic elements concern the rate of introduction of new technology and the extent to which traffic growth and economic growth can be decoupled,[3] whilst the contextual elements concern the level of cooperation between different levels of decision-making.

Table 4.2 Nine Images of the Future obtained by Combining 'Contextual' and 'Strategic' Elements

		'Strategic' Elements ↓	
'Contextual' Elements ↓	Technology+/ Decoupling+++	Technology+++/ Decoupling+	Technology++/ Decoupling++
Local, Regional + EU cooperation	**D1**	T1	TD1
Global + EU cooperation	D2	**T2**	TD2
Local-Global cooperation	D3	T3	**TD3**

Source: Banister *et al.* (2000)

Three Images of the Future were chosen for further development (bold in Table 4.2):

- Image I EU Coordination of Active Citizens (D1) – this involves local, regional and EU cooperation, together with a high degree of decoupling and a lower level of technological innovation. This is a bottom-up approach and requires strong action and support from individual citizens and changes in lifestyles;
- Image II Global Cooperation for Sustainable Transport (T2) – this involves global and EU cooperation, together with a high level of technological innovation and some decoupling. This is a top-down approach to policy making, and depends on strong leadership from the EU and other national and international agencies; and
- Image III Accord on Sustainability (TD3) – this has both global and local cooperation and a moderate level of decoupling and technological innovation. There is a combination of action from both directions, top-down and bottom-up, so that the targets in this Image can be achieved.

Identifying Policy Measures

Having developed policy targets and specified Images of the Future, the next stage is to develop policy paths from the present (1995) to the future (2020) – this is achieved through a 'backcasting' process (see Dreborg, 1996; Robinson, 1990). Policy options for each of the Images of the Future must be consistent with the strategic and contextual elements and contribute to the achievement of one or more policy targets. A first stage in identifying possible policy options for different futures is the generation of a comprehensive inventory of policy measures, followed by an assessment of compatibility against the policy targets and the Images of the Future (for compatibility analysis see Dekker *et al.*, 1973). This procedure provides a list of possible policy measures for use in each Image of the Future.

Generating Policy Packages

Certain combinations of policies may work well together and give rise to synergies, leading to impacts greater than the sum of their individual parts. Other combinations of policies may conflict with each other. The generation of policy packages is based on maximising potential synergies and minimising potential conflicts. There is increasing recognition for the need to identify packages of measures rather than individual policies at the local, national and European level, if effective action is to be taken to achieve sustainable mobility.

A recent communication from the European Commission states that land-use policies are likely to be more effective in reducing CO_2 emissions if they are complemented by a package of transport policy measures (European Commission, 1998). Potential conflicts and synergies between policies can be explored using a matrix approach, as in the UK Department of Environment's guide to the environmental appraisal of development plans (UK Department of Environment, 1994).

In this project, a great deal of emphasis has been placed on strengthening this basic concept of policy packaging through the creative generation of composite groups of measures that complement each other and can strengthen the overall likelihood of achieving the targets set for the Images of the Future. The generation of successful policy packages also relies on identifying the timing of component policies and suitable initial measures. These initial measures should have widespread support and be fairly easy (and quick) to implement. Other measures outside the remit of the specific sector of policy being considered (transport in this case) might also be considered as part of the policy package, particularly where they have an important role in increasing the effectiveness of other policies in the package of measures. Ten of the policy packages are summarised below as illustrations: each follows a similar format of construction logic, description and main policy measures. Impacts on stakeholders were also considered for each of the policy packages but have not been included here for reasons of brevity (for more details, see Banister *et al.*, 2000).

Putting the Policy Packages Together in Policy Paths

The analysis framework allows us to conceive of a large number of policy Paths with different characteristics that could possibly be used for reaching the Images of the Future defined earlier. None of these Paths can be described in all its details here. Most measures allow for considerable flexibility in their application and continuous assessments would be necessary to regularly adjust the strategy and reach the policy targets. A further development of the approach described here is the development of a database management tool that allows new targets and policy options to be set, monitored and evaluated (Banister *et al.*, 2000). To give an impression of the possible variety of Paths and their respective difficulties, two different Paths have been constructed for two Images of the Future (Figure 4.2). Each of the two Images reflect a different starting point, one from the bottom up with a focus on decoupling strategies (Image I), and the other from the top down with a focus on technological strategies (Image II). In the previous section, we have outlined ten Policy Packages to give a feel for the range and depth of the alternatives available. From these packages, in combination with additional individual policy measures, it is possible to construct the policy Paths to meet the targets set for sustainable mobility (Table 4.3).

Policy Package 1: Ecological Tax Reform

Construction Logic

The transport market and our economy in general is distorted by externalities such as resource depletion and environmental damage that are not adequately reflected in overall costs, and taxation on labour has to compensate for a large share of externalities. An ecological tax reform is a way of internalising these external costs of transport.

Description

Internalising externalities is a basic market-oriented policy strategy to reduce unwanted side-effects of economic activities. An application of this approach to the transport sector alone would help to improve the structure of this sector, changing the nature of transported goods by only slightly increasing transport costs. An ecological tax reform applied to the whole of the economy would further lead to a general reduction of the material and energy intensity of our economies and reduce the need for transport. The ecological tax reform proposed in this package is a more general approach. The introduction of such a package will not only be motivated by considerations concerning transport policy. Trends in Europe over recent years indicate that this direction is quite probable.

Two important considerations in the ecological tax debate are the utilisation of the new tax revenues for alleviating fiscal pressure in other fields and the stability of tax revenues. Suitable bases for increased taxes on externalities are the consumption of energy and materials, CO_2 emissions and the use of land. The ecological tax reform proposed here is aimed at being fiscally neutral across society as a whole. That is, labour taxes should be reduced correspondingly. However, this interpretation does not imply that an Ecological Tax Reform should be fiscally neutral for every sector of society. On the contrary, the transport sector which is resource intensive would have to face substantially higher taxes, while labour intensive sectors would be taxed less.

Variant A In Image I, where cooperation at the global level is not prevalent, there is still some room for shifting taxes from labour to resources at the EU and/or the national level. In addition the revenues from local road pricing could be used to lower local labour costs in some cases. Congestion pricing will provide stable revenues.

Variant B This variant is aimed at Image II, in which comparatively high taxes could be levied on energy, material and CO_2 emissions since there is global cooperation on these issues. Global consensus makes it possible to levy even higher taxes on air transport (compared to Variant A) and to introduce taxes on fuel for shipping. This considerably enhances the base for the CO_2 tax and increases economic efficiency, so that a certain reduction of CO_2 can be accomplished at a much lower cost.

Main Policy Measures

- Lowering taxes on labour.
- Increasing taxes on energy, materials and CO_2 emissions at the national or the EU level (Variant A).
- Introducing local road pricing (Variant A).
- Imposing much higher taxes on energy, materials and CO_2 emissions at the national, EU or global level (Variant B).

Policy Package 2: Liveable Cities

Construction Logic

This package aims at making cities more attractive by reducing the dependence on the car. Strategic measures include better conditions for walking, cycling and public transport, decreased space for cars and parking, land use planning favouring mixed use areas, local services and amenities and decentralised concentration. Intensified IT plays an important role.

Description

The use of public space in cities is the main issue in this policy package. Reducing the volume and impact of car traffic has a high priority and is achieved by simultaneously improving alternatives to the car, limiting road and parking space for cars, limiting the environmental impact of motor vehicles (emissions, noise, accidents) and reducing the need for travel, particularly by the car.

The use of IT to replace trips plays a crucial role. Reduced space for cars is difficult to achieve without alternative access to the activity required. If public transport is the alternative, it cannot be fast and reliable if car use is not restrained (potentially resulting in a 'locked' position). IT presents a major opportunity to achieve an initial decrease of car travel which could make it possible to increase space for walking, cycling and public transport. Tele-working facilities and e-commerce play an important role.

Environmental zones are established in which only clean low speed cars are allowed access. The progressive extension of these areas create growing markets for such vehicles and new technologies such as electric, hybrid and fuel cell vehicles. Low speed zones in residential areas make walking and cycling more attractive. More generally, quality of life is increased in these areas.

Land-use planning measures, such as decentralised concentration and high densities around public transport nodes, enhance the efficiency of public transport. Less car parking space helps to facilitate higher density development which in turn helps to suppress car ownership. Mixing residential, working and shopping/service areas reduces the need for commuting and shopping travel by bringing origins and destinations closer together.

Main Policy Measures

- Improved conditions for walking, cycling and public transport.
- Progressive reduction of space available for cars.
- Low speed zones (30-40 km/h) in residential areas.
- Environmental zones reserved for clean slow speed vehicles.
- Schemes for car-pooling, car sharing and car rental.
- Improved opportunities for telecommuting, tele-services, tele-shopping and doorstep delivery.
- Land-use planning supporting decentralised concentration, mixed land uses, neighbourhood services and public transport.
- Provision of urban amenities and recreational facilities.
- More extensive and coordinated distribution systems, using cleaner vehicles.

Policy Package 3: Low Impact City Vehicles

Construction Logic

This policy package aims at a better match between transport demand and the type of vehicle used. This could significantly increase resource efficiency.

Description

The average all-purpose car is currently designed to transport five people with luggage at speeds above 100 kilometres per hour. The same car is used in city traffic for transporting one person at much lower speeds. High speed not only requires larger engines but also more complex, heavy construction. To better match performance with demand a new category of Low Impact Vehicles (LIV) is created. These vehicles would typically be small (2-seater) cars with a maximum speed of 50 km/h and low emission motors – mainly electric. They would be cheap, easy to handle, clean and require less parking space. Spaces perpendicular to the streets could be used. Lower safety requirements are acceptable when their use is restricted to areas where the maximum speed for all vehicles is 50 km/h. On the other hand their use could be allowed in environmental zones where only bikes and low impact freight vehicles have access. Lower driver requirements could widen their use to elderly and disabled people, thereby considerably enhancing their mobility.

However, even these vehicles have an excessive capacity. For one person with little luggage, a cycle may in most cases be sufficient. Therefore safety and convenience for cyclists is of prime importance in order to better adjust transport services to demand. The low speed zones is one measure that improves cycling conditions. Wider use of electric cycles may also be possible. High costs for car use, restricted parking space and different types of cars for different uses would raise the attractiveness of car rental and car sharing compared to traditional car ownership (additional incentives like a lower sales tax or subsidised parking space for non private cars could also be used). This in turn would lead to a more intensive use of equipment and to more efficient management of the car fleet. More durable vehicles (in terms of passenger kilometres), quicker innovation due to shorter life-cycles and lower material intensity would be additional positive effects.

Cheap rental of LIVs would be an ideal complement to fast public transport in less dense areas. With changing transport habits and growing markets, LIVs could even become a viable option for local transport in rural areas.

Main Policy Measures

- Introduction of a new category in vehicle registrations for Low Impact Vehicles (LIV).
- Measures to support car pooling, car sharing and car rental.
- Action to promote very efficient and clean vehicles for taxi-fleets, rental-fleets and public car fleets.
- Dedicated parking space for LIVs and a stepwise reduction of parking space for conventional cars.
- Low speed zones in residential areas (30-40 km/h).
- Environmental zones only for very clean vehicles in central areas.
- Improved conditions for walking, cycling and public transport.

Policy Package 4: Long Distance Links – Substituting for Air Travel

Construction Logic

This policy package is directed at reducing long-distance passenger travel by substituting highly energy intensive modes with less energy intensive modes and other forms of communication. It also involves the reduction of travel distances.

Description

Long-range leisure travel and airborne freight transport is growing at about 5-6 per cent per annum. As important economic structures rely on cheap air transport, attempts to internalise at least a part of the considerable externalities will become increasingly difficult in the years to come. Rapid action to correct market distortions and to provide alternatives is therefore necessary. However, additional measures may also be needed to limit growth of air travel.

Given existing capacity problems, restrictive policies on airports may offer another opportunity. Although environmental pressures near airports are high and expansion plans always cause strong local resistance, employment opportunities often lead to decisions in favour of further airport development. Restrictive policies at the local and regional level would require a high degree of coordination. Limitations within the European flight control system are more promising. Among other transport modes, only rail has the potential to offer a serious alternative. Faster rail services on existing infrastructure (with tilting technology for example), technical harmonisation, organisational cooperation and improved conditions for competition, Europe-wide operating carriers could all help make better use of unexploited potentials on long-distance routes. Considerable innovation for improving passenger comfort, flexibility, freight tracking and handling will be necessary. The present conservative rail culture needs to change (perhaps quite radically) in order to be able to answer to these challenges. Long range air transport of some goods may also be substituted by maritime transport.

Main Policy Measures

- Steadily increasing tax on air fuel (possibly implemented inside the EU).
- Restrictive policy on airport development.
- Organisational improvement of European railway links (including EU regulations enhancing co-operation between operators, providing a framework for competing and European wide acting rail carriers).
- Technical harmonisation of European railways.
- Better use of existing rail infrastructure (achieved through innovative rolling stock, electronic controls and organisational measures).
- Demonstration of teleconferencing facilities.
- Promotion of local leisure activities.
- Making residential areas and their surroundings more attractive for leisure and recreation.

Policy Package 5: Fair and Efficient Distribution of Mobility – Tradable Mobility Credits

Construction Logic

Increasing transport costs creates social and spatial equity problems. Differentiated approaches are required which avoid these problems. This policy package provides a flexible solution combining simple market mechanisms with new information technology.

Description

Spatial equity problems might be addressed by differentiating mileage-related taxes between different areas: urban areas will require higher rates than rural ones. Differentiated electronic road pricing is one potential solution to this problem. Where revenues from road pricing are hypothecated, local authorities would be free to fix road fees which would depend on variables such as the level of congestion, air quality, vehicle occupancy, and so on.

Effective incentives for decreasing overall mileage cannot be directly coupled with monetary costs because this would create unacceptable social inequities. Introducing 'tradable mobility credits' (TMCs) might solve the social distribution problem: every person gets a limited number of credits for paying road fees and other mobility services at reasonable prices, corresponding to slightly less than present average mileage. Establishing a market for these credits will lead to higher costs for those who travel further and to extra income for those driving less. A similar system was intensively discussed in Switzerland in the 1980s and numerous variations on such a system are conceivable.

Encouraging the use of public transport may be coupled with a similar system of TMCs as they could also be used for paying public transport services. This would effectively decrease car mileage if public transport is attractive. Smart-cards would present an excellent form for realising a system of TMCs. The cards could easily be sold (or recharged) by public authorities according to allocated quotas. These could also be used for the payment of road pricing fees, public transport journeys and traded between individuals. A strong differentiation in taxes (road pricing fees) for vehicles depending on geographical area and vehicle emissions becomes easier to implement with such a system. The introduction of TMC could be a strong incentive for the use of clean vehicles such as proposed in the 'Low Impact City Vehicles' policy package.

Main Policy Measures

- Replacement of car taxes and basic insurance (except CO_2 tax on fuel) by differentiated road pricing.
- Introduction of Tradable Mobility Credits (TMC) for the payment of road fees.
- Extension of the TMC system to public transport journeys.

Policy Package 6: Promoting Subsidiarity in Freight Flows

Construction Logic

Policies for decoupling freight transport from economic growth cannot limit themselves to traditional transport policy. Structural approaches are required to reduce the travel distance of goods. This policy package focuses on these approaches.

Description

Reducing the travel distance of goods might be achieved through a strategy of 'regionalising' material flows. As different approaches are needed at different scales for different products, subsidiarity may be a better term to use. The policies address the spatial patterns of production and consumption and the impacts are only likely in the medium and long term.

Information systems and declaration requirements are developed by public authorities in order to allow for responsible consumer choices. European agricultural policy is reformed to promote opportunities for purchasing regional products. Changes in land-use planning policies create advantages of more flexible small-scale structures of production and consumption. In terms of the production, economic development policies at all levels encourage regional networking and cooperation of companies. Differentiated pricing of transport according to regional contexts (by differentiated road pricing for example) widen the margins of action for attributing real costs.

Variant A This is mainly lifestyle and market-oriented in which price mechanisms are widely used. In agricultural policy, regional marketing is encouraged by differentiated subsidies. Structural development programmes favour companies that use local products and services. Road pricing and increases in transport costs also play a role. There is a strong information campaign aimed at changing lifestyles and consumer preferences.

Variant B This has a stronger emphasis on regulation and service-oriented policies. Here price mechanisms are less important. A strong emphasis is placed on the rapid introduction of product labelling, showing the origin of the product and its transport content. Standards for public procurement also play an important role.

Main Policy Measures

- Promotion of 'regional' consumer markets through public awareness and information campaigns, reform of the Common Agricultural Policy, product labelling, flexible subsidiarity in internal market regulations and changes in land use planning policies.
- Promotion of company networking and industrial districts through economic incentives, regulation and the provision of specialised infrastructure (such as training centres).
- Information systems on the transport content of all goods (parallel to the Environmental Management and Audit Scheme - EMAS).
- Transport impact assessment for major political decisions.
- Differentiated road pricing and increases in road transport costs, particularly for road transport in sensitive areas (Variant A).
- Changes in public procurement to allow exchange of knowledge and information, whilst limiting flows of goods in the spirit of local production and subsidiarity (Variant B).

Policy Package 7: Promoting Dematerialisation of the Economy

Construction Logic

A basic strategy for reducing the need for freight transport is to reduce the material throughput of the economy. This requires approaches which go far beyond traditional transport policy and these form the focus of this policy package.

Description

Three sub-strategies can be used to promote dematerialisation if the economy: substituting products with services; increasing the durability of products; and miniaturising products. This policy package addresses all three strategies.

The substitution of products by services can be encouraged by changes in the economy. Shifting the tax burden from labour to material consumption, shifting development policy priorities away from infrastructure and hardware investments to the improvement of the human and social capital could have a significant impact. A series of more specific changes (such as labour regulations, insurance for borrowed or rented equipment and professional service standards for example) could support a general shift in the service dimension of consumption.

The internalisation of external environmental costs will help to curb the material intensity of the economy. Full life-cycle responsibility of manufacturers for their products will increase the durability of products and stimulate the more intensive use of them. Systems for sharing and rental of equipment will lead to more intensive use, and this may in turn lead to technical development towards more durability.

Encouraging car-free lifestyles by improving public transport, facilitating car sharing and rental or providing home delivery services would not only reduce private car use and ownership but may also change the attitude towards the everyday consumption of materials.

Variant A This variant is mainly market and lifestyle-oriented, in which economic policy plays a dominant role.

Variant B This variant relies more on regulation and public services. It emphasises manufacturer responsibility for recycling and disposal of goods after use, the introduction of increasingly stringent standards and a shift in structural development policies towards human and social capital investments.

Main Policy Measures

- Incentives for the rental and sharing of goods and services – tax and other polices aimed at encouraging hardware investments are linked to incentives that allow intensive use of equipment.
- The tax burden is shifted from labour to materials, energy and emissions of CO_2 and European taxes on energy and waste policies are coordinated (Variant A).
- Development policy (including structural funds) give priorities to human resources (Variant B).
- Life-cycle product responsibility for manufacturers is introduced, making manufacturers responsible for all recycling, dismantling and/or disposal costs of their products after use (Variant B).
- Standards which affect material consumption (such as cars and building) are revised (Variant B).

Policy Package 8: Minimising Specific Emissions

Construction Logic

This policy package aims at a significant reduction of specific emissions from road and air transport. It is particularly intended for Image II, where the all purpose car has a strong role.

Description

Emission standards are related to specific test cycles but deviations from these occur in practice due to high speeds, accelerations, cold starts and other causes. Actual emissions are in fact often much higher than those observed in test cycles, particularly for conventional cars. Stricter emission standards only affect a (decreasing) part of actual emissions and may not necessarily be the most cost-effective measure.

To ensure durability of exhaust treatment systems manufacturers must have long-term responsibility for their proper functioning. Regular control of emission levels should be made compulsory. An option may be to use on-board engine diagnostics which are now common in new cars. Information about the benefits of a smooth driving style should be disseminated. Education of drivers combined with economic incentives for fuel efficient driving could have significant benefits both for CO_2 and other emissions.

If diesel engines do not comply with the strong measures needed to reach emission targets, they must be phased out from use in city traffic. This does not seem unlikely although it is difficult to predict technology development in this area. They may still be used for inter-city freight but not in local distribution.

Hybrid vehicles, which are less sensitive to driving style, could be promoted by more flexible certification levels or by lower sales taxes for example. All measures leading to reduced vehicle weight will also have beneficial effects on emissions. However, more fuel-efficient engines do not necessarily imply lower emissions. Higher combustion temperatures may decrease fuel consumption but, ceteris paribus, tend to increase emissions of NO_X. This is especially problematic for aircraft because treatment of exhaust gases is not possible.

Main Policy Measures

- Long-term producer responsibility for emission levels.
- Information regarding the effect of driving style on emissions and fuel consumption.
- Introduction of more realistic test cycles.
- Promotion of hybrid vehicles, which do not have the same problem with off-cycle emissions.
- Reduction of the sulphur content of diesel fuel.
- Fee rates on new cars, dependant on emissions and fuel consumption.

Policy Package 9: Resource Efficient Freight Transport

Construction Logic

This policy package aims to increase the resource efficiency of freight transport and reduce haul distance.

Description

This policy package is mainly intended for Image II. In order to meet sustainability targets, the use of combined transport is increased considerably. Promoting European standards and technologies for automatic flexible freight handling and tracing will therefore have a high priority.

Substituting individual shopping travel by home-delivery is another important strategy in this package. Coordination of distribution including home delivery will be encouraged in order to increase load factors. Information technologies and e-commerce will contribute significantly to this. Integrated information systems may lead to shorter supply chains.

Integrated logistic services between the production and distribution stages of products will be based on information systems. An important political task will be to support the development of standardised interfaces that ensure interoperability of different company systems in order to avoid new monopolies, ensure the access of SMEs to such systems and improve the acceptance of these technologies.

Two variants of this package have been developed: Variant A is more market-oriented. An important component is increased costs for road transport. In variant B, which is more regulation and public service oriented, direct support for railways is more important.

Main Policy Measures

Variant A

- Support for the development of technologies and standards for automatic flexible freight handling and tracing.
- Promotion of integrated logistical systems.
- European ruling on common standards for railways, improved regulatory framework for Europe-wide operating carriers.
- Introduction of mileage-related taxes for road freight vehicles which raise transport costs (achieved with GPS-systems) - taxes may depend on time of the day or geographical area (see also policy package 5 - fair and efficient distribution of mobility).

Variant B

- Standards for automatic flexible freight handling and tracing (hardware and software).
- Introduction of an IT-system for the exchange of logistics related information for the operation of integrated logistics systems by companies or networks.
- European ruling on common standards for railways.
- Public investment in additional infrastructure, including tracks and intermodal nodes.
- Improvements to the regulatory framework for Europe-wide operating carriers .
- Priority given to home-delivery using clean vehicles in local traffic management schemes.

Policy Package 10: Customer Friendly Transport Services

Construction Logic

This policy package aims at making public transport and intermodal travel more convenient. Intensive use of IT makes public transport more flexible and accessible.

Description

Technological innovation allows the development of personal communicators with smart card facilities. Each person will have a dedicated multipurpose personal communicator (MPC) that can be used for all forms of communication and information services. The MPC will have real-time information on travel services and facilities, including multimodal travel so that journeys can be planned in advance and modified as circumstances arise.

This requires co-operation of all public transport providers so that door-to-door journeys can be booked with a single transaction. Car rental firms should also be integrated into the system. The intention is to encourage multimodal journeys which are flexible and convenient. Standardisation and full compatibility between functions and locations is necessary. The MPC has an advisory role in that it can suggest alternatives, in terms of where to go, when to go, special deals, or even linking with other people. The MPC can also be used for individual banking facilities, shopping, booking leisure and other activities.

Main Policy Measures

- European standards for mobility information between transport companies and personal communication devices.
- European public transport information system, combining local, regional, national and European systems.
- Increased flexibility of local public transport with the help of information systems.
- Priority for public transport in local transport planning.
- Improved opportunities for cycling and walking.
- Luggage deposit facilities at major public transport interchanges.
- Improved integration of public transport, taxis, car rental, and car sharing.
- Car pooling with the help of integrated information, booking and payment systems.

Figure 4.2 Policy Paths – Uncertainty and Choice

<table>
<tr><td></td><td></td><td></td><td colspan="2">UNCERTAINTY:
Different futures</td></tr>
<tr><td></td><td></td><td></td><td>Image I:
Focus on
decoupling,
Bottom-up</td><td>Image II:
Focus on
technology,
Top-down</td></tr>
<tr><td>CHOICE:</td><td>→</td><td>Market and lifestyle orientation</td><td>Path 1.1</td><td>Path 2.1</td></tr>
<tr><td>Different Strategies</td><td>→</td><td>Regulation and service orientation</td><td>Path 1.2</td><td>Path 2.2</td></tr>
</table>

Paths Towards Image I – Path 1.1

This Policy Path includes five of the Policy Packages developed in the earlier part of this chapter:

- Ecological Tax Reform Variant A (Policy Package 1);
- Long Distance Links – Substituting Air Travel (Policy Package 4);
- Fair and Efficient Distribution of Mobility (Policy Package 5);
- Promoting Subsidiarity in Freight Flows Variant A (Policy Package 6A);
- Promoting Dematerialisation of the Economy Variant A (Policy Package 7A).

In Image I, transport intensity is considerably lower than today. Decoupling strategies are therefore most important in the policy Paths. Both Paths 1.1 and 1.2 rely mainly on bottom-up initiatives. This is slightly more pronounced in Path 1.2 where local initiatives on local/city level are crucial, not least to achieve more 'liveable cities' with diminished reliance on car travel. In Path 1.1, there is greater emphasis on using market incentives, while the dominant policy orientations in Path 1.2 are regulation and public services. In both cases, policy is intended to facilitate environmentally benign lifestyles (common in Image I – see Tables 4.3 and 4.4).

Table 4.3 Combining the Policy Packages into Paths

		Path 1.1	Path 1.2	Path 2.1	Path 2.2
	Image	**I**	**I**	**II**	**II**
	Lifestyle	X		X	
	Market	X		X	
	Regulation		X		X
	Services		X		X
1A	Ecological Tax Reform A	X			
1B	Ecological Tax Reform B			X	
2	Liveable Cities		X		
3	Low Impact City Vehicles		X		
4	Long Distance Links - Substituting for Air Travel	X	X		
5	Fair and Efficient Distribution of Mobility – Tradable Mobility Credits	X			
6A	Promoting Subsidiarity in Freight Flows A	X			
6B	Promoting Subsidiarity in Freight Flows B		X		
7A	Promoting Dematerialisation of the Economy A	X			
7B	Promoting Dematerialisation of the Economy B		X		
8	Minimising Specific Emissions			X	X
9A	Resource Efficient Freight Transport A			X	
9B	Resource Efficient Freight Transport B				X
10	Customer Friendly Transport Services			X	X

Table 4.4 Path 1.1: Focus on Decoupling and Bottom-up: Market and Lifestyle Orientation

Policy Packages		Targets	Key elements	transport type: Passenger: urban	Passenger: inter-urban	Passenger: rural	Passenger: long range	Freight: urban	Freight: short-range	Freight: long-range	Policy Orientation	Government level	time horizon: Start	time horizon: Effect
1 A	Ecological Tax reform A	ENV EFF REG	DPA DFR	x	x	x	x	x	x	x	M	EUR NAT LOC	2000 2010	2010 2020
4	Long Distance Links – Substituting Air Travel	ENV EFF	DPA ORG				x			x	M R L	EUR NAT REG LOC	2000	2010
5	Fair and Efficient Distribution of Mobility	EFF ENV	DPA ORG	x	x						M	EUR NAT REG LOC	2010	2020
6 A	Promoting Subsidiarity in Freight Flows A	ENV EFF	DFR					x	x	x	M L	EUR NAT REG LOC	2000	2020
7 A	Promoting Dematerialisation of the Economy A	EFF ENV	DFR					x	x	x	M L	EUR NAT REG LOC	2000	2020
	Path 1.1	**ENV** **EFF** **REG**	**DPA** **DFR** **ORG**	**x**	**x**	**x**	**x**	**x**	**x**	**x**	**MM** **LL** **R**	**EUR** **NAT** **REG** **LOC**	**2000**	**2020**

Targets	ENV	Environment	Key Strategy Elements	TEC	Technology
	EFF	Efficiency		DPA	Decoupling Passengers
	REG	Regional Development		DFR	Decoupling Freight
Government Level	LOC	Local		ORG	Organisation
	REG	Regional	Policy Orientation	L	Lifestyle
	NAT	National		M	Market
	EUR	European		R	Regulation
	GLO	Global		S	Service

The widely used market incentives, such as local road pricing, could induce distributional conflicts, if complementary measures were not also introduced. If cars become cleaner and more fuel efficient, it is likely that the least affluent (those with the oldest vehicles), will have to pay the highest costs in any road pricing system. In the context of an ecological tax reform, this can be compensated through labour tax reductions. Another solution which has been included is the introduction of tradable mobility credits. However, the introduction of this would probably take some time, so that careful introduction of measures in the transition phase is very important. A wide range of policy measures and packages make it more probable that the targets can be reached. However, efforts to reduce freight transport intensity are essential and will not be an easy task. Some elements of the 'liveable cities' Policy Package could be added to help through the transition phase before the more market-based measures have an impact.

Paths Towards Image I – Path 1.2

This Policy Path again includes five of the Policy Packages developed in the earlier part of this chapter:

- Liveable Cities (Policy Package 2);
- Low Impact City Vehicles (Policy Package 3);
- Long Distance Links – Substituting Air Travel (Policy Package 4);
- Promoting Subsidiarity in Freight Flows Variant B (Policy Package 6B);
- Promoting Dematerialisation of the Economy Variant B (Policy Package 7B).

Regulation allows for more differentiated interventions than market-oriented policy measures but careful evaluation of the results is necessary to avoid unwanted effects. Urban policies are very important in this path.

Table 4.5 Path 1.2: Focus on Decoupling and Bottom-up: Regulation, Public Service and Lifestyle Orientation

	Policy Packages	Targets	Key elements	Transport Type: Passenger				Transport Type: Freight			Policy Orientation	Government level	Time Horizon	
				urban	inter-urban	rural	long range	urban	short-range	long-range			Start	Effect
2	Liveable Cities	ENV EFF	ORG DPA DFR	x x	x	x		x x	x		R S	LOC REG EUR	2000	2010
3	Low Impact City Vehicles	ENV EFF	TEC ORG	x				x			R S M	EUR NAT LOC	2000 2010	2010 2020
4	Long Distance Links – Substituting Air Travel	ENV EFF	DPA ORG				x			x	M R L	EUR NAT REG LOC	2000	2010
6 B	Promoting Subsidiarity in Freight Flows A	ENV EFF	DFR					x	x	x	R L M	EUR NAT REG LOC	2000	2020
7 B	Promoting Dematerialisation of the Economy A	EFF ENV	DFR					x	x	x	R L M	EUR NAT REG LOC	2000	2020
	Path 1.2	**ENV EFF REG**	**DPA DFR ORG**	x	x	x	x	x	x	x	**R S LL M**	**EUR NAT REG LOC**	**2000**	**2020**

Targets	ENV	Environment	Key Strategy Elements	TEC	Technology
	EFF	Efficiency		DPA	Decoupling Passengers
	REG	Regional Development		DFR	Decoupling Freight
Government Level	LOC	Local		ORG	Organisation
	REG	Regional	Policy Orientation	L	Lifestyle
	NAT	National		M	Market
	EUR	European		R	Regulation
	GLO	Global		S	Service

Comparison of Paths 1.1 and 1.2 (Image I)

The outcome of both Paths is not very different. The widespread use of market instruments in Path 1.1 may cause less resistance than the many regulations in Path 1.2, which would require extensive debate at the local level. As local regulation, especially in urban transport policy, plays a more important role in Path 1.2, it is a more bottom-up approach than Path 1.1, which requires a good framework for road pricing at the European level. In both Paths, old material-intensive industries will have to make considerable changes to be able to adapt and this will be a source of resistance. As these industries are often regionally concentrated, this may also cause political tensions between regions. On the other hand, knowledge-based and service-oriented industries will clearly be on the positive side. Both strategies correspond to an acceleration of the structural changes that are already going on. With the growing strength of the service sector and IT industries, chances of political feasibility for these policies will increase. Employment arguments will play a major role in the public debate on these policies. Therefore it will be very important to give evidence for new employment opportunities arising from these strategies in both Policy Paths.

Paths Towards Image II – Policy Path 2.1

This Policy Path includes four of the Policy Packages developed in the earlier part of this chapter:

- Ecological Tax Reform Variant B (Policy Package 1B);
- Minimising Specific Emissions (Policy Package 8);
- Resource Efficient Freight Transport Variant A (Policy Package 9A);
- Customer-Friendly Transport Services (Policy Package 10).

As this package uses mainly market mechanisms, the 'Minimising specific emissions' Policy Package may be enhanced by including the introduction of tradable permits or feebates for new cars and aircraft and according to fuel consumption or weight. Decoupling strategies may be too weak for achieving the targets alone. Therefore some elements of other Policy Packages (such as 'Promoting Subsidiarity in Freight Flows' and 'Promoting Dematerialisation of the Economy' developed for Image I) could be included, particularly if it is realised that the basic group of four Policy Packages is not sufficient to achieve the policy targets (Table 4.6).

Table 4.6 Path 2.1: Focus on Technology and Top-down: Market Orientation

Policy Packages		Targets	Key elements	Transport Type: Passenger: urban	Passenger: inter-urban	Passenger: rural	Passenger: long range	Freight: urban	Freight: short-range	Freight: long-range	Policy Orientation	Government level	Time Horizon: Start	Time Horizon: Effect
1 B	Ecological Tax reform B	ENV EFF	DPA DFR	x	x	x	x	x	x	x	M	EUR NAT	2000 2010	2010 2020
8	Minimising Specific Emissions	ENV EFF	TEC ORG	x	x	x	x	x	x	x	M R	EUR	2000	2010
9 A	Resource Efficient Freight Transport A	EFF ENV	ORG					x	x	x	M R	EUR NAT REG	2000	2020
10	Customer Friendly Transport Services	EFF ENV	TEC ORG	x	x						R S M L	EUR NAT REG LOC	2000	2010
	Path 2.1	**ENV EFF REG**	**DPA DFR ORG**	**x**	**x**	**x**	**x**	**x**	**x**	**x**	**M R S L**	**EUR NAT REG LOC**	**2000**	**2020**

Targets	ENV	Environment	Key Strategy Elements	TEC	Technology
	EFF	Efficiency		DPA	Decoupling passengers
	REG	Regional Development		DFR	Decoupling freight
Government Level	LOC	Local		ORG	Organisation
	REG	Regional	Policy Orientation	L	Lifestyle
	NAT	National		M	Market
	EUR	European		R	Regulation
	GLO	Global		S	Service

Paths Towards Image II – Policy Path 2.2

This Policy Path includes three of the Policy Packages developed in the earlier part of this chapter:

- Minimising Specific Emissions (Policy Package 8);
- Resource Efficient Freight Transport Variant B (Policy Package 9B);
- Customer-Friendly Transport Services (Policy Package 10).

In order to strengthen the ‘Minimising Specific Emissions’ Policy Package, a regulation-oriented approach might also be included, including:

- CAFE standards or uniform reductions of average specific fuel consumption for cars and aircraft;
- Introduction of methanol, by, for example, funding research and development and by public procurement of methanol vehicles.

As in Path 2.1, the decoupling strategies may be too weak for achieving the policy targets with just the Policy Packages included here. Therefore some elements of other packages (such as ‘Promoting Subsidiarity in Freight Flows’ and ‘Promoting Dematerialisation of the Economy’ Policy Packages developed for Image I) could also be included here (Table 4.7).

Table 4.7 Path 2.2: Focus on Technology and Top-down: Regulation and Public Service Orientation

Policy Packages		Targets	Key elements	Transport Type: Passenger: urban	Passenger: inter-urban	Passenger: rural	Passenger: long range	Freight: urban	Freight: short-range	Freight: long-range	Policy Orientation	Government level	Time Horizon: Start	Time Horizon: Effect
8	Minimising Specific Emissions	ENV EFF	TEC ORG	x	x	x	x	x	x	x	R	EUR	2000	2010
9B	Resource Efficient Freight Transport B	EFF ENV	ORG					x	x	x	R S	EUR NAT REG	2000	2020
10	Customer Friendly Transport Services	EFF ENV	TEC ORG	x	x						R S M L	EUR NAT REG LOC	2000	2010
	Path 2.2	**ENV EFF REG**	**DPA DFR ORG**	x	x	x	x	x	x	x	**R S M L**	**EUR NAT REG LOC**	**2000**	**2020**

Targets	ENV	Environment	Key Strategy Elements	TEC	Technology
	EFF	Efficiency		DPA	Decoupling Passengers
	REG	Regional Development		DFR	Decoupling Freight
Government Level	LOC	Local		ORG	Organisation
	REG	Regional	Policy Orientation	L	Lifestyle
	NAT	National		M	Market
	EUR	European		R	Regulation
	GLO	Global		S	Service

Comparison of Paths 2.1 and 2.2 (Image II)

Paths 2.1 and 2.2 are both directed towards Image II. Although some policy elements are similar they have quite different policy orientations. The general potential for decoupling is better in Path 2.1, mainly due to ecological tax reform which also affects transport volumes. It is uncertain whether the same technological progress can be achieved if market mechanisms are not widely used as in Path 2.1. The consequence is that it will be impossible to reach the targets by following Path 2.2 without introducing a renewable fuel, such as methanol, on a wide scale. In Path 2.1, there is some chance that this step could be postponed. This, however, appears to be a rather costly strategy. As measures for decreased fuel consumption of new cars and aircraft, such as CAFE or uniform relative reductions, are relatively inefficient from an economic point of view, it may be concluded that it will be significantly more costly to follow Path 2.2 as compared to Path 2.1.

In both cases, rather severe measures will be necessary in order to reach targets in time. In Path 2.1, which relies more on price mechanisms, this may also lead to distributional problems. However, measures such as the tradable mobility credits in Path 2.1 does not seem to have much chance in the general political climate in Image II. Some elements of ecological tax reform, as currently discussed in many European countries, will be necessary in both Paths. Furthermore, it is assumed that tele-activities will develop substantially in the years to come and provide some alternative to physical transport.

Conclusions on Policy Paths

It has only been possible to sketch the character and briefly compare the different policy Paths in this chapter. However, it is clear that there are different ways to reach the policy targets for sustainable mobility. Different political constituencies with preferences for different policy orientations may all find their path to a sustainable mobility future. This opens opportunities for political agreement about targets without already defining the specific strategies how to reach them. However, the Paths have also shown that the technically oriented top-down approaches in Image II open fewer options for a flexible policy than the more comprehensive approaches that are possible in Image I.

Important lessons must be learnt from this process of policy packaging and the development of Policy Paths. It is noticeable that there are some common elements to several Paths. These common elements should perhaps be given special attention, as they are likely to be components in all futures that might help achieve more sustainable mobility. These common elements should be implemented early, as they will also have greatest impact and need to be carefully structured so that their expected impacts match their actual outcomes.

Carrying out Validation and Assessment

The process of validation and assessment is crucial to understanding the role of different policy measures and packages in alternative futures. This can be carried out in a number of ways using workshops, interviews and/or questionnaires (further discussion of these techniques can be found in Becker, 1997). All three of these techniques were used to carry out validation and assessment of the policy scenarios and the policy packages in this research (Figure 4.1). These techniques allowed exploration of issues, such as:

- the levels of acceptability of different policy measures and paths amongst decision-makers and transport users;
- potential barriers and obstacles of individual policy measures and policy packages;
- possible regional differences in impacts of different policies;
- the robustness of different policy options under different possible futures.

Summary

This account of scenario-building has attempted to encapsulate the main features of a process which might be used in other sectors of policy analysis, i.e., not just in the transport sector. Very few other policy scenario studies appear to have developed such a detailed and systematic approach. The eight stages of the process outlined above may therefore be a useful guide for the generation of policy scenarios in other studies. In this chapter, we have outlined in brief the early parts of the research covered in stages one to five, with a clear and detailed focus of the innovative extended backcasting methodology to detail the policy packaging process and the establishment of paths from now (1995) to our future year (2020). A full and comprehensive discussion of all the elements of the scenario building process is given in Banister *et al.* (2000).

Policy Conclusions

One of the main aims of this research has been to advise decision makers on possible policy packages to achieve sustainable mobility in Europe in 2020. Here we highlight some of the main results of the process to complement the detailed description of the policy packages and the policy paths.

Decoupling

If transport is to become more sustainable, then positive policy action is required along two main dimensions, namely technology and decoupling (Table 4.2). Even if the strongest priority is given to technology, this is not sufficient on its own to achieve the targets or Images. This conclusion is based on the notion that transport volumes, both passenger and freight, are expected to continue to grow. Strong decoupling in both the passenger and the freight sectors is therefore also essential to achieve sustainable mobility. This means that a decrease in transport intensity of Gross Domestic Product (GDP) is needed.

- A wide variety of policies is available for decoupling both passenger and freight transport from economic growth. This seems possible without limiting economic growth (further analysis is however needed), but policies would need to accelerate some existing trends of structural change and lifestyle change. However, as decoupling can be regarded as a shift in the transport paradigm, such changes may result in opposition from those who perceive they may lose from these changes. Accelerated decoupling strategies will bring benefits to the overall economy, but may temporarily increase political conflicts.
- To reduce these political conflicts, two important further actions are required. First, the nature of decoupling and its pivotal role in achieving sustainable mobility needs to be presented to, and discussed among decision makers at all levels. Secondly, the implications of decoupling have to be discussed with the public as well as with business and industry to think through the necessary actions in terms of travel and activity patterns. The first is an information activity, the second a public acceptance activity.
- This conclusion is already generating considerable interest in Europe. The achievement of targets for sustainable mobility requires a fundamental reassessment of the links between transport growth and economic growth.

Technology

Technology has a key role to play in moving policy in the direction of sustainable mobility, particularly in the longer term. In the shorter term firm action and direction is required at the European level to promote best practice and to help push particular technological paths. For example, should research be directed at new technology (hydrogen) or at an intermediate technology (methanol); what should be the role of diesel fuel in urban areas; and how can cleaner technology and fuels be introduced in cities, together with the necessary infrastructure? These actions need to be accompanied by strong decoupling. It may be necessary to protect the market in the short term so that the appropriate conditions for technological innovation are encouraged. In the longer term there should be an open market with pricing and regulation determining which technologies are consistent with sustainable mobility.

Action is Needed Both Within and Outside the Common Transport Policy

The analysis of different aspects of decoupling transport volume growth from economic growth clearly shows that a Common Transport Policy must be supplemented by measures outside the transport sector (and consequently outside the CTP). Some of these non-transport policy actions are related to structural changes in society (like the consequences of IT or increased interest in local-regional markets). Other actions are a matter of more general macro-economic policy intervention (like a tax shift from labour to resource use). Some developments in line with decoupling will be driven without policy interventions (like the rapid growth in the use of information technology). Here actions may be needed to cope with drawbacks, like increased urban sprawl. Increasingly, the solutions to the problems raised by sustainable transport extend beyond the traditional boundaries of transport analysis.

The Time Element

The time horizon taken for the scenario-building process is 2020, but this is only an intermediate stage in the process towards sustainability. As decoupling is a necessity and those measures often have a long lead-time (particularly with the use of market based measures), it is important that they start early. Technology will also be important, but measures can be taken stepwise. However, this does not mean that no action should be taken now as clear guidance is required on standards for technology (e.g. on fuel consumption and emissions), and on whether investment should take place in intermediate technology (e.g. methanol) or whether encouragement should be given to 'jump' to the ecotechnology (e.g. hydrogen fuel cells). The uncertainty about changes over time should be recognised so that flexibility permits modifications in measures and Targets. The issues raised here are crucial to the whole arguments relating to sustainability. Actions are required now if the challenging targets are to be achieved, not just within the EU but more generally. Failure to act now means that there is no chance of achieving sustainability by 2020.

The Regional Dimension

Much of the discussion here and at the validation sessions has concentrated on the city and the urban transport problems. Different problems exist in rural areas and in the peripheral regions of Europe (including the CEEC and CIS countries). The differences in conditions across the EU and wider Europe requires different measures, different processes of implementation and phasing. Uniform policies concerning regulations and taxes do not produce optimal results and can create unnecessary conflicts. Ways must be found to adapt measures to local conditions while maintaining overall EU targets and consistency of policies. Differentiated road pricing may provide a useful approach to achieve Targets with regionally based policies. In Europe, the regional dimension is of key importance as much of the budget is invested in those locations seen as disadvantaged.

The Trans-European Networks (TENs)

The TENs form an important component in the achievement of cohesion within Europe, but in terms of sustainable mobility, their role may be more limited. The main purpose of the TENs in the context of sustainable mobility is to achieve a significant modal shift from road (and air) to rail. If the TENs only increase the supply of transport and encourage more travel overall, then sustainable mobility targets will not be achieved. This means that the TENs must form part of an integrated transport strategy that packages increases in supply of rail with reductions in supply of other modes. The opportunities for the TENs are substantial, particularly if they include the new telecommunications networks which can reduce levels of physical movement. The problems of the TENs extend to the role for freight transfer to rail, and the question of European standardisation and harmonisation in the freight sector. Consideration should also be given to designing more regional and locally based networks that fed into and are complementary to the TENs. This would allow subsidiarity, with local and regional networks being decided at the appropriate decision level.

Air Travel

The dramatic increase in passenger and freight travel by air (about 6 per cent growth per annum or a doubling every 12 years) is a major constraint on the achievement of sustainable mobility targets, as it is both long distance and energy intensive. Although not central to this research project, this growth makes decoupling much harder. The development of new technology with larger aircraft and later hydrogen powered engines may help to reduce energy use and emissions per passenger kilometre but the effects of certain emissions at high altitudes is still not clear. The volume growth has also to be addressed. At present the air industry benefits from an advantageous tax situation as there is no tax on kerosene. Equal tax treatment would help raise costs and prices in the air sector, but more action is required. The low cost of air travel on shorter European routes may also affect the potential for high-speed rail. But, if rail takes over from shorter air routes, it may only release more air space for long distance air travel. Achievement of sustainable mobility objectives requires careful consideration of the future of air transport (Banister, 1999).

Support for Sustainable Mobility

Throughout this project, questions have been raised about the nature and scale of change required to achieve sustainable mobility. It is essential to achieve support both for the principles and for the practice of sustainable mobility. Many people are constrained by current value systems and conventions. In the validation process it has been found that there is strong support for the principles of sustainable mobility, but equally strong barriers to real change. It has also been found that there are different views from the EU countries and professions, with no clear commonality. One prerequisite for the implementation of the proposed policy packages is a gradual shift in attitude towards increasing importance of values in line with sustainable development.

Complementary Actions

Although the primary elements for the policy packages are taken from the transport sector, there are many complementary actions needed in other sectors. These include the important role that land use and development factors have in reducing transport intensity. It also includes the new technologies within transport (e.g. telematics), new technologies as they impact on transport (e.g. telecommuting), and the possibilities of an ecological tax reform. In addition, the research has also found that new institutional and organisational structures may be necessary to achieve sustainable mobility. Included here are partnerships between the public and private sectors to facilitate technological innovation, the development of partnerships at all levels with involved people (including the general public) to gain support for change (and to inform), new means to encourage and disseminate best practice, and the means by which progress can be monitored over time.

Common Elements

Whatever the starting point of the scenarios or the path to be followed, there are certain common actions necessary. These include consideration of ecological tax reform (coupled with CO_2 tax, fuel, vehicle and car ownership tax reform), emissions standards (including off-cycle performance, long term responsibility, automatic monitoring of emissions, etc.), actions to provide integrated information systems (including the personal communicator), and the promotion of teleactivities.

Lifestyle Changes

Over the next 20 years, the amount of time available for leisure activities will dramatically increase, particularly within the demographic context of an ageing population. Much of this new leisure time may involve long distance energy intensive travel as people wish to see the world. The question here is whether there is anything that can (or should) be done to reduce this expected growth since it will again severely impact on sustainable mobility. For much of the year people may be 'sustainable' with local travel being undertaken on low energy modes, but once (or twice) a year may travel round the world, thus negating any overall notion of sustainability. This means that changes in lifestyle are essential to meet sustainable mobility objectives, and that actions in the passenger sector may be harder to achieve than those in the freight sector.

Possibilities of Both Strong Decoupling and Technology

Image I was characterised by co-operation on local and regional levels (mainly bottom-up politics). Image II on the other hand was characterised by a good climate for global co-operation (mainly top-down politics). If both these frame conditions materialise, then Image III is a feasible option. Originally, it was argued that strong decoupling may not be possible to combine with strong technological development as the costs would be too high. However, under certain conditions, a 'win-win' situation may be possible, i.e. a focus on both strong decoupling and technology (a new Image IV). In this case there is a good base for later achieving more far-reaching sustainability goals. To reach such an Image requires a high level of commitment and intervention of decision bodies across all sectors. The capacity for preparing decisions and implementing them is likely to be a bottleneck in realising this Image. Transport policy at the EU level is only one of many competing areas of action.

Choosing Initial Measures

If Governments and the EU commit themselves to the long-term goal of sustainable mobility in Europe, then a consistent policy should be developed. This policy will have to evolve and be adapted to contextual factors that are more or less impossible to predict and control. We suggest a few guiding principles for choice of *initial measures* to be included in a start-up package:

- the measure should not be too controversial today (*the principle of acceptability*);
- measures that are essential to goal fulfilment but will have a delayed effect should be implemented early (*the principle of inertia or long lead-times*);
- measures that will set dynamical processes in motion should be implemented early (*the principle of dynamic effects*); and
- measures that tend to retain freedom of action in the future are often to be preferred to measures leading to lock-in solutions (*the principle of adaptability*).

In some areas the system dynamics governing development is only roughly understood. The predictability is low, at least in the longer term. For example, this is true for the interdependence between travel behaviour, infrastructure development and spatial patterns of production and residential areas. The same can be said for the development and dissemination of new technology, such as cleaner and more energy efficient vehicles. Economic incentives, city planning and supply of good public transport certainly will have an impact on trips by private cars in urban areas, although it is hard to say how much. Also, there may be unpredictable and unwelcome side effects of the policy actions.

The dimensions of uncertainty and potential impact can be combined to form a framework for discussing political strategy. Several issues concerning sustainable mobility can be characterised by large potential impact of policy and large uncertainties. A testing and learning strategy is then required. A Common Transport Policy should accept this lack of predictability and proceed in small steps and have frequent follow-up activities. It is also preferable to try several solutions in order to gain experience and learn. The role of public policy is then to promote variety and to set targets that play the role of selection mechanisms. It is also to catalyse a new dynamic that may lead to a more favourable development.

In the past, transport has mainly been seen as having a serving function for the economy and leisure activities. Where sustainable mobility is a major policy objective, transport cannot fulfil these demands in an unlimited way. Transport has to be integrated with other policy. Transport is at a turning point, and it is clear that transport interventions alone will not move policy in the direction of sustainability. The role of transport policy among other policies must be given a stronger emphasis, together with the different policy strategies that are required. More emphasis has to be placed in influencing economic, structural, agriculture, tourism and other policies to find the means to decouple transport growth from economic development.

Notes

1 The POSSUM Consortium has members from University College London, The Free University of Amsterdam, The National Technical University of Athens, The Environmental Strategies Research Group in Stockholm, EURES - Institute for Regional Studies in Europe in Freiburg, VTT - Technical Research Centre of Finland in Helsinki, The Warsaw University of Technology, and the Scientific Centre for Complex Transport Problems in Moscow.

2 A fuller description of the different scenario-building approaches can be found in Rienstra (1998) and Becker (1997).

3 The concept of decoupling in the transport sector is used to denote a situation where the assumed link between transport growth and economic growth is broken. The objective is to promote economic growth (good), but not transport growth (bad).

References

Banister, D. (1999), 'Some Thoughts on a Walk in the Woods', *Built Environment*, Vol. 25, pp. 162-167.

Banister, D., Stead, D., Steen, P., Dreborg, K., Åkerman, J., Nijkamp, P. and Schleicher-Tappeser, R. (2000), *European Transport Policy and Sustainable Mobility*, E and FN Spon., London.

Becker, H. (1997), *Social Impact Assessment*, UCL Press, London.

Commission of the European Communities (1992), *The Future Development of the Common Transport Policy: A Global Approach to the Construction of a Community Framework for Sustainable Mobility*, CEC, Brussels.

Commission of the European Communities (1994), *Strategic Transport Glossary*, CEC, Brussels.

Commission of the European Communities (1998a), *Communication on Transport and CO_2 - Developing A Community Approach*, COM 204 (1998), CEC, Brussels.

Commission of the European Communities (1998b), *The Common Transport Policy - Sustainable Mobility: Perspectives for the Future*, Communication from the Commission to the Council, the European Parliament, the Economic and Social Committee and the Committee of the Regions, COM 716 (1998), CEC, Brussels.

Dekker, F., Mastop, H., Verduijn, G., Bardie, R. and Gorter, L. (1973), 'A Multilevel Application of Strategic Choice at the Subregional Level', *Town Planning Review* Vol. 49, pp. 49-162.

Dreborg, K. H. (1996), 'Essence of Backcasting', *Futures* Vol. 28, pp. 813-828.

ECMT (1997), *Trends in the Transport Sector*, ECMT, Paris.

EUROSTAT (1997), *EU Transport in Figures - Statistical Pocketbook*, EUROSTAT, Luxembourg.

Godet, M (1986), 'Introduction to la Prospective', *Futures*, Vol. 18, pp. 134-157.

Johansson, T.B., Steen, P., Fredriksson, R. and Bogren, E. (1983), 'Sweden Beyond Oil: The Efficient Use of Energy', *Science*, Vol. 219, pp. 355-361.

Khakee, A. and Strömberg, K. (1993), 'Applying Futures Studies and the Strategic Choice Approach in Urban Planning', *Journal of the Operational Research Society* Vol. 44, pp. 213-224.

Löhnroth, M., Johansson, T.B. and Steen, P. (1980), 'Sweden Beyond Oil: Nuclear Commitments and Solar Options', *Science*, Vol. 208, pp. 557-563.

May, G. (1982), 'The Argument for More Future-Oriented Planning', *Futures*, Vol. 14, pp. 313-318.

OECD/ECMT (1995), *Transport and Sustainable Development*, OECD, Paris.

Olson, R.L. (1994), 'Alternative Images of a Sustainable Future', *Futures*, Vol. 26, pp. 156-169.

POSSUM Consortium (1999), *POSSUM Project Final Report*, University College London, London.

Rienstra, S. (1998), *Options and Barriers for Sustainable Transport Policies: A Scenario Approach*, Netherlands Economic Institute, Rotterdam.

Robinson, J.B. (1990), 'Futures Under Glass - A Recipe for People who Hate to Predict', *Futures*, Vol. 22, pp. 820-842.

UK Department of the Environment (1994), *Environmental Appraisal of Development Plans. A Good Practice Guide*, HMSO, London.

5 The Value of Time in Transport

BARBARA ADAM

In previous chapters references were made to timely or untimely policy decisions and participation processes; the iterative nature of decisions; or the inherent contradictions between policy objectives due to, among other things, their different timescapes. This latter point is particularly relevant for the objectives of environmental protection and social/ regional cohesion which together (or in opposition) with the objective of economic growth and development form the cornerstones of sustainable mobility.

This chapter deals explicitly with the theme implicitly running through many of these discussions, namely the time dimension. Making time an explicit dimension in transport policy can help innovative solutions towards sustainable mobility. In line with the more general argument of this book about the equivalent importance of both the contents of policy and its form, i.e. the decision process, we discuss time with reference to both.

Time and Sustainable Mobility

Transport time is tightly locked into the dominant perspective on time of industrial societies. It is irreducibly tied to a time that is globalised, standardised, decontextualised, quantifiable, and measurable. Within that time, individual modes of transport are scheduled; intermodality is planned and organised; the Common Transport Policy is conceived; individual projects are executed. Moreover, transport time is inextricably tied to the economic perspective from which time is conceived as an economic good, that is, a resource with use value and a resource with exchange value that is inseparably bound to money, efficiency and the production of profit. This association of time with money and profit links, in turn, to a high value of speed. In the first instance, speed means progress as exemplified in the development of ever faster means of transport. Thus, Peter Freund and

George Martin (1993, p.89) suggest that 'Speed *is* the premier cultural icon of modern societies'. In the second instance, speed saves time – labour time and capital time – and this in turn saves money. When time is equated with money, therefore, speed means not just progress but profit.

The conception changes dramatically, however, when we foreground different relations: when we understand, for example, speed with reference to the time-space relation and when we bring energy consumption into the picture. This alternative conception entails, first, an explicit acknowledgement that speed consumes not just time but space, and that speed, time and space are inversely related. This means, the faster the transport (i.e. the shorter the time to cover distance) the more land it requires or, to express the relation differently, the higher the speed of travel the bigger the quantities of space consumed. High-speed travel, in fact, only makes sense over large distances since time and the consumption of space are inversely related. It entails secondly the explicit recognition that time and energy too are inversely related. It means first, that the shorter the time to cover a given distance, the more energy is needed and second, that the more energy is needed, the higher becomes the proportion of non-reusable energy that is involuntarily dissipated into the environment. That is to say, the demand on energy resources increases with rising transport speeds. A number of consequences thus follow from this shift in perspective: time as tempo/speed comes to be inextricably linked to the consumption of space/land, the depletion of resources and to the production of pollution.

Experience has shown, moreover, that time saving through speed has not facilitated more profitable use of time but has encouraged instead more mobility and travel over further distances (Brög, 1996; Whitelegg, 1993 and 1997; Weizsäcker, 1994). Furthermore, since miles used (i.e. distance travelled) indicate economic activity and are taken as a measure of economic prosperity, and since there is a limit to the hours in a working day, the goal of more distance/prosperity has to be achieved through ever greater speeds with ever increasing costs to the environment. Currently, industrial societies' hope is pinned on better and more efficient technology, i.e. technology that can achieve more distance, at greater speeds and with less pollution. Thus, whilst the link between transport, speed and pollution is generally acknowledged, the issues of space consumption and resource depletion tend to feature much less in the envisaged/proposed technological solutions.

This brings us to the issue of sustainability and time and to the question what sustainable mobility and sustainable transport might mean from a timescape perspective. At the most general level, sustainability relates to the past-present-future extension of a particular process or phenomenon. In the widest sense, *sustainability means meeting the needs of the present with resources evolved in the past without compromising the ability of others in distant times and places to meet their needs.* Concern with sustainability thus shifts the focus from economic concern with the environment as *producer* of economic wealth and surplus value to the environment's *re*-productive capacity.

According to Herman Daly (1991, in Whitelegg 1993, p.5) a 'sustainable society should satisfy three basic time-based conditions:

- its rates of use of renewable resources do not exceed their rates of regeneration;
- its rates of use of non-renewable resources do not exceed the rate at which sustainable renewable substitutes are developed;
- its rates of pollution emission do not exceed the assimilative capacity of the environment.'

With respect to industrial societies' modern transport, John Whitelegg produces a table that shows that the first and third condition are not met but that the second condition has the potential, at least, to be met. 'It is perfectly possible', he suggests, 'to carry out the same set of activities but over shorter distances and to switch from environmentally damaging modes to modes which are relatively benign' (Whitelegg, 1993, p.5). Sustainable transport, therefore, means not just a change in technology but in speed, distance, and mode of transport. From this perspective we can see that sustainable mobility and sustainable transport are not primarily a question of technology but of basic assumption/approach to time and space, speed and consumption. Moreover, no matter how amiable the general goal and specific targets, sustainability in transport cannot be achieved, for example, if the rate of emission reduction is constantly overtaken by the rate of growth in vehicle numbers and miles consumed, in the speed of the various transport modes and in the number of trips taken.

Despite this contradictory relation, this combination of speed, growth, technology and sustainability is pursued in the European Union's Common Transport Policy. In the 1992 White Paper on Transport Policy, the CTP is defined as a policy designed to ensure the proper functioning of the Community's transport system that eliminates remaining restrictions and distortions of closed markets, improves the potential for competitiveness, financial performance and efficiency, whilst taking account of environmental challenges. The document recognises transport as a growth industry (p.6) which is expected to continue to grow in the future (p.20) and it views transport growth as crucial for the 'continued health of the community's economy' (p.10). It acknowledges:

- that demand for the transport of goods and services tends to run parallel to GNP;
- that economic activity is dispersed over wider social areas, thus is no longer concentrated in major cities;
- and that the trend is towards reduction in shipment size and increase in frequency.

The stated, recognised impacts on the environment are:

- energy consumption at 30 per cent of total final energy consumption of EU (p. 35);
- global warming and operational pollution of air, soil, water and marine life;
- land intrusion: roads, for example, make up 1.3 per cent of total land area of the EU;
- risks associated with transport of dangerous goods;
- and congestion associated with raised energy consumption, pollution and environmental inefficiency (p. 35).

At the same time, the document insists that the CTP will have to function in accordance with the Maastricht Agreement which means not only a transport system that strengthens the Community's economic and social cohesion but also one that integrates environmental protection requirements (p. 13).

This balancing act is to be achieved by 'demand management mechanisms' (p.25) ensuring that 'all transport users ... pay the full costs – internal and external – of the transport services they consume' (p. 14). In order to avoid imbalances for competitiveness the charging has to be done at EU level; and through BATNEEC – best available technology not entailing excessive costs.

In this way, it is argued, the Community's actions already contribute to both the economic prosperity associated with transport growth and the pursuit of environmental protection. That is to say, in addition to the technological developments, it is argued that the internal market and the internalisation of full transport costs; intermodal competition and complementarity; as well as interoperability and the integration of systems and networks, already address the economic, operational, social and environmental efficiency of the transport system.

Time is not absent from the document, but it is there implicitly rather than explicitly. The document takes time to be unproblematic and given. It assumes time to be merely the abstract framework within which transport is scheduled and policy developed. Assumptions about and approaches to time, therefore, are not empirically available but have to be inferred. The implicit understanding of time contained in this document can be summarised as follows:

- time is a quantity to be measured by clocks and calendars;
- time is abstract, absolute, globally standardised and context-independent;
- time is a personal and public resource with use value;
- time is a commodity and economic resource with exchange value;
- time is money, time saved is profit, speed means progress and efficiency, faster means better and more cost-effective.

The valorisation of speed and associated social issues related to equity in transport needs and use are of particular relevance in transport policy.

Irrespective of whether we are focusing on transport policy issues related to road, rail, water or air, speed seems to be a priority at European as well as at national level, with time saving being an unquestioned dominant factor in transport policy. The implicit stance on speed is thus as follows:

- speed is universally valorised above all else;
- speed justifies developments in each of the transport sectors;
- the technological developments associated with increase in speed are valued as progress;
- speed is assumed to be inescapably tied to economic competitiveness and profit;
- more fundamentally still, the consumption and compression of distance in ever faster times is thought to be a precondition for economic growth;
- finally, speed is implicitly tied to status: high speed and high technology equals high status – air travel and high speed trains are prime cases in point – and no/low-tech, slow movement carries low status as is demonstrated by the position of walking and biking on the inter/national policy agenda.

From a temporal perspective this cluster of assumptions about speed requires further exploration. There is a need to take a more critical and nuanced perspective, ask some pertinent questions and dismantle some myths about speed as socio-economic cure-all (Adam, 1995 and 1998).

First, we need to ask 'what happens to the saved time'? Clearly, if the time saved through increased speed is quite small then it tends to be difficult to reallocate that time in a meaningful way. Alternatively, if the convenience of a new road, for example, results in more trips, then the original time saving is negated.

A study relevant to this point, conducted by Werner Brög in 1996, shows that the time spent travelling per day per person has stayed remarkably constant over time and across a large number of cultures, countries and continents. The conclusion of Brög's study is that the increased speed of daily transport has not resulted in more disposable time but instead has been absorbed by travelling over ever longer distances.

Second, we might ask 'what, apart from time-saving *per se*, has to happen for people and goods to actually get faster from A to B'? Increased speed in conjunction with increased numbers of travellers brings inevitable increases in delays. That is to say, speed of and in itself does not avoid congestion, delays and waiting times. Instead it has a tendency to create these unwanted side effects. With air travel within Europe, for example, the time spent on the ground checking in and out tends to far exceed the high-speed travel time spent in the air.

Speed therefore needs to be understood not in isolation but in the wider context of complex social interactions, time-use and waiting patterns, intersections of people, technology and travel modes, as well as rhythmically patterned structures of traffic networks and flows.

Third, we need to query the universal relevance of speed. While there is no question that high-speed travel by train, for example, is preferable on environmental grounds to travel by car or aeroplane, it has disadvantages from a regional travel and haulage perspective. High-speed train travel means as few stops as possible, thus satisfying the needs of long-distance travel and haulage but not the requirements of the many people (and goods) who would like to join this high-speed service on the numerous possible intersection points along the way. This is also the reason why high-speed travel by train does not contribute to policies aiming to relieve the pressure from urban centres by promoting re-housing in suburbs or smaller cities where bigger and cheaper housing is available and where the environmental quality is better – this presupposes a reduction in commuting time which in theory is possible but which only materialises if stops are scheduled.

Fourth, we need to pay attention to the assumption that high-speed, trans-national travel networks bring economic growth to local economies located along their corridors. There is much evidence to the contrary that is well documented in John Whitelegg's (1997) book *Critical Mass; Transport, Environment and Society in the Twenty-first Century*. Economic growth in local economies, he points out, depends on a number of essential conditions to be fulfilled: trains have to stop; motorways have to have intersections; airports have to be serviced by efficient public transport; the high-speed service has to be used to come to the places rather than a convenient means to escape them. TEN may fulfil some of those conditions but economic growth of local economies can by no means be guaranteed *a priori*.

Fifth, and closely related, we need to attend to the assumption that TEN and the capacity to travel further in less time has improved accessibility. Again, Whitelegg's (1997) research provides evidence to the contrary. It shows that local and regional accessibility has suffered under this overall trend toward the compression of distance and time. The Swedish transport policy recognises this difficulty and, accordingly, suggests that rural needs and not the needs of the largest cities should provide the benchmark for services. Cities should be considered as special cases, the exceptions to the rule, whose needs will have to be assessed and served on a case-by-case basis.

Sixth, we need to address the myth that speed is a good thing for everyone. From the points raised so far we can already see that there is an equity issue associated with the valorisation of speed, time compression and space expansion. We need to ask 'who benefits from high speed travel and at whose expense'?

Whilst the largest cities along main routes and priority corridors have benefited, smaller towns away from industrial centres are worse off with respect to mobility, accessibility and speed of travel now than they were at the turn of the century. In the UK, for example, rail travel times between such smaller towns have in fact substantially increased and the number of trains running has decreased (Whitelegg, 1997, p.73). In the UK, the country whose privatisation of the railway is most advanced, a number of additional matters of equity between large urban centres near main transport corridors, smaller towns and isolated rural communities have worsened: the synchronisation and time-tabling between companies and trains have suffered with the result that it is increasingly difficult to make connections between trains. Reliability and punctuality have deteriorated. The number of trains running has been rationalised and uneconomical lines closed with the results that at increased cost to the traveller there are less trains running to ever fewer destinations.

Beyond locational equity concerns, there is an equity issue about which groups of people benefit most from the high speed, high cost, long distance transport. Whilst advantaging those with business between distant cities such a service offers little to those who require good and extensive local public transport – local commuters, children and their carers, the elderly, the disabled, the poor – all those who do not need, want or cannot afford long-distance, high-speed transport.

This equity issue between social groups is intimately tied to temporal matters since the poorest members of society – the unemployed, pensioners, non-earning parents/carers, people with disabilities, and children – tend to be poor in financial terms but rich in time whilst the wealthy have money but tend to be short on time, that is, poor in time. With respect to transport, this creates the following time-based social inequity: the wealthy are able to use money to buy time through transport – the higher the speed (time saving) the more costly tends to be the transport. For the poor the opposite exchange is not possible: their time cannot be exchanged for money to buy them access through transport. Thus, the pursuit of speed and its implicit valorisation benefits the totality of individual transport stakeholders in very unequal terms.

For societies there is an inescapable social time-based dimension of inequality linked to distance and speed which is similar to the one of individual wealth. In the EU, the societies at the Southern periphery tend to be the poorer members of the community. Yet their distance from the centre in the North-West is the greatest which means in order to overcome the temporal disadvantage of distance they would need to spend extra on speed. While the wealthier nations are able to 'buy speed' this tends not necessarily to be a viable option for the poorer members. Such socio-temporal transport inequality therefore can only be actively compensated for at EU level. Similar problems can often be observed within country borders, the notorious North-South Italian divide being the most prominent example.

From a timescape perspective, therefore, the success of high-speed rail travel would not be established exclusively with reference to how well it competes with the environmentally more damaging modes of private car and aeroplane. Instead, it would also be assessed with reference to issues of socio-temporal equity. This means, a socio-temporally aware assessment would be concerned to ensure that a high speed rail service is not developed at the expense of the less profitable rural lines and the slower regional and local modes of public transport. This requirement should not detract in any way whatsoever from the important environmental considerations but it asks for a wider perspective that embraces issues of social equity with equal commitment.

Seventh, the issue of transport speed is further tied to changes in the culture of production and with it new organisational forms of road haulage. Thus, just-in-time transport, currently the dominant form of freight transport, is inextricably tied to just-in-time production (cf. Martin and Schumann, 1997; Whitelegg, 1997). This system of production entails a highly synchronised and tightly timed system of manufacture and an equally fined tuned system of delivery which reduces not just the waste of storage time but also the waste of storage space. This in turn transfers the warehousing onto the motorways and byways of society with devastating environmental consequences.

Following the time-compressing logic of time is money, the just-in-time transport system requires both flexibility and 24-hour cover as a precondition to achieving the necessary sensitivity to the peaks and troughs in the market. This increase in the speed and precision of timing and synchronisation of the delivery of goods is clearly accompanied by a number of pluses and minuses.

On the positive side, there is no question that this new logic of production and delivery brings extensive savings for the producing companies; that it decreases the need for warehousing space; and that it provides a substantial volume of extra work for haulage companies.

On the negative side, we need to recognise that just-in-time production externalises company costs associated with 'unproductive' time and places the burden on the haulier in the first instance, and on the environment and society in the second instance. Moreover, there is no doubt that this system dramatically reduces the potential for rail to provide this haulage service. This means, just-in-time transport brings with it not only an extensive increase in lorries on the road but also an equivalent rise in fuel consumption, both of which do not bode well for the environment.

The gains for business, therefore, are unambiguously tied to losses for the environment and people's health. Clearly, this system of time compression is a powerful instigator for reactive transport policy at all levels of policy formation.

From a timescape perspective, therefore, it becomes pertinent, with respect to the valorisation of speed in general and high-speed transport in particular, not to take as given that speed *per se* is a good thing and therefore not to pursue the increase in speed at any cost. Who gains and loses with a proposed high-speed service becomes a pertinent consideration, and not to trade one against the other an important commitment. Thus, high-speed, trans-national trains, for example, should not replace high quality local, regional and national rail and other public transport services. Equally, questions about who is and who is not catered for by a particular service should not be left out of the equation. With these issues explicitly addressed, transport policy is moving towards a comprehensive socio-economic appreciation of what effects it might have not just on the physical but the social environment.

Time in Policy

Time is in yet another way important for transport policy, namely with reference to policy rather than transport:

- policy is about planning the future in a context of past decisions and present constraints;
- it is about conceiving of change within specific or open time frames;
- it is about timing and synchronisation locally, nationally and transnationally;
- it is about planning schedules and the specification of target dates;
- it operates with implicit and/or explicit temporal frames of reference and time frames;
- it entails particular visions of the future that guide policy formation in the present;
- it encompasses national self-perceptions about being ahead of partners or in urgent need of catching up;
- assessment of the success or failure of a policy can only be evaluated if it is placed in a temporal frame against which it can be compared and judged to be un/successfully implemented.

Another complicating factor is that the time planning of a government in power regularly exceeds its competency in terms of its period of election. That is to say, governments elected for four to five years and shorter put in place policies that affect their county's future for much longer periods. Transport planning is one of those areas of governance where long-term decisions are being made which commit successor governments or involve them in very costly changes of direction.

In the absence of any body or institution responsible for the long-term future of a nation, it is essential that the public at large are extensively involved in any planning and decision-making processes concerned with policies that far exceed the mandate of the government of the day. Although not formalised in any way with respect to the time argument, the importance of public involvement in policy is gradually being recognised and ways are searched to implement it in practice.

Taking time seriously would not just involve explicit recognition of and compensation for the democratic deficit of bringing about a long-term future based on four to five year political mandates and associated financial decisions. It would also have to recognise that the different levels of a nation's politics and policy making may have very different temporal concerns regarding their level-specific transport which may or may not complement each other.

A local authority, for example, may primarily be concerned with current urban traffic congestion and therefore be inclined towards building ring-roads, car-free city centres, and providing the best possible local public transport system. Alternatively, it may be preoccupied with con/serving a particular locality and environment. Such restructuring of priorities may not fit with national and EU (long-term) emphases on high-speed trains and motorway systems that simply move trough local territories in order to connect all of Europe and beyond.

The higher the speed, the larger the space involved and the longer the time frames of planning incurred and its public economic and environmental effects. With respect to the financing of transport policies and specific projects, a grave conflict is that of allocating finance over very long periods, often shared between a number of public and private institutions, and the annual budgets of national and local governments.

In Italy, for instance, the large debts incurred by previous administrations made any allocation for large-scale, long-term projects almost impossible to achieve unless there were external EU money available to part-fund specific and particularly expensive trans-European projects. In the Italian case, it seems, the lack of national moneys determines national transport policy and skews it in a particular direction of large, trans-European, high-finance projects, and increased future debt. TEN as a national transport policy is embraced most enthusiastically by the countries who can least afford it since the financial assistance through the Structural Fund does by no means cover all the socio-environmental costs that will be incurred.

Equally illuminating on this issue are the French and UK situation where administrations with very different political cultures and visions of the future from those of their predecessors had to make investments as a result of the previous administrations' decisions. In such situations, it seems, governments' policies and decisions are heavily 'marked by the legacy of their predecessors'.

A closely related issue links to countries' transport policy histories, that is, to their identity in relation to the past, present and future. Some member countries of the EU pride themselves in and identify with their long history of spatial planning of which transport is an important aspect. One can also conclude that the more established and bureucratically embedded a country's transport policy, the less likely is the country to merely fit in with the EU's vision of a CTP and the TEN. Thus, Germany, France and the more recent members Austria and Sweden, for example, see themselves shaping rather than merely adopting EU policy. Italy, Greece and Spain, in contrast, see the adoption of EU policy as an opportunity to bring about coveted modernisation of their countries' transport system. For the former countries, their transport history forms a positive part of their self-perception and identity whilst for Italy, Greece and Spain the EU's directives constitute the potential for a new future identity.

A further set of issues to be mentioned under the policy framework relate to the prioritising, phasing, staging and synchronising of plans and decisions of policy within and between the different levels of transport policy. The prioritisation of policies is essential in a context of scarce resources. Given that not everything is possible, in other words, choices have to be made about the order of importance. This order, in turn, is dependent on a great number of past, current and future-related matters ranging from established policies and traditions, via the political stability and bureaucratic structure, to financial resources and economic-political decisions.

Closely related is the issue of the speed of policy implementation. The speed of change has to be appropriate to the political context, the economic context, the policy history, as well as the policy and its associated projects. Due to the political and economic instability of post-war Italy, for example, some projects had a thirty year history as conceptions and plans before recent EU involvement got them off the drawing board and, in a compressed time frame, through the phases of decision making and on the path towards realisation.

Finally, most countries appear to work towards a specified time frame within which their transport plans and policies are to be effected and implemented: Belgium 1996-2000; Denmark till 2005; Germany till 2010; Sweden till 2007; the UK till 2000. These time frames for transport policy, however, do not necessarily overlap with or match the time frames associated with respective countries' environmental policy objectives. Yet, transport policy is meant to centrally take account of the environmental issues involved.

Moreover, these variable time frames of national transport policy clearly are not compatible transnationally and thus an obstacle to the achievement of a European-wide Common Transport Policy. The long-term nature of transport policy needs extensive future planning and this in turn requires elaborate and reasonably stable political structures in conjunction with an appropriate political culture on the one hand and the financial will and determination to honour such temporally extended investment commitments on the other, especially if they involve a change of government and therefore radically new perspectives on transport policy.

Irrespective of the existence of transport plans with time frames, therefore, effective implementation of such plans depends on a suitable economic-political context that allows for the future projection and predictability that is necessary for putting long-term policies and plans into action.

Conclusion

With respect to the Common Transport Policy, taking account of time involves a reconsideration of the relations between transport, economic growth, the valoratisation of speed and social equity. For the planning of transport projects it means recognising, on the one hand, time-based differences and time-based roots of barriers to their successful realisation and, on the other, the time intensive nature of co-ordination and synchronisation of action across administrative levels and national boundaries. It entails further that we acknowledge the importance of the past and future for concerted action in the present the variable history of knowledge and skills, the differences in priorities, objectives and goals and the inequity in the power to define what is real, relevant and valuable.

It entails, finally, that in our plans, policies and assessments we allow for the spatial and temporal disaggregation of impacts, or as Anthony Giddens (1990) calls it, their time-space distantiation. That is to say, with respect to plans, policies and appraisal, we need to consider that the impacts of transport policies and projects (positive, negative and indifferent) have effects that are dispersed in time and space and thus do not display a direct cause-and-effect relationship. It means those processes and their potential effects cannot be understood and/or evaluated adequately through classical linear models.

With a temporal focus and a timescape perspective therefore, we make the implicit explicit. We complexify transport theory, research and practice; and we engage to a large extent with the qualitative dimension of the subject matter of transport. The temporary, processual, emergent nature is emphasised and its contextuality highlighted. We acknowledge that there is no single time but multiple times, no space without time, no territory without a past, present and future and no consumption of distance and time without a social and environmental price to pay.

Taking time seriously, therefore, entails that we recognise its subtle structuring of transport theory, practice and research. For a Europe-wide Common Transport Policy, this means extending the planning of space, territory and spatial mobility to encompass temporal mobility, time planning and a time politics as precondition to achieving a sustainable and equitable transport future.

References

Adam, B. (1995), *Timewatch: The Social Analysis of Time*, Polity, Cambridge.

Adam, B. (1998), *Timescapes of Modernity. The Environment and Invisible Hazards*, Routledge, London/New York.

Brög, W. (1996), Presentation at *Car-Free City Conference*, Commission of the European Communities in May, Copenhagen.

Daly, H. (1991), *Steady State Economics*, Island Press, Washington, D.C.

European Commission (1992), *The Future Development of the Common Transport Policy – A Global Approach to the Construction of a Community Framework for Sustainable Mobility*, COM (92) 494, European Commission, Brussels.

Freund, P. and Martin, G. (1993), *The Ecology of the Automobile*, Black Rose Books, London/New York.

Martin, H.P. and Schumann, H. (1997), *The Global Trap*, Zed Books, London/New York.

Weizsäcker, E.U. v. (1994), *Earth Politics*, Zed Books, London/New Jersey.

Whitelegg, J. (1993), *Transport for a Sustainable Future. The Case for Europe*, Belhaven Press, London.

Whitelegg, J. (1997), *Critical Mass. Transport, Environment and Society in the Twenty-First Century*, Pluto Press, Chicago/London.

6 Understanding Accessibility

STEVEN NEY

Introduction

Accessibility is a key, if not *the* key concept in transport policy-making. Common sense would suggest that investment into roads, rail, public transport, and aviation infrastructure should increase and widen individuals' ability to access locations.

Yet, accessibility, in keeping with transport policy objectives in general, is an ill-defined and multi-faceted concept. There is little or no consensus in the wider policy debate that accessibility is a policy goal worth pursuing. Even among those who agree that accessibility is a 'good' (as opposed to a 'bad'), the concept shows remarkable resilience to concrete application, a characteristic it shares with other concepts both in transport policy and in other policy arenas. What is more, the notion of accessibility is closely linked to notoriously difficult policy concepts such as mobility, need, and well-being.

Depending on the policy context and the level of policy argument, accessibility means different things to different types of policy actors. Understanding the role the term accessibility plays in transport policy deliberation means that we come to grips with two dimensions of transport policy-making: first, the different possible uses of the term, and, second, the socio-institutional policy contexts in which policy actors apply the idea of accessibility. After briefly outlining the European transport policy issue in the first section, in the second section we will disaggregate the use of the term accessibility on two analytical levels:

- Semantic: what set of problems and issues does the term accessibility highlight?
- Normative: what are the different explicit and implicit normative assumptions that underlie the concept of accessibility?

An analysis of this type is, however, insufficiently dynamic. In a very real sense, the state of confusion that characterises transport policy debates (Banister and Button, 1993; Banister, 1995) relates to changing perceptions concerning the social benefits of modern transport, in particular, and of industrial society, in general. The impact of what Ronald Inglehart (1990) calls 'post-material' values on transport policy deliberation has thrown some of the central concepts of transport policy-making into sharp relief. Whereas policy-makers would not have questioned the inherent desirability of increased mobility, accessibility, and increased average journey speeds twenty-five years ago, it is not at all clear that accessibility, say to a wildlife reserve for recreational purposes, is a policy goal worth striving for today. In short, the entrance of a new institutional discourse into the political fray has undermined conventional certainties in transport policy-making. The third section, then, will look at the institutional framings of the transport policy debate.

The final section looks at the ramifications of these institutional constructions of the transport issue for transport policy-making. Essentially, this section will re-examine transport policy-making against the backdrop of scientific uncertainty and socio-institutional diversity.

The European Transport Policy Issue

As a public policy issue, transport in Europe has much in common with many other policy spheres. Like many currently disputed issues, the developments in European transport that policy-makers, researchers, and the public alike welcomed as firm evidence of socio-technical progress not even two decades ago are now disputed, contentious, and politically divisive. Unlike many other policy spheres, such as Global Climate Change, the problems in transport policy are, it would seem, fairly evident and immediate (anyone who lives in a European city will readily agree). Indeed, most contemporary transport policy literature, whether it be a EU policy-document, a critical scholarly analysis, or a populist call to arms, begins by pointing to very similar phenomena.

There are four sets of phenomena that characterise developments in the European transport sector: the rapid growth in transport demand, the modal shift that satisfies this demand, the changing patterns of land use, and the increasing social costs of these developments.

Increasing European Demand for Transport

Transport demand in Europe (including Eastern Europe) has experienced rapid growth since WWII. 'Our welfare societies', contend Himanen *et al.* (1993), 'have apparently generated a complex array of contact patterns (material and immaterial) which require physical interaction at an unprecedented scale'. They describe the spatial development of Europe in terms of a 'geography of movement': the demand for the movement of goods and people in Europe is at a historically unprecedented level and will continue to rise in the future.

Passenger transport, the European Commission surmises, has become a growth industry. Not only has the passenger transport sector consistently outperformed the economy as a whole (growing faster than average GDP by about one percentage point), it has also increased its spatial scope with average journey distances virtually doubling from 16.5 km in 1970 to 31.5 km in 1993. At present, transport constitutes about 7 per cent of EU GDP (European Commission 1995b, p. 2).

The figures for freight transport are very similar. Over the past three decades or so, demand for the movement of goods has increased from 700 thousand million tonne-kilometres in 1981 to around 1,100 thousand million tonne-kilometres in 1994 (ECMT, 1998a). This trend is set to continue: the European Commissioner for transport, Neil Kinnock, foresees a 70 per cent rise in freight movement in the next seven years (p. 1).

Meeting Demand on the Road

The expansion of road transport, both in terms of privately owned cars and heavy goods vehicles, has absorbed most of the spectacular rise in transport demand to the detriment of other transport modes (Himanen *et al.* 1993; Banister and Button 1993; European Commission 1995b). The flexibility and independence a private car affords has led to a situation where cars are responsible for three quarters of all passenger kilometres travelled in the European Union (European Commission, 1995b, p. 1). By the same token, the changing nature of logistics and stock management (e.g. just-in-time distribution) confer a comparative advantage onto road haulage (Banister and Button, 1993, p. 3).

The numbers are impressive. In Britain alone, the Department of Transport (DoT) predicts an increase in road traffic of 83 per cent to 142 per cent in the next thirty years (Schofield, 1993, p. 117). A three-fold increase in car ownership in Britain, Bert Morris (1993) argues, will meet increasing demand for passenger transport. In Austria, the traffic on motorways is set to increase by 37 per cent between 1993 and 2000

(ECMT, 1998b). At the European level, Kinnock (1997) maintains that road haulage will take the lion's share of the predicted 70 per cent growth in demand thus increasing its share in freight transport from 70 per cent to 80 per cent. At the same time, he continues, railways' share of passenger and freight transport has fallen from 10 per cent to 6 per cent and from 32 per cent to 14 per cent respectively.

Changing Patterns of Land-Use

Another distinct feature of the European transport policy are the changes in land-use patterns that have both caused and exacerbated present transport trends. All major European cities, maintains Peter Hall (1995), have decentralised since WWII. David Banister and Kenneth Button (1993) argue that extortionate prices for inner city housing, a general increase of income levels and the consequent desire to own a car, as well as people's (somewhat abstract) desire for space have depopulated urban areas. This suburbanisation and de-urbanisation of residential housing and employment has fundamentally altered transport behaviour. As a result, complex and longer car journeys have replaced the 'simple journey-to-work pattern' (p. 2) leading to more road-based traffic. The net result, Hall (1995) maintains, has been a significant increase in journey lengths with no obvious savings in journey times despite ever increasing capacities for speed in all transport modes.

The Social Costs of Rapid Transport Growth

Whereas policy-making conventionally assumed that the inherent benefits of transport systems invariably outweighed their costs by several orders of magnitude, the public, researchers, and some policy-makers have gradually become more critical. In the last two decades, there has been a growing awareness that the benefits of transport may no longer justify the costs it incurs. In general, the transport literature identifies three types of social costs, associated with the transport system: congestion, pollution, and accidents.

The combination of rapid growth in transport demand, the modal shift towards road transport, and the changing patterns of land-use have produced significant congestion on European roads. Himanen *et al.* (1993) speak of congestion as a 'post-modern transport problems' because conventional transport policy options, that is increasing road capacity, are no longer open to policy-makers. European cities are close to their absolute capacity and observers (Banister and Button, 1993; Himanen *et al.*, 1993; European Commission, 1995a) increasingly point to the ineffectiveness of new road investment in reducing congestion. The European Commission (1995a, p. 16) maintains that it:

> is sometimes argued that the best remedy against congestion is to simply provide more infrastructure. Notwithstanding the need for additional infrastructure in Europe for other reasons, this statement is generally untrue: as motorists are discouraged from using a congested road there is a 'latent' demand which is triggered once extra capacity becomes available. In the long run congestion will persist.

Congestion incurs a cost: it hinders the mobility of people and goods. The European Commission estimates these costs to the EU economy to be in the region of 2 per cent of EU GDP.

Another interrelated set of social costs of transport emerge from increased pollution. The transport system, argue Banister and Button (1993), causes environmental problems at the local, trans-boundary, and global level. At the local level, the noise from vehicles, be they cars, Heavy Goods Vehicles, trains or aeroplanes, has matured from being a mere nuisance to an environmental problem of significant proportions. At the transboundary and global levels, the emissions from road vehicles, aeroplanes, ships, and trains (in this case, indirect emissions) significantly contribute to phenomena such as acid rain, stratospheric ozone depletion, concentration of tropospheric ozone, and global climate change (Banister and Button, 1993, p. 4). In terms of human health, the European Commission (1995a, p. 1) maintains that:

> [a]ir pollution problems (e.g. ozone) in summer are requiring that, on more and more occasions, citizens across Europe have to refrain from outdoor activities. It is estimated that thousands of European citizens die each year from just one form of air pollution (particulate matter) – according to some studies air pollution from transport kills more than 6000 people in the UK alone.

Again, these developments represent a cost to society. The European Commission estimates that, excluding the costs of climate change, costs from air pollution amount to 0.4 per cent of EU GDP and that noise pollution costs Europe 0.2 per cent of aggregated European income.

Last, European accident statistics show that increased transport demand, coupled with increasing vehicle capacities, has come at a grim price: the Commission (1995a) reports that about 50 000 people are killed in transport accidents in Europe each year. The estimated financial costs of transport accidents is about 1.5 per cent of EU GDP (European Commission 1995a, p. 22).

The Concept of Accessibility

Understanding how different policy actors respond to the problems identified in European transport means that we have to come to grips with the basic terms used in the policy debate. In what follows, we will analyse the concept of accessibility both in terms of its differing semantic meanings and in terms of the different normative contents implied in varied uses of the idea.

Defining Accessibility: the Semantics of the Term

Ideally, policy discourse, in its broadest sense, should be based on terms and concepts that are clear to all policy actors. In reality, however, policy communication is more complex: basic ideas and concepts in transport discourse are vague and thereby always open to interpretation. The idea of accessibility is no exception. Yet, policy actors often deploy the term as if there were a hardened consensus on what accessibility means. Closer inspection, however, reveals that there is no clear, let alone unambiguous, definition of accessibility in the literature. In fact, policy actors more often than not will refer to accessibility without providing any definition.

At a very general level, accessibility refers to 'the ease with which people can travel to and from a particular location' (Hall and Banister, 1995, p. 278). Accessibility, then, is a characteristic or property of a location, an object, or a service. Work, shops, the public transport system, medical care, legal aid, and leisure facilities are things that can be more or less accessible. The European Commission (1995b, p. 6), while discussing public passenger transport, refers to 'system accessibility' as a desirable property of public transport systems:

> Access to passenger transport is crucial. Improving *system accessibility* covers a wide range of areas. This includes the design of rolling stock and (intermodal) stations, linking residential areas to central trip-attracting activities (work places, shopping, leisure activities), serving rural and peripheral areas and meeting the needs of people with reduced mobility.

At a general level, then, it would appear as if accessibility is a structural phenomenon: it is an attribute of objects such as locations and services.

Yet, as the last passage indicates, accessibility also describes individuals and groups of individuals. Researchers often use the term to discriminate between groups of individuals who, for a variety of reasons, have less accessibility to locations and services than others. For example, David Denmark (1996) speaks of the 'transport disadvantaged': these are people who 'have mobility and access problems' (Travers Morgan, 1992 quoted in Denmark, 1996, p.2). Who are these individuals? Denmark identifies them as being the 'poor, the elderly, the handicapped (sic) and especially those from minority groups'(p. 2). The European Commission (1995b, p. 2) similarly uses accessibility to outline a particular social group. 'Public passenger transport', the Commission argues,

> is particularly important for those who have no access to private cars, if they are to have access to employment, services such as shops and schools, to leisure activities, holiday destination and to family and social contacts.

Here, accessibility is something that certain individuals and groups possess and others do not: it is, in short, a second order level of accessibility referring to individual capabilities. Whereas structural accessibility assumes that individuals have access to suitable means of transport, this level of accessibility focuses on individual problems, due to disability or poverty, with access to transportation.

However, the neat distinction between structural (first-order) and individual (second-order) accessibility breaks down when policy actors apply accessibility to macro-level phenomena. In transport modelling, researchers are fond of using the concept to describe particular geographical and socio-economic regions. The SASI model (Bökemann *et al.* 1997), along with many other transport models, defines accessibility as 'the relative locational advantage of each region with respect to relevant destinations in other regions and in the region as a function of travel time or travel cost (or both) to reach these destinations by the strategic road and rail networks.' (p.12). Intransparent wording aside, who or what exactly is more accessible is unclear. Is it the locations in a specific region? Or is it the individuals and groups of individuals (such as, say, enterprises, political groups, or families)? Is it the services this region offers? Or the region's labour supply? Arguably, regional accessibility refers to both structural and human resource features simultaneously: regions have a comparative advantage because their individuals can access to means of transport and because their locations are embedded in a functioning transport infrastructure.

In sum, the literature is unclear about what the term accessibility means. On the one hand, the term depicts characteristics of locations and services. On the other hand, researchers also use the term to distinguish different social groups: those with full accessibility to services and locations and those with restricted accessibility to desired locations due to restricted access to transport. However, policy actors rarely keep these levels of aggregation and definition apart: often, as the SASI model illustrates, accessibility, when applied to socio-economic rather than purely geographical regions, points both to structural characteristics and individual capabilities.

Accessibility and Mobility

The idea of accessibility is very close to the concept of mobility both in terms of meaning and function in the transport policy discourse. Like the term accessibility, mobility plays a pivotal role in transport policy debates, be they of political or academic nature. Like accessibility, the meaning of mobility is fluid and fuzzy. What is more, the relationship between these two ideas in the literature is less than clear. A sensible 'division of labour' between the two concepts could mean that while accessibility predominantly describes the social and structural features of a particular location, mobility would be an indicator for the individual's ability to reach certain destinations.

A cursory overview of the literature, however, reveals that there are at least four different relationships between the concept of accessibility and the concept of mobility.[1] First, some researchers use the terms mobility and accessibility interchangeably. Denmark (1996), while quoting Altshuler (1979), suggests that 'mobility is most usefully conceived in terms of the ease with which desired destinations can be reached.' (p. 3). This definition of mobility is very similar to Hall and Banisters' (1995) definition cited above. Here, accessibility implies mobility and vice versa (Banister and Button, 1993; Hall and Banister, 1995): there is no necessary uni-directional causal link from one to the other. Accessibility is a precondition for mobility to the same degree as high mobility will indicate high accessibility.

A second relationship between the two terms forges a direct causal link between the two terms. Here accessibility is a precondition of mobility. Access to transport, Downie (1994) argues, makes abstract concepts such as access to activities meaningful. Here, accessibility becomes a functional condition (or, more philosophically, a transcendental argument) for mobility: without access (to, say, a car or to public transport) individuals cannot be mobile. Denmark (1996, p. 5) similarly, if somewhat less forcefully, identifies mobility as:

> a complicated function depending on a range of variables including access to a car as a driver or passenger; public transport availability, accessibility and relevance; location of residence in relation to required services and social outlets; the health of the person involved; the availability of

paratransit or community transport; ability to pay for a suitable transport mode; and the existence of user or supply-side subsidies.

Although Denmark understands accessibility as one of many ingredients that make up mobility, the direction of causation is clear: the structural variable (accessibility) determines the individual variable (mobility).

A third relationship between accessibility and mobility in the literature reverses this causality. Rather than mobility depending on the accessibility of locations and services, it is accessibility that is shaped by the degree of individual or collective mobility. Quoting an NRMA (1995) study, Denmark (1996) surmises that transport disadvantage 'most commonly results in reduced mobility. This in turn, reduces access to essential services and resources including employment, shops, commercial and community services, and cultural and leisure facilities' (p. 5). The logic of this relationship is as follows. A particular condition, such as disability or poverty, impairs individuals' mobility. Since individual's are not mobile, they cannot access desired locations and services: thus, mobility (individual variable) determines the accessibility (structural variable).

Last, Himanen *et al.* (1993), arguing in terms of welfare economics, conceive of accessibility and mobility as expressions of two incompatible economic principles: efficiency and distributional equity. Mobility, they maintain, 'concerns the Spatial Movement (sic) of people and goods.' Mobility is a crucial factor in balanced economic growth: it matches input factors in the production process as well ensuring an efficient distribution of final products (p. 10). Conversely, accessibility 'refers to the ease with which people can reach desirable facilities (e.g. schools, hospitals, work, recreation areas), and has as such direct distributional aspects.' This, they continue, means that facilities such as schools, hospitals, shops, etc. ought to be equally accessible to all: in short, accessibility is a public good. However, the policy objective of providing efficient mobility as well as universal accessibility are ultimately contradictory: a Pareto-optimal distribution of transport resources will, in terms of welfare economics, not necessarily imply equal access to all locations and services.

Why do policy actors and researchers conceive of and deploy the term accessibility so inconsistently, even within the same article or policy document?

Accessibility, Well-Being and Equity: Normative Implications

Policy actors define and use the concept of accessibility in fundamentally divergent ways because the concept is inherently value-laden. Throughout the transport policy literature, the link between transport (and the accessibility that accompanies it) and human well-being is a recurring theme. In the *White Paper on Employment, Growth and Competitiveness*, the European Commission (1993, p. 34) argues that Europe's:

> ascendancy in the past was due to the quality of its communications networks, which gave its inhabitants easy access to natural and technical resources. By developing the movement of people and goods, Europe has been able to marry economic prosperity, quality of life and commercial efficiency.

What is true for regions is also seems to be true for individuals: Denmark (1996), quoting Martin Wachs, argues that mobility is 'an "essential service" for the elderly..., critical to their physical, social and psychological well-being' (p. 5).

Yet, not all transport commentators agree that the relationship between modern transport and human well-being is positive. In his forceful polemic, Hermann Knoflacher (1997) points to modern transport 'madness' as the root of all contemporary human misery. The proliferation of motorways, coupled with incompetent town and city planning, have created misanthropic ('*menschenfeindlich*') environments: traffic noise deprives people of their right to a good nights rest, transport related emissions are poisoning humans and nature, and transport infrastructure not only insults the eye but also strangles local economic growth.

Well-being, particularly the distribution of well-being, is inextricably linked to questions of equity and fairness. As Himanen *et al.* (1993) suggest in the passage above, accessibility, or the lack of it, has implications for an equitable distribution of burdens and well-being in a society. But what would an equitable distribution of costs and benefits look like in terms of accessibility? Again, different policy-actors resolve this question in various ways.

For some researchers and policy actors, equity means the fair allocation of costs between individual transport users. Here, there are no a priori differences between individual transport users: just as rational individuals enter the market on equal terms, there is nothing that intrinsically distinguishes one transport user from the other. This notion of transport equity, which Todd Litman (1996) calls 'horizontal equity', 'incorporates the concept that consumers should "get what they pay for and pay for what they get"' (p. 1). Conversely, having others pay for the costs one incurs is inequitable. The European Commission (1995a, p. 5), while addressing transport externalities, concludes that external costs:

> imply that individual transport decisions no longer lead to an outcome that is desirable from the point of view of society as a whole. Moreover, the external costs are paid by others: tax payers implicitly end up footing the bill of road maintenance and health care due to damage from air pollution, whilst damage to buildings and crops results from acidification and other forms of pollution is paid by house owners, businesses and farmers. This is unfair and inefficient.

The message is clear: the more accessibility one wants, the more one has to pay.

Yet, is equity in accessibility always a question of matching demand and supply (or matching wants to purchasing power)? Other transport commentators point out that accessibility is more than a commodity: accessibility is a levelling device and therefore is synonymous with equity. Litman (1995, p. 1) summarises this form of equity in the somewhat cumbersome term 'vertical equity with regard to needs and ability'. In particular, it is a measure:

> of whether an individual is relatively transportation disadvantaged compared with others in the community. It assumes that everyone should enjoy at least a basic level of access, even if people with special needs require more resources per mile, per trip or per person.

Here, providing equity means providing accessibility. By the same token, the absence of accessibility creates inequities. There is, then, a role (or even a duty) for transport policy in rectifying these perceived inequities. In this context, Denmark (1996, p. 7) surmises:

> Certainly, if a lack of appropriate transport is preventing some disadvantaged people from getting to government, commercial or community services it would seem reasonable that transport provision should be used as a tool to deliver equitable access.

The same normative implications of accessibility reappear at the macro-level: when discussing regional socio-economic disparities, policy actors apply the same line of argumentation. In the EU, the idea of cohesion expresses interregional equity. Again, the tool for achieving socio-economic equity, or cohesion, is providing accessibility. The European Commission (1995, p. 3) clearly links cohesion with accessibility when it maintains that:

> if Europe is to reach its goal of regional cohesion, then each region should have access to the major markets of the European Union. This is particularly important for developing small and medium sized towns as a

> network of regional centres required for ensuring the availability of essential public services such as education and vocational training.

Unlike market-oriented approaches that conceive of equity as the fair distribution of costs incurred by accessibility, this view understands equity as a function of accessibility. What is more, the implications for transport policy differ considerably from more market-based ideas. Whereas the latter would rely on the 'invisible hand' to provide equity, the former envisages a strong role for active policy action: policy actors can deliver equity by providing accessibility via the transport system.

A third approach to accessibility and equity, however, is less optimistic. Rather than relying on the market or transport policy, this perspective identifies the locus of inequity within modern transport systems themselves. The Austrian transport expert Hermann Knoflacher (1997), a vociferous proponent of this approach, perceives transport systems to be inherently inequitable. Transport infrastructure, he argues, intrinsically favour large-scale, centralised economic activity. Motorways, high speed rail links, and airports link strong economic centres thus bypassing small-scale local economic activity. The result, Knoflacher contends, is economic, social, and cultural dependence of peripheral regions on more central regions as transport saps local labour supply, destroys local businesses, and flattens regional cultural diversity. Accessibility, Knoflacher maintains, means little more than the appropriation of the small and indigenous by the large and centralised.

In sum, the term accessibility is extraordinarily difficult to pin down. In some contexts it refers to structural qualities, in others it describes individual attributes. In others still, accessibility characterises both structural features and individual capabilities. Yet, these differences do not stem from an inherent confusion or incompetence in the transport research community: indeed, these differences are not even random. As the preceding section has hopefully shown, accessibility is a value-laden concept inextricably intertwined with ideas of human well-being and equity. Values, in turn, are not empirically falsifyable and thus open to interpretation. If we are to believe the post-modern sociology of knowledge, interpretation does not take place in a social vacuum. In order to understand what the various definitions of accessibility mean for policy-making, we have to understand the socio-institutional discourses from which these definitions emerge.

Socio-Institutional Contexts: Three Ideal-Typical Discourses

Where, then, do the differing definitions and interpretations of the concept of accessibility originate?

A possible explanation could be that phenomena in transport policy-making are interpreted through what Graham Allison (1971) called different 'perceptual lenses'. Martin Rein and Donald Schön (1994) make a very similar point when they contend that policy controversies are based on differences in 'policy frames'. These are the conceptual and cognitive tools that allow individual policy actors to filter, order, and make sense out of the plethora of policy-relevant data, phenomena, and events. In short, policy frames act as selective perceptual filters and, in this way, structure policy-relevant knowledge.

This is what Paul Sabatier (1993) calls 'policy belief systems'. Sabatier argues that these policy belief systems function like ideologies: they set value priorities, they structure perceptions of causal relationships, they mould perception of states of the world, and they affect how an individual policy-maker views the efficacy of different policy tools. Policy belief systems allow policy actors to interpret data and thus create plausible stories, or narratives, from policy events: they enable policy actors to construct coherent and rational explanations of the transport policy issue with a beginning and a resolution, with protagonists and antagonists, and, of course, with a moral.

The important point here is that there is no way of validating or falsifying these 'perceptual lenses'. What is to count as a right or wrong, as a fact or myth, as a problem or non-issue is structured by these policy-frames. Rein and Schön (1994) argue that 'if *objective* means frame-neutral, there *are* no objective observers' (Rein and Schön, 1994, p 30). This is not to say that transport planning based on the bio-cycle of the South American Bullfrog is as valid as planning based on a carefully constructed econometric model.[2] It does, however, suggest that transport policy debate, be it at political or academic level, operates on a 'contested terrain': what is obvious, scientific, and objective to one policy actor may, for very good reasons, not be so clear for another.

Policy frames or policy-belief systems do not hang in mid-air. They emerge from and are embedded in specific institutional and organisational contexts. Institutions and organisations, in turn, are the different patterns of social co-operation we use for solving policy problems such as transport. What is more, these patterns of co-operation are not value-neutral: in order to enable co-operative interaction, institutions rely on shared norms and values. These normative structures provide the foundations for the policy-belief systems actors deploy for understanding policy problems.

Policy-belief systems thus fulfil a double-function: not only do they provide the conceptual tools for understanding complex policy problems, they also provide for institutional continuity. Institutional structures that persistently fail to provide policy solutions will, one suspects, not be terribly successful. Institutional policy-belief systems, by highlighting certain aspects of a problem and backgrounding others according to their shared norms and values, define policy problems so that they can be solved in terms of the available institutional mechanisms. As a result, we can expect that the way policy actors define and deploy the term accessibility will vary with the socio-institutional context they operate in.

Within the transport policy discourse, we can identify three distinct, albeit ideal-typical, stories. Each has a distinct diagnosis of the transport issue which is based on a characteristic set of assumptions. Each story constructs links of cause and effect; each story suggests a particular course of action. More significantly, each story defines accessibility in a different way.

Accessibility as Regional Development and Cohesion: The Classical Transport Planning View

For the most part of the post-WWII era, rational planning approaches, typically but not exclusively found in government hierarchies, have dominated the transport policy debate. Based to a large degree on engineering and economic models, the classical view of transport planning has defined the transport issue in terms of a purely technical problem to be conquered by the application of increasingly sophisticated technologies. On the conceptual level, these technologies comprise transport models with increasing numbers of variables; on the concrete level, the high speed railways, the high-tech aviation hardware, and the ever-increasing efficiency of motor cars bear witness to transport planning's belief in technology. Yet for all the apparent objectivity and rationality inherent in the classical transport perspective, the approach is based on some very strong assumptions concerning accessibility.

The assumptions The basis of rational transport planning approaches is that there is a strong positive link between accessibility, i.e. the ease by which individuals can reach desired locations, and economic growth. Banister and Lichfield (1993) see the clearest expression of this assumption in the logic of Classical Location Theory. Here, the (monetary or utility) values of different locations depend on the location's degree of accessibility. Transport costs, this approach argues, are a key determinant of land and rental values. Moreover, land use is tied to the rent level in the market: changes in transport costs lead to changes in rental values which, in turn, affect land use. As a result, the more transport costs have fallen, the less people are averse to longer journey distances: this logic explains the increasing suburbanisation trends in industrialised countries (p. 7).

The underlying rationale of this approach was developed in the US of the 1950s where researchers first started to systematically analyse the relationship between spatial organisation and location. Hansen's (1959) analysis of transport in and around Washington D.C. found that accessible locations were more likely to attract development than inaccessible locations. These findings suggested there was 'land-use transport feedback cycle' meaning that land-use patterns depended on the location of human activities such as work, shopping, or leisure. The distribution of these activities implied a strong role for transport systems: in order to partake in desirable activities, individuals had to use the transport system (Wegener, 1993, p. 157). The classical transport management approach, then, accords a strong role to transport in spatial development. The common wisdom that emerged from these early transport studies was that:

- transport shapes cities;
- transport policy affects the spatial organisation and development of cities;
- transport is a function of land-use;
- land-use policy influences transport (Wegener, 1993, p. 159).

Moreover, these conclusions foresaw a strong role for rational transport planning. Since journey and location decisions were co-determinate, US planners concluded that they had to consider transport and land-use planning together (Wegener, 1993, p. 157). If transport determines the development of locations, then the rational planning of transport could induce land-use patterns that would lead to economic growth. Conversely, a deterioration of transport systems leads to economic decline. The European Commission (1993, p. 19) expressed these sentiments by arguing that transport networks:

> are the arteries of the single market. They are the life-blood of competitiveness, and their malfunction is reflected in lost opportunities to create new markets and hence in a level of job creation that falls short of our potential.

Increasing traffic volume, brought about by improved accessibility, necessarily becomes a sign of economic prosperity. For example, Bert Morris (1993) points to the strong positive relationship between income and car ownership (p. 148). The European Commission's Common Transport Policy (CTP) aims to promote regional cohesion, meaning the harmonisation of economic performance across different European regions, by producing, improving, and upgrading transport links: in short, cohesion is a function of economic growth which in turn depends on the provision of accessibility.

The diagnosis How do the assumptions of the classical planning view affect the way policy-actors perceive transport policy problems?

From this perspective, transport problems are little more than technical management problems. Bert Morris (1993), a representative of the British Automobile Association (AA), somewhat predictably contends that car ownership is the key variable in the transport policy debate. In Britain alone, he continues, car ownership will dramatically increase in the coming years. In the light of an increasing number of cars on the road, future transport problems will emerge from congestion and system inefficiencies (p. 149): he argues that urban congestion is the result of illegal parking and poorly planned roadwork (p. 152). Similarly, the European Commission (1993) bemoans the slowing of transport infrastructure investment in Europe. What is more, they continue, the networks that do exist are poorly co-ordinated interregionally, internationally, and intermodally. 'The fact that not enough attention has been paid to developing infrastructures', the Commission avers, 'is one of the reasons for the deterioration in the quality of life' (European Commission, 1993, p. 22).

In short, the classical planning view sees present transport problems as a purely technical issue of providing increasing degrees accessibility. On the one hand, lack of physical transport infrastructure not only jeopardises economic growth (in terms of the costs of congestion), but also individual well-being (pollution, loss of income) and regional cohesion. On the other hand, these tendencies are exacerbated by inefficient management of existing transport structures.

Policy prescriptions The diagnosis of transport problems in the classical planning view leads to clear policy prescription: the provision of more infrastructure and the efficient management of existing networks.

This is reflected in the objectives of the EU's Common Transport Policy. First, the policy aims to reinforce the internal market by facilitating the free movement of goods and persons, an aim that can only make sense if there is a positive link between accessibility and growth. Second, the EU plans to eliminate regulatory obstacles, hoping to encourage the development of a coherent and integrated transport system based on the best available technology. Third, the Commission will reduce regional disparities by providing accessibility to land-locked, island, and peripheral regions. Fourth, this development must be environmentally sustainable in terms of Global Climate Change. Last, the new and improved transport system must be safe (Rienstra *et al.*, 1997, p. 273). In sum, the European Commission (1993, p. 39) proposes to promote:

- new and better designed infrastructures, accessible to all citizens;
- will permit better, safer travel at low costs, and thus an increase in trade, while reducing costs and distances and creating scope for other activities;
- effective planning in Europe in order to avoid a concentration of wealth and population;
- bridge-building towards Eastern Europe, which is essential in order to meet requirements, step up investment, and promote trade.

What does this mean in practice? Since accessibility means economic growth, of which increasing traffic volumes are an indicator, the policy-maker must maximise the full economic potential inherent in the growth of transport. In short, the classical transport approach leads to more roads, railways, and waterways. The Trans-European Networks (TENs) Project of the EU foresees:

> 70,000 kms of rail track, including 22,000 kms of new and upgraded track for High Speed Trains; 15,000 kms of new roads, nearly half in regions on the outskirts of the Union, to complete a 58,000 km or improved network already largely built; combined transport corridors and terminals; 267 airports of common interest and networks of inland waterways and sea ports. (European Commission, 1998, p. 1)

The total cost of the project, the European Comission estimates, will be no less than 400 billion ECU by 2010.

Instruments and indicators Efficient management of transport necessitates suitable rational planning instruments and tools. The assumption that policy-makers can direct regional development and economic growth by manipulating accessibility means that these phenomena must be amenable to quantification, modelling, and prediction. The tools, instruments and indicators of the classical planning approach reflect this belief.

Planning and allocation decisions in transport policy-making heavily rely on quantitative models based on discounting techniques such as Cost-Benefit-Analysis (CBA) and Multi-Criteria-Analysis (MCA).[3] The goal of transport models, such as the EUNET model sponsored by the European Commission, is to 'measure the impacts of transportation policies in general and specific transportation system investments in particular' (SASI, 1997, p. 9). Exact measurement and quantification of the socio-economic impacts associated with increased accessibility is necessary if planners are to assess the degree to which accessibility fosters economic growth. Furthermore, given the volume of expenditure in transport projects such as 'the Trans-European Networks (TETN) program, the need for consistent prediction and rational and transparent measurement of the likely socio-economic impacts of major transport system improvements becomes obvious' (Bökemann *et al.*, 1997, pp. 8-9). Three things are important here: first, the belief that transport systems are controllable; second, that complex transport phenomena are amenable to quantitative modelling and prediction; third, that rational models imbue the transport planner with control over highly complex social, economic, and political processes.

How do planners know they have fulfilled their objectives? In other words, how do planners define accessibility in the concrete terms of quantitative indicators? Again, the SASI project provides a good example of how planners translate the basic assumptions into functional model parameters. The SASI project aims to measure both the social and economic impacts of transport infrastructure investment as well as its contribution to European regional cohesion. Since accessibility means economic growth, the only logical indicator for the degree of accessibility is regional GDP per capita (Bökemann *et al.*, 1997, p. 12). Regional cohesion in turn, Bökemann *et al.* (1997) argue, is a more difficult concept to quantify: that is why 'the cohesion measures used in this study reflect the even- or unevenness of the spatial distribution of socio-economic and accessibility indicators among the regions' (p. 34). There are, then, three sets of indicators to cover both the social and the economic aspects of accessibility. The economic measure of accessibility is, as mentioned, GDP per capita. Regional unemployment, in turn, measures the social availability of jobs. Last, the SASI project uses both income and regional unemployment as cohesion indicators on the European scale.

These indicators reflect the basic assumptions of the classical planning view. In the SASI model, accessibility *is* regional GDP: the more accessibility, the higher GDP. The qualitative dimensions of accessibility, such as the social exclusionary effects of poor public transport, low car ownership, etc. have been faded out of the analytical perspective. In sum, the set of indicators are tied to a structural conception of accessibility.

Accessibility as Horizontal Fairness: The Market and Transport

In recent years, voices critical of the assumptions and policy prescriptions of the classical planning approach have increasingly found their way into the transport policy debate at all levels. Many of these voices question the validity of the classical planning ideology both in terms of its understanding of transport problems and in terms of its policy solutions. It may very well be, these critics argue, that the entire assumptional edifice on which planners have based transport policy for the past three decades is fundamentally flawed. In particular, many of these voices contend, the classical planning approaches have taken insufficient account of market mechanisms.

Is accessibility synonymous with economic growth? The market-based approach starts by questioning the positive relationship between transport infrastructure investment, accessibility, and economic growth (Banister and Lichfield, 1995). Whereas, Banister and Lichfield maintain, there is little doubt that infrastructure investments impact on land and rental values, the effects are not nearly as simple as Classical Location Theory would predict. Often, infrastructure investments do not create new economic activity in a region, but merely displace activities from other regions: rather than efficiency gains, investment leads to shifts in the Pareto optimal distribution (p. 4). Even where there are efficiency gains, they argue, the scale of measurable impact may be very small and highly localised.

A major reason, contend Banister and Lichfield, why the positive relationship between economic growth and accessibility does not hold is that transport costs make up a small part of production costs. Firms look to other factors, such as land value, labour costs, or tax structures, in their location decisions. Additionally, transport infrastructure investment is subject to diminishing marginal returns: every new (and expensive) transport link in Europe yields less and less in terms of accessibility. These two factors in combination, they conclude, may mean that lower transport costs are a marginal factor in firms' location decisions (p. 5).

What is more, at the regional level, the classical planning approach systematically plays down the costs of transport infrastructure investments. More often than not, Banister and Lichfield continue, investments such as high speed rail links provide more benefits to central regions than peripheral areas thus undermining urban/ rural regeneration policy objectives (p. 4). Further, increases in journey lengths, the accompanying pollution, and congestion may outweigh the benefits associated with increased accessibility.

The assumptions Rather than understanding accessibility and the transport system as a simple systems amenable to prediction and quantification, this approach suggests that accessibility is more complex. In this perspective, transport infrastructure investments exist within a dynamic system of complex exchanges where participants react and adapt to signals from other actors: this, of course, is a market. This is not to say that transport investment does not imply economic growth: it means, however, that there are always other, possibly unintended, outcomes that accompany infrastructure investments. As Banister and Lichfield note,

> [t]he changes in accessibility resulting from new investment in an already dense and congested network will not be of a sufficient scale to have a major long-term impact on the local economy. They are unlikely to be of a sufficient scale to attract major new employment into the city. Their impact may encourage longer distance travel out of the city as the new investment will make other locations more accessible; accessibility works in both directions. (p. 280)

Accessibility, then, better understood in terms of complementarity of diverse competitive networks. Rather than analysing investment in terms of a single transport sector, such as rail, Banister and Lichfield suggest we comprehend 'the impact of one new link on the network as a whole' (p. 280). In contrast to the uni-directional, mechanistic logic of the classical planning approach, the market-based view advocates a more relativist and flexible approach to accessibility: not the narrow impact on a particular sector but the impact of infrastructure investment on the relative competitive positions of particular *networks* is important. Banister and Lichfield conclude by stating that new:

> concepts of networks and accessibility are required to determine under what conditions the competitive position of one network will be changed as compared with another on at least three dimensions – to influence expectations, to facilitate co-ordination and to ensure compatibility. (p. 280)

How can a market-based approach fulfil these requirements? The basic assumption of market-oriented approaches to transport policy is that, in general, markets are efficient when left alone. This means that as long as prices accurately reflect the underlying costs of any particular resource or service, the market will efficiently allocate resources according to demand and supply. What is more, phenomena in transport emanate from the complex interaction of individual and self-interested decisions: transport users are rational utility maximisers who adapt their behaviour to market signals.

When, however, markets fail, resource prices will not reflect the underlying costs. Since market-behaviour depends on price signals, distorted prices lead to inefficient market-behaviour. Individuals will over-consume resources priced below their true costs and, likewise, under-consume resources that are over-priced. This, in turn, can lead to economically inefficient producer behaviour such as rationing and price-dumping. The net result is an inefficient allocation of resources and, put plainly, waste.

Why do markets fail? When left to their own devices, markets, in theory, automatically adjust as individuals adapt their behaviour to changing price signals: markets form expectations and co-ordinate compatible transactions. Yet, if policy-makers tamper with the complex web of individual transactions that make up the market, this self-equilibrating mechanism breaks down.[4] Thus, market-based approaches, quite unlike the classical planning approaches, perceive a very different role for public policy. Rather than actively regulating and directing transport policy decisions, market-based approaches imply leaving as much decision-making as possible to consumers. The rationale, as Banister and Lichfield outline above, is that individual behaviour in markets is too flexible, adaptive, and complex to predict with any certainty, let alone postulate a uni-directional link between accessibility and income. Accessibility, then, is not so much a cause of economic growth as it is one of many factors that influence individual transport decisions.

The diagnosis The view from the market interprets the present transport issue in industrialised countries in a fundamentally different way than the classical planning approaches. For years, market advocates maintain, planners and policy-makers justified transport infrastructure investment, meaning predominantly roads, in terms of economic growth and the subsequent regeneration of depressed regions. Yet, the advocates of market-oriented approaches argue, there is very little evidence of these alleged benefits (Banister and Lichfield, 1995, p. 5; Banister and Hall, 1995).

Instead, more roads invariably mean more traffic. With increasing traffic volumes, they continue, comes more pollution, less accessibility for those without cars, and the relocation of industrial, leisure and shopping facilities into green belts. Not even car-users have profited: increasing road traffic coupled with suburbanisation have generally increased the journey distances, congested the roads, increased pollution, and have exacted a gruesome price in terms of accidents. The European Commission (1995a, p. 4), when commenting on fair and efficient road pricing, argues that:

> [r]educing pollution and congestion by means of increasing road capacity is – in many cases – not the best option. The cost of construction of road (and parking) capacities in densely populated areas continues to increase. Studies indicate that improving and extending infrastructure results in *more* journeys overall as road users make use of the new or improved facilities. The environmental impacts both of these extra journeys and of the construction of the road infrastructure may outweigh any benefits in improved traffic flows.

Why have transport policies so spectacularly failed? The answer, contend market advocates, is simple: the transport market is distorted. Transport prices, particularly road transport prices, do not reflect the full social and environmental costs it incurs (Himanen *et al.*, 1993; Banister and Lichfield, 1995; European Commission, 1995a). This leads to signal failures and to inappropriate consumer behaviour (Himanen *et al.*, 1993): individuals consume 'too much' road transport compared to other modes to which the explosion in car-ownership and road congestion bears witness.

What is more, misguided policies exacerbate these signal failures. Insufficient information about individual market behaviour leads to what Himanen *et al.* (1993) call public 'response failures': regulation to charge the transport consumer the marginal social costs often misses the mark because 'most actors appeared to have creative talents in circumnavigating intervention measures'. Similarly, the European Commission (1995a, p. 2) reflects on the disadvantages of transport regulation:

> Most policies that have been devised so far do not influence these [transport] decisions directly and, therefore, overlook an important factor – human behaviour. Transport choices are influenced by transport prices and there is evidence that for many journeys there is a mismatch between transport prices paid by individual users and the underlying costs. The result is that decisions are distorted and too much of the wrong sort of transport occurs at the wrong place and the wrong points in time.

The bottom-line, this view informs us, are external costs (that is, costs that a transport user incurs but someone else pays) for which, as Section 1 indicated, consumers are increasingly unwilling to pay.

Policy prescriptions and instruments In order to re-establish the self-equilibrating market mechanisms in transport, policy-makers must make transport prices reflect their true social and environmental costs. NeilKinnock (1995), the European Commissioner for Transport maintains that efficient pricing of road transport 'can consequently be a valuable complement to other policies for trying to ensure a better distribution of transport within and across modes, space and time. Or to put it simply: we won't get transport right if we don't get the price right' (p. 2).

How can policy-makers 'get the prices right'? A number of policy tools are available for internalising external transport costs. In theory, policy-actors can fall back on command and control regulations such as subsidies. However, as Himanen *et al.* (1993) point out, regulation may exacerbate market distortions. Furthermore, argue the market advocates, tools that work with market forces are more flexible, efficient, and less costly than command and control measures. Assuming that policy-makers can tie costs closely prices, market based instruments are more effective if the policy-problem varies across space and time as does the European transport issue (European Commission, 1995a, p. 8).

The European Commission outlines five reasons for adopting pricing strategies in the EU. First, regulation cannot tap into all the mechanisms needed for changing transport consumer behaviour. Second, the costs of regulation have increased so that replacing regulation with pricing may bring about efficiency gains. Third, technical advances, such as electronic telematics, would allow the introduction of pricing strategies. Fourth, liberalisation in the framework of internal markets means that market distortions across modes and operators will disappear. Last, the present transport issue calls for integrated and flexible responses that only pricing can offer (p. 10).

There are two main economic instruments open to policy-makers: charging users directly and fiscal measures. Tackling congestion means using both strategies: whereas telematics allow the policy-maker to charge the costs directly to the user, fiscal measures attempt to create an incentive structure in which the 'right kind' of transport consumption takes place. Examples are differentiated vehicle taxes based on the environmental characteristics of the vehicle, differentiated fuel taxes, and the removal of diesel subsidies.[5]

In sum, the market-based approach suggests that accessibility plays a relatively minor role in regional economic growth. It is merely one of the many factors that influence individual transport decisions. Transport prices, or, more precisely, the correspondence of prices and underlying costs, are far more significant in determining transport and locational decisions. Accessibility, regional economic growth, and regional cohesion will fall into place once policy-makers 'get the prices right'.

Accessibility as a 'Bad': Sustainability, the Environment, and Industrial Society

Although classical transport planning and market-based approaches interpret the transport issue very differently and arrive at divergent conclusions, both of them are grounded in the socio-economic system of advanced capitalism: although both perceive the relationship between accessibility and regional economic growth differently, both assume that they are socially desirable.

This is precisely where both classical transport planning and market-based approaches differ from what we will call the 'holistic post-materialist' approach.

The assumptions The holistic post-materialist view of transport policy is the voice of protest. Current theory and practice of transport policy in industrialised countries, it argues, is hopelessly confused, irrelevant to real human needs, and fundamentally immoral. Misguided transport and land-use policies have left us with environments that cannot fulfil our basic social and biological needs. Congestion, accidents, commuting, long journey distances, and, particularly, pollution are depriving people of their basic human rights to a liveable and healthy life.

Why, then, do planners and policy-makers continue to destroy the natural and social world with environmentally rapacious and socially disastrous transport infrastructure? The reason, this view maintains, is because policy-makers are both ideologically and structurally trapped in a socio-economic system that systematically sets the wrong priorities. Pollution, congestion, or accidents are not the root cause of present transport problems: they are mere symptoms of a deeper social malaise. Advanced capitalist systems, this voice proclaims, are fundamentally inequitable: what we experience as traffic problems are the results of an economic, social, and political system that inequitably distributes costs and benefits across society. It is no coincidence, argue proponents of this view, that the women, elderly, ethnic minorities, and the poor have accessibility problems: it reflects the low value the capitalist system places on these groups. It is also no coincidence that transport policy is biased in favour of road transport: powerful economic interests, such as the automobile industry and the construction industry, have long captured the political decision-making process.

Tinkering with the system, as the classical transport planning and market-based approaches suggest, is less than useless; it merely reproduces existing inequalities. Addressing transport problems means fundamentally rethinking our economic, political, and socio-cultural values: in short, it requires a holistic approach to socio-economic change so that we can live in harmony with ourselves and with nature.

The diagnosis In terms of accessibility, the holistic approach suggests we have to overcome prevailing transport ideologies. Knoflacher (1997) argues that current transport thinking amounts to little more than ideological obfuscation of the facts and downright deception of the citizen. Conventionally, policy-makers justify transport infrastructure investments in terms of time saved on journeys. This, however, is an illusion stemming from an overly particularistic approach to transport analysis. A holistic approach shows, contends Knoflacher, that there are in fact no time savings across the entire system. Transport is a zero-sum game: ten minutes saved on one individual's journey imply that someone else's journey time increases (pp. 43-48). Yet, since journey times are distributed inequitably, the illusion that modern transportation saves time survives and flourishes.

This logic, supported by deceptive theoretical constructs such as CBA and MCA (Knoflacher, 1997, pp. 84-87) leads to a transport system geared for ever increasing speeds. Policy-makers, captured by the road construction lobby (Knoflacher, 1997, pp. 33, 83, 86), commission the whole-sale destruction of the natural environment by building more and more motorways and high speed rail links. Yet, contends Knoflacher, policy-makers and conventional transport researchers have fundamentally confused cause and effect. Knoflacher here contrasts micro- to macro-mobility: the former is slow, life-sustaining, and environmentally sustainable mobility within small regional areas, the latter is high speed, socially and environmentally damaging movement of people and goods across vast distances. Whereas policy should be promoting micro-mobility and thus reducing the speed of the transport system, policy-makers constantly seek to increase speeds thus destroying humans' social and environmental habitats.

Rather than being a boon to regions and society, Knoflacher (1997) maintains that accessibility is the cause of human misery in industrialised countries. Improvements in accessibility always means the relative devaluation of a weak region compared to a strong area. High speed links between small and central locations usually spell the social, cultural and economic death of the weaker region. As work and services, such as shopping, health care, and government services shift from the periphery to the centre, the indigenous transport patterns that sustained a fragile socio-cultural network are brutally torn apart. As a result, not only employment and labour supply leaves the region but also the indigenous cultural patterns of social interaction are irretrievably destroyed (pp. 57-58).

Consequently, rural dwellings have deteriorated from places where people lived, worked, and socialised to mono-functional residential communities with little or no horizontal interaction. What is more, local suppliers, and with them local economic activity, collapse under the pressures of having to compete with large, centralised economic units. The bottom-line is that, as transport links enable people to by-pass locations at very high speeds, weaker regions deteriorate further. In this view, accessibility implies the centralisation and, more significantly, the homogenisation of human activities; it is, in short, the exploitation of the weak by the strong.

How could it have come to this? Here, Knoflacher (1997) points to a unholy alliance of politics, big business, and research. For years, the researchers in this iron triangle have provided the conceptual tools to hide the special interests behind transport policy: those of the motor vehicle industry and the construction industry. Here, laments Knoflacher, logic is turned on its head to suit big business interests.

An example he cites is the Austrian legal process in disputes over rural land for prestige transport projects. He recounts how a skewed administrative processes, corrupt politicians, and the archaic legal system conspire to force small land-owners to sign over their land for transport infrastructure projects. Public hearings amount to little more than sham democracy since the methods used to evaluate projects (CBA, MCA) favour those in control of defining the parameters of the evaluation (these, Knoflacher adds, are exclusively hand-picked to assure conformity to dominant interests) (p. 87). In court cases, the 'independent' evaluations originate from consultants that are anything but independent (p. 103).

These developments, however, are symptomatic of wider social developments. The structure of advanced capitalist societies are failing to meet real human needs. Indeed, the demand for mobility, argues Knoflacher, is a sign of unsatisfied need. It is no surprise that people who are cooped up in poorly planned, dirty, dangerous, and unpleasant cities and towns feel the desire to leave at the week-end. What is more, the increasing trend of individual atomisation caused by advanced capitalist labour markets exacerbates the desire for mobility: a person who has a functioning social network and healthy interpersonal relations does not need to travel. The demand for increased mobility is a result of social pathologies such as single-parent families and single households.

These developments, in turn, emerge from a socio-economic system that is based on morally dubious principles. Knoflacher maintains that the principle liberal capitalism stands for, factor mobility, in reality legitimates the savage exploitation of the weak by the strong. Our perception of economic development, he contends, is dictated by the winners of this unfairly structured game: the losers, by and large, have little say. What is more, the modern transport system is the medium with which the fast, strong, and centralised hunt down the slow, weak, and indigenous. 'The price of today's economic growth', Knoflacher avers, 'will be paid by the workers, the social system the "Third World" and the next generation that will have to inherit a destroyed planet' (p.119).

Policy prescriptions Policy prescriptions within the holistic post-materialist view concentrate on two levels: the conceptual level and the policy level. At the conceptual level, this view suggests we fundamentally alter the way we think about transport. Transport systems must place the human person into the centre of consideration. Yet, humans are more than rational individuals: they have a right to a healthy social and natural environment. Thus, the reconceptualisation of transport policy thinking must aim to harmonise human needs and the natural environment.

On the concrete level, the holistic post-materialist view suggests radical changes to transport systems. The primary concern here is to radically reduce the volume of road transport (Knoflacher, 1997; *Die Grünen*, 1994). For this purpose, the German Green Parliamentary Party (1994) outlines a comprehensive set of policy proposals that aim to tackle the transport problem from a variety of angles. In order to favour rail transport, bicycles and pedestrians the German Greens foresee a number of both supply side and demand-side measures. On the supply-side, the German Greens believe that massive investment in public transport as well as improved accessibility (in terms of price structures) is of eminent importance. Further, they reject prestige transport projects such as the 'Transalpin' in favour of systematically upgrading existing systems. Last, land-use policy should, they argue, favour high density settlements to reduce the need for travel. Add to this the diverse traffic calming measures Knoflacher suggests, and one obtains a fairly comprehensive restructuring of current transport priorities.

On the demand-side, the German Greens envisage what more conventional policy-actors would consider as draconian measures. In order to discourage the use of motor vehicles, the Greens suggest the internalisation of external costs by drastic increases in fuel taxes and a lifting of the subsidy on diesel fuel. Further, they intend to lower the legal speed limit on all roads (30km/h in built locations, 80km/h on country roads, and 100 km/h on motorways). Tight regulations on transit freight traffic will accompany these measures. Last, the Greens foresee road bans tied to air quality thresholds.

The important aspect of the policy prescriptions of this perspective is that policy uses a wide spectrum of policy instruments. This holistic approach envisages the use of both command and control as well as economic instruments to curb road transport. In addition, the holistic approach aims at changing attitudes towards transport and mobility. This approach is exemplified in the *Guiding Principles of the European Federation of Green Parties*' (1993, p. 4) vision for European transport:

> The environmental impact of transport will be reduced through investment in clean public transport, sensible land-use planning, and taxation of fossil fuels in all sectors, including air traffic. Car-free cities and taxation on fossil fuels will be the rule. Massive motorway projects designed to facilitate road freight between the regions of Europe will be abandoned and investment in the reconstruction in railways preferred.

In sum, the holistic post-materialist view of transport policy aims at restructuring both the central assumptions and tools of transport policy as well as effecting a cultural change. Transport problems are a symptom of fundamental inequities inherent to advanced capitalism. Solving transport problems, advocates of this view argue, means fundamentally changing inequitable socio-economic structures.

The Triangular Policy Space

The previous sections demonstrated that policy actors define accessibility in terms of their respective 'perceptual lenses'. As we have seen, these policy belief-systems, starting from different initial assumptions, interpret the transport issue in very divergent ways and suggest different policy prescriptions.

This does not mean that every policy actor in the transport arena neatly falls into one of the three categories. These policy belief-systems are institutional discourses that emerge form specific socio-institutional settings. The classical transport planning discourse is typical for hierarchically structured organisations: the need for hierarchies to control their environments (Schmutzer, 1994) requires that participants believe that environments can, ultimately, be controlled. Likewise, markets work best when individuals are free to form contractual relationships and when there is a minimum of social control:[6] it is not surprising that markets value freedom from interference. Last, the holistic view is characteristic of egalitarian groups: the rejection of all domination and the emphasis on equality distinguishes them from the other social forms.

In the transport policy debate, then, these three institutional ideal-type discourses fulfil a specific function. The three policy belief-systems make up the apices of a triangular discursive policy space. This policy space delineates the fault lines of the debate but, more importantly, it also outlines the external boundaries of the transport policy debate. These three discourses, constantly pulling in opposite directions, provide the discursive framework in which any thinking and policy debate on transport can take place: in short, they mark the 'contested terrain', in which policy-actors think and dispute about transport issues.

Figure 6.1 The Triangular Policy Space

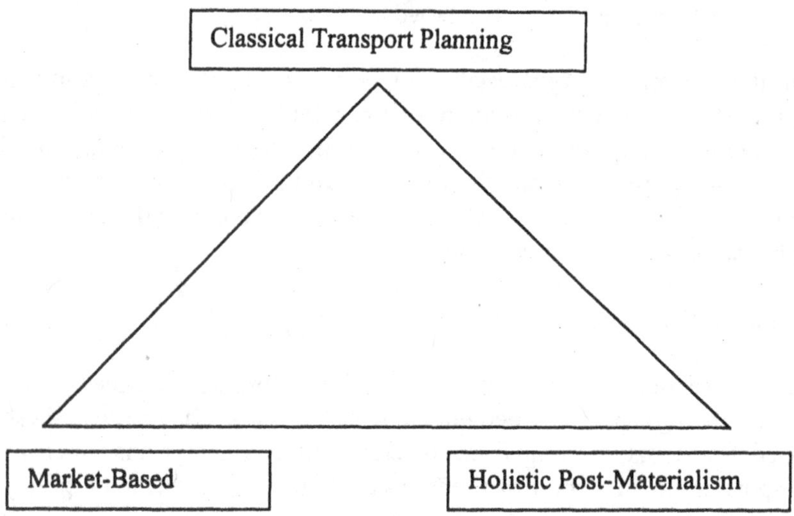

The triangular policy space is a map of socio-institutional discourses: it is not a map of individual attitudes towards transport policy. Of course, these policy belief systems significantly affect and shape the policy-actor's attitudes towards transport policy. However, since policy-actors operate in many socio-institutional contexts, we can expect them to move around within the confines of the policy space and use policy belief-systems selectively as well as strategically.[7]

This section has introduced three institutional policy discourse on the transport issue. We have seen how the different assumptions inherent in each approach lead to very different interpretations and solutions of the present transport problems. These discourses form a triangular policy space in which transport policy debate takes place. But what does this mean for transport policy-making?

Implications for Transport Policy-Making

The fact that socio-institutional discourses filter policy debate in the transport issue has some profound ramifications for the structure of transport policy-making. In particular, the socio-institutional policy belief-systems imply that:

- transport policy deliberation always takes place under conditions of uncertainty and complexity;
- conflict in transport policy debates is endemic; and
- policy-maker must learn to constructively deal with policy conflict.

Uncertainty and Complexity in Transport Policy-Making

Socio-institutional belief-systems play a prominent role in the transport policy debate due to the inherent complexities and uncertainties that surround many transport phenomena. For example, whereas researchers and policy actors for many years virtually took the 'land-use transport feedback cycle' for granted, Robert Cervero and John Landis (1992) show that infrastructure investments (in this case rail stations) in the US have not led to increased development in the recipient areas. They even go on to demonstrate that the largest proportion of suburban development has taken place in cities without motorway links (Wegener, 1995, p. 158).

However, Wegener (1995) maintains, Cervero and Landis' findings apply only to the US. Given the socio-economic framework, in which the US transport system is embedded, it is 'not surprising that, under conditions of ubiquitous accessibility, incremental transport improvements have little effects on location' (p. 159). Tokyo, Wegener avers, provides a counter-example: development in the city is driven by rail development. Consequently, the distance to Tokyo Central Station determines land-values. Wegener concludes that in situations where 'commuting by rail of more than one hour one-way being common, accessibility remains a primary value strongly determining all location and travel decisions' (p. 159). In short, transport is a highly complex system in which any 'attack – however apparently intelligent – on a single element or symptom generally leads to a deterioration of the system as a whole' (Forrester, quoted in Himanen *et al.*, 1993).

With complexity, however, comes uncertainty. Peter Hall (1993) points out that the relationship between accessibility and development is 'one seamless web'. However, he contends the 'trouble is that this combination is so subtle, no one anywhere seems to have completely understood how to make it work at a fine-tuned level' (p. 75). Himanen *et al.* (1993) argue that, like the sorcerer's apprentice, transport experts helplessly face the transport demons they have summoned (p. 21). The uncertainties in transport planning theory and methodology are so significant, Banister and Lichfield are forced to admit that the:

> precise relationship between transport investment and urban development are not well known, even theoretically. There seems to be no single methodology available to test the relationships, the counterfactual situation is difficult to determine and the question of causality not addressed. Decisions have been made based more of faith than understanding. Even where clear methodological approaches have been tried, problems arise concerning available data and the inherent complexity of many relationships. The links between land use, transport and development are much more profound than just an examination of the physical, social and economic relationships might produce. (p. 15)

.Yet, what does this mean for policy debate?

Conflict in Transport Debates is Endemic

If knowledge is inherently incomplete and certainty is a scarce resource which, of course, it always is, then human judgement and interpretation play a prominent part in policy deliberation. Policy-makers facing complex and uncertain problems need plausible interpretations on which to base policy: they need conceptual tools that will allow them to navigate through the complexities and uncertainties. The socio-institutional discourses, in turn, provide these interpretations (Haas, 1992).

However, interpretations come at a cost. If policy-actors interpret transport phenomena in terms of policy belief-systems, they invariably introduce normative aspects into the debate: there is then, no 'value-free' ground on which policy debate could take place. This, in turn, means that policy conflict, far from being an aberration of the policy process, is endemic.

Since the socio-institutional discourse emanate from fundamentally different forms of social organisation, the values reflected in the policy belief systems are necessarily incompatible. Thus policy debate becomes a process of claiming and blaming: policy belief systems claim to have solutions for problems and they apportion blame to the perceived culprits. As we have seen, there is considerable tension between the different approaches: transport planners reject market solutions as unfair and inequitable (Morris, 1993), advocates of market-based approaches blame inefficient regulation for the current transport dilemma and accuse the holistic view of adventurism (Pearce *et al.*, 1991), and the holistic view accuses the other positions of deception and immorality. This is because each policy-belief system, despite the hue of rationality and objectiveness, is based on very fundamental normative principle about how people should organise their social relations.

Knowledge, then, partly becomes a rhetorical resource. Rather than providing objective data on transport phenomena, policy actors use transport models, scenarios, and indicators as ammunition in a highly value-laden policy debate. This is what Rein and Schön (1994, p. 29) refer to as an 'intractable policy controversy' where:

> two or more parties contend with one another over the definition of a problematic situation and vie for control of the policy-making process. Their struggles over the naming and framing of a policy situation are symbolic contests over social meaning of an issue domain, where meaning implies not only what is at issue but what is to be done.

Here, policy actors develop 'a remarkable ability, when embroiled in a controversy, to dismiss the evidence adduced by our antagonists' (Rein and Schön, 1994, p. 5). These types of policy conflicts are divisive, contentious and exceptionally immune to resolution.

Against this background, we have to re-evaluate the role of transport research in the transport policy debate. In the transport debate, no amount of methodology, objectivity, and rationality will prevent a particular piece of knowledge from becoming politicised. Even the most rational transport model contains a strong normative assumptions: the implication that policy-makers can solve transport problems within the regulative structures of planning and government agencies. The notion that a particular piece of transport knowledge will convince policy actors *on its own merits* is, at best, illusionary: policy actors are bound to disagree, often for very good reasons. All transport knowledge is embedded in a socio-cultural context; if two or more policy-actors do not share this context, as is common in democracies, then normative policy conflict is inevitable.[8] The task of the policy-maker, then, is to profit from policy conflict.

Reflexivity and Policy-Oriented Learning

The fact that all policy knowledge is contextual and that transport policy debate is inherently conflictual does not mean that constructive policy debate is impossible. Socio-institutional policy belief-systems are not irrational nor are they inaccurate: each policy frame merely foregrounds certain issues and backgrounds others.[9] It follows that each particular perspective has its strengths and weaknesses.

This is not to say, however, that the road to effective transport policy-making lies in uncritically accepting any form of analysis. Just because we cannot conclusively prove any one policy belief system to be 'wrong' does not mean that all diagnoses and policy recommendations must be 'right'. Since we must distinguish socio-institutional discourses not by what they include into their analytic frameworks but by what they exclude or filter out, policy belief-systems create socio-institutional 'shutters'. Policy actors who rely on one policy-belief system alone (or, alternatively, do not encounter serious criticism from proponents of other policy belief-systems) will introduce a systematic bias[10] into their analysis of transport problems: this, as Collingridge (1992)[11] has demonstrated, can lead to myopia, poor analysis, and, ultimately, poor policy decisions.

We can tentatively point to the problems of each policy belief-system in the transport debate. The discourse with most to answer for is the classical transport planning approach. Having dominated transport policy-making for nearly three decades, classical planning has not succeeded in coping with ever-increasing traffic volumes. Arguably, transport modellers and planners have exacerbated transport problems by clinging to the central assumption that accessibility means economic growth. Yet, as we have seen above, there is very little empirical evidence that increasing accessibility has any noticeable impact on regional economic development (Banister and Lichfield, 1995). Rather than abandoning or even reformulating the basic assumptions in the light of empirical evidence,[12] the classical transport planning view stubbornly maintains that it is not the central assumptions that are incorrect, but the means of measurement. This invariably leads to the search for an ever bigger and technically sophisticated transport model with which to measure socio-economic impacts of transport infrastructure investments.

But what are transport planners measuring? To take the SASI transport model as one example of many, the model purports to provide indicators for regional cohesion and thus allow policy-makers to assess the socio-economic impacts of transport investments. However, the model reduces regional development and cohesion to GDP per capita and regional unemployment respectively: as we have seen, Bökemann *et al.* (1997) seem to believe that this covers economic as well as social impacts. At best, however, these indicators measure an economic *impact* of transport infrastructure investment: there is no social dimension to these indicators whatsoever. The indicators leave income distribution, the access to public and private services, the socio-cultural fabric, to say nothing of social exclusion, ethnic, and gender issues completely untouched. Surely, indicators of regional cohesion should have something to say about horizontal social, cultural, and political ties between two locations. Yet all the SASI indicators tell us is whether transport infrastructure investment has succeeded in harmonising regional unemployment rates which really indicate the degree of social exclusion within a community.

The strength of the classical planning approach is also its greatest weakness. Transport planners are very adept at formalising, quantifying, and modelling certain transport processes. However, the strictures formal models impose on researchers causes transport planners to spectacularly miss the point. By excluding all factors not amenable to exact and objective measurement, transport planners invariably fail to grasp the inherent complexity of transport policy processes. As a result, most transport models fail to produce conclusive results even within their highly restricted analytical scope.

Last, and most significantly, the classical transport planning approaches systematically deny the political nature of transport models. Cloaked in the veil of science and objectivity, transport planners maintain the illusion that they stand aloof from the political fray of transport decision-making. Rigid methodology, strict quantification, and hard data ensure, so the story goes, that research is objective. Transport planning methods do not explicitly provide policy options: they merely provide the 'facts' and let these speak for themselves. Yet, these underlying assumptions themselves are a political act. By insisting that policy be informed by 'objective' analysis and then proceeding to define what 'objective analysis' entails, the transport planning approaches *a priori* disqualify any alternative form of analysis. Defining the transport policy issue as a technical problem amenable to technical solutions precludes any other approaches.

Similarly, market-based approaches also have decisive weaknesses. The entire market argument is based on the assumption that markets are efficient in allocating resources. This assumption is problematic for a variety of reasons. First, the concept of a perfectly competitive market is an ideal-type model: there are no perfectly efficient markets in the real world. Second, although neo-classical economics would readily agree that markets always are imperfect, the causes for market failure the discourse identifies is either too one dimensional or too general. There are many reasons apart from government interference that may cause markets to fail. Like all other forms of social co-operation, markets depend on a favourable institutional and environmental framework. Markets may fail because prevailing socio-cultural values are unfavourable to market-type transactions (for example the belief in equivalent exchange values). Alternatively, markets may collapse because transaction costs unrelated to production or marketing costs are prohibitively high.[13] Another reason for market failure may be an insufficient legal and administrative framework that can effectively implement sanctions. There are, in short, a plethora of cultural, social, and political reasons for market failure: the catch-all phrase of 'government interference' is either too all-inclusive to provide an adequate grasp of all possible sources of market failure or it is too limited if it refers to government intervention alone.

More significantly, the market-oriented approaches to transport policy-making are grounded in some very strong assumptions about human behaviour. The conception of Economic Man, the rational utility maximiser who not only knows but also can rank his preferences, is also an ideal-type. Assuming markets are efficient in order to analyse distributive efficiency of transport policy is one matter; asserting that market-oriented policies will actually change individual transport behaviour is quite another. Although cost and prices certainly influence human behaviour, they are by far not the only factors likely to influence an individual's or a firm's transport decisions.[14] Further, it is not at all clear that internalising the external transport costs will lead to a reduction in road transport: individuals and firms may simply reallocate resources from other areas to accommodate the higher costs of road transport. In this case, economic measures aimed at relieving congestion and reducing CO_2 emissions would clearly fail.

Last, the market-based approaches have little to say about equity. As Himanen *et al.* (1993) point out, an efficient distribution of mobility may not necessarily be equitable. The market-based approaches avoid the issue of what happens to those individuals unable to pay for the full costs of their mobility. Given that there are, as yet, no financially viable alternatives to road transport, the question arises of who will shoulder the burdens of adaptation. One is left to suspect that those who are already economically disadvantaged will be disproportionately hit by increased road prices while they shift from one mode to the other.

The holistic post-materialist view, like the other socio-institutional discourses, also has serious deficiencies. In particular, the holistic approaches have rather low tolerance for other modes of thought. First, the advocates of the holistic post-materialist approach claim to understand people's real human needs better than individuals do themselves. Rather than the false needs the corrupt system imposes on humans, such as a desire material goods, striving for status, or conforming to social pressures, the holistic view points to real human needs: life in harmony with the natural and the social world. Unlike the other approaches, the holistic post-material perspective aims not only to change societal structures but also to alter the way individuals think. Within the holistic post-materialist view there is a definite moral 'right path': all other modes of thinking are polluted, corrupt, and immoral.

Second, the holistic post-materialist approach has little respect for the civil liberties that uphold a morally corrosive political and economic structure. Knoflacher (1997) explicitly states that the freedom of mobility as well as the freedom of settlement contravene real human needs such as a right to a healthy life, a right to personal development and a right to a home (*Recht auf Heimat*) (p. 126). Additionally, Knoflacher introduces a virulent strain of xenophobia into his argumentation. Transit traffic through the Austrian alpine regions, he avers, is little more than 'an alien body in the organism of the state. A healthy body will, if it is to survive, will reject all alien bodies' (p. 121). The upshot of his argument is that regional and local freight and passenger transport is justified because it is 'life-sustaining' to a particular community. Conversely, transit transport, which benefits those outside a community, is an evil to be eradicated.

This is not to say that all proponents of the holistic post-materialist view are inherently xenophobic. However, many advocates of this perspective are obsessed with moral pollution from a corrupt outside world. This is reflected in the elaborate and indiscriminate conspiracy theories this view constructs to explain transport policy problems. The unholy alliance of big business, corrupt government, and dishonest researchers conspires to maintain adequate profit levels at the cost of human well-being (Knoflacher, 1997). What is more, not only has big business captured government agencies and university departments, it also has succeeded in poisoning the minds of most people.

Although there can be no doubt that transport policy-making in the past and at the moment is significantly, and perhaps unduly, influenced by commercial interests, sweeping generalisations of the Knoflacherian type are inaccurate. Closer inspection of transport policy-making reveals that, like all policy spheres in advanced capitalist states, the state is fragmented, fissiparous, and highly specialised.[15] In short, policy-making takes place in a complex web of policy-networks and policy communities. The sheer number and variety of policy actors in these networks undermines the credibility of any general conspiracy theory. Often, government agencies in different policy networks will pursue contradictory policy goals. What is more, presently there is little evidence of iron triangles in transport policy-making (unlike in, say, agriculture). For example, the European Commission, often regarded as the lackey of big business interests by the holistic views, is forcefully pushing road pricing policy options (European Commission, 1995a) which run counter to the economic interests of large scale commercial enterprises.

We can see that if policy-making were left in the metaphorical hands of one socio-institutional perspective alone, we would be left with rather one-sided policy solutions. The classical planning approaches would continue to construct transport infrastructure without regard to social or environmental effects. The market-based approaches would let market mechanisms allocate resources without regard to the potential social exclusionary effects thus creating a 'transport underclass'. Last, the holistic post-materialist approach would, in the extreme, install an eco-dictatorship in which civil liberties are sacrificed at the altar of environmental sustainability.

Policy conflict, that is the mutual critical exchange between the discourses, rather than being an aberration of policy dispute, is vital both in a normative and an instrumental sense. Instrumentally, the critical scrutiny of policy arguments by other discourses is important because rival discourses can point out the perceptional blind-spots inherent in each policy belief-system: the net result is more balance and more informed policy decisions. Normatively, conflict indicates that institutional views are not marginalised or excluded from policy debate. What is more, the mutual criticism and scrutiny of policy actors facilitates what Sabatier calls policy-oriented learning. By pointing out the normative dimensions of rival policy arguments, policy actors problematise underlying assumptions of policy arguments. Double-loop learning occurs when policy actors begin to question the assumptions of their own socio-institutional discourses (Sabatier and Jenkins-Smith, 1993).

This, however, necessitates that policy-makers create a policy environment in which criticism and policy conflict is fostered rather than suppressed. In short, policy-makers must become reflexive in order to profit from the inherent conflict in transport policy.

Conclusion

The concept of accessibility is defined in many different way by diverse policy actors. These divergent definitions, however, are not random or irrational, they merely reflect the differing socio-institutional belief system through which policy actors interpret transport phenomena.

There are three ideal-typical policy discourses in the transport debate which emerge from very different institutional contexts and have divergent implications as to how transport policy ought to be organised. The first, the classical planning view, defines accessibility as economic growth: in order to assist regional development, it argues, policy-makers need to provide more infrastructure investment. The second discourse points to the inherent inefficiencies of planning and regulation. Instead, it favours a market-based approach to solving transport problems: accessibility here is a function of efficient market transactions. Last, the holistic view rails against both 'systemic views': both state and market have conspired to provide social and natural environments that no longer satisfy real human needs. What is more, present transport dilemmas are merely a symptom of a fundamentally flawed, inequitable, and misanthropic socio-economic system: here, accessibility stands for the exploitation of the weak by the strong.

These ideal-typical discourses delineate the boundaries of the transport policy debate: they enable thinking and argument about transport policy. Since the socio-institutional discourses are inherently normative (they legitimate fundamentally divergent forms of social organisation), and since transport is a complex and highly uncertain policy domain, conflict in transport policy debates is inevitable and endemic.

This, however, need not be exclusively negative. Since policy-belief systems highlight certain aspects of policy issues, the exclusion of a particular view form policy deliberation may lead to poor policy: the critique and scrutiny policy conflict implies is a strong corrective to poorly planned policy measures. However, in order to fully profit from socio-institutional policy conflict, and to avoid the transport debate deteriorating into an 'intractable policy controversy', policy makers must become aware of the different normative assumptions that underpin policy frames.

Policy oriented learning (Sabatier and Jenkins-Smith, 1993) in transport policy, as indeed in any policy domain, is an iterative and arduous process. The past thirty years, congested roads and increased pollution have shown that there are no easy fixes to the problems of a complex transport system. One thing, however, is certain: if policy-makers insist on keeping transport policy debates away from the broader public scrutiny (meaning away from critique from other policy belief-systems), then the transport policy debate will, similar to nuclear energy, indeed become an unsalvageable and intractable policy controversy.

Notes

1 Denmark (1996), perhaps unwittingly, illustrates the fluidity of the two terms. Within one page, he refers to three different possible analytic relationships between mobility and accessibility.

2 This raises the issue of credibility of technical knowledge, see Jasanoff and Wynne (1998).

3 For a critique of the use of such models in transport policy-making, see Adams (1994) or Knoflacher (1997).

4 There can, of course, be very good reasons for introducing market distortions.

5 For a full discussion of market-based measure, c.f. Pearce (1989, 1991).

6 Technically speaking, this social form is low grid, low group, Douglas (1982, 1992, 1996).

7 For a more detailed discussion of triangular policy spaces in the GCC debate, see Thompson and Rayner (1998); Thompson, Rayner and Ney (1998).

8 One can, of course, argue that policy conflict is desirable and is an indicator of a democratic policy process, c.f. Ney and Thompson (1999).

9 In fact, policy belief-systems, if they are to survive scrutiny, must be credible. Credibility, in turn, has a lot to do with the predictive and explanatory powers of a particular approach, c.f Jasanoff and Wynne (1998).

10 Mary Douglas (1982, 1992, 1996) speaks of 'cultural biases' which are, in effect, socio-institutional discourses.

11 Collingridge (1992) reviews cases such as the Space Shuttle disaster, high rise building schemes in the UK, and nuclear power. Unfortunately, he does not address transport although the analysis and conclusions of his case studies equally apply to transport policy-making.

12 Which of course would be very difficult because a change in the assumption that economic growth is a function of accessibility would question the role of planners in the transport policy process. If transport policy does not affect regional economic growth, what do we need transport planners for?

13 See the literature on common pool resource (CPRs). Here, transaction and monitoring costs are sufficiently high, as are the incentives to renege on contracts, that efficient market transactions are impossible (Ostrom, 1990).

14 See Pollitt (1990) for a discussion of incentive structures in public management. Arguing against the Public Choice approach, he point out that monetary incentives are one of a wide range of motivations for public servants.

15 For a discussion of the policy network literature see Richardson and Jordan (1979); Rhodes (1990); Atkinson and Coleman (1992); Smith (1993).

References

Adams, J. (1994), *Risk*, UCL Press, London.

Allison, G. T. (1971), *The Essence of Decision: Explaining the Cuban Missile Crisis*, Little Brown, Cambridge, Mass.

Altschuler, A. (1979), *The Urban Transport System*, The MIT Press, Cambridge, Mass.

Atkinson, M. and Coleman W. D. (1992), 'Policy Networks, Policy Communities and the Problem of Governance', *Governance: An International Journal of Policy and Administration*. Vol.5, No.2. pp. 154-180.

Banister, D. (ed.) (1995), *Transport and Urban Development*, E& FN Spon, London.

Banister, D. and Button, K. (eds.) (1993), *Transport, the Environment and Sustainable Development* E & F.N. Spon, London.

Banister, D. and Button, K. (1993), 'Environmental Policy and Transport: An Overview' in D. Banister and K. Button (eds.) (1993), *Transport, the Environment and Sustainable Development* E &F.N. Spon, London, pp. 1-15.

Banister, D. and Lichfield, N. (1995), 'The Key Issues in Transport and Urban Development' in D. Banister (ed.) (1995), *Transport and Urban Development*, E& FN Spon, London, pp. 1-15.

Banister, D. and Hall, P. (1995), 'Summary and Conclusions' in D. Banister (ed.) (1995), *Transport and Urban Development*, E& FN Spon, London, pp. 278-287.

Bökemann, D., Hackl, R. and Kamar, H. (1997), *Socio-Economic and Spatial Impacts of Transport Infrastructure Investments and Transport System Improvements*. Socio-Economic Indicators Model Report, EUNET Project, Vienna.

Cervero, R., Hall, P. and Landis, J. (1992), *Transit Joint Development in the United States*. University of California at Berkeley, Institute of Urban and Regional Development, Berkeley.

Collingridge, D. (1992), *The Management of Scale: Big Organisations, Big Decisions, Big Mistakes*, Routledge, London.

Denmark, D. (1996), *The Outsiders: An Essay on Transport Planning Method*, Institute of Transport Studies Working Paper, Sydney.

Die Grünen/ Bündnis 90 (1994), *Bundestagsprogramm 1994*, Bonn.

Douglas, M. (ed.) (1982), *Essays in the Sociology of Perception*, Routledge and Keegan Paul, London.

Douglas, M. (1992), *Risk and Blame: Essays in Cultural Theory*, Routledge, London.

Douglas, M. (1996), *Thought Styles: Critical Essays on Good Taste*, Sage Publications, London.

Downie, A. (1994), *Target 2015: A Vision for the Future, Access to Transport in Australia for all Australians*. Disability Advisory Council of Australia, Australian Government Publishing Service, Canberra.

ECMT (1998a), *Statistical Trends in Transport 1965-1994*. OECD Publications Service, Paris.

ECMT (1998b), *Transport Infrastructure in ECMT Countries: Profiles and Prospects*. OECD Publications Service, Paris.

European Commission (1993), *White Paper on Growth, Competitiveness, and Employment: The Challenges and Ways Forward into the 21st Century*. COM(93) 700 Final, European Commission, Brussels.

European Commission, (1995a), *Towards Fair and Efficient Pricing in Transport: Policy Options for Internalising the External Costs of Transport in the European Union*. COM(95)691, European Commission, Brussels.

European Commission (1995b), *The Citizen's Network: Fulfilling the Potential of Public Passenger Transport in Europe*. COM(95)601. European Commission, Brussels.

European Commission (1998), 'Outline of the European Transport Network', European Commission, Brussels (http://Europa.eu.int.//).

European Federation of Green Parties (1993), *Guiding Prtinciples of the European Federation of Green Parties.*

http://utopia.knoware.nl/users/oterhaar/greens/europe/princips.htm

Haas, P. (ed.) (1992), 'Knowledge, Power and International Policy Cooperation', *International Organization*, Vol. 43, pp. 377-403.

Hall, P. (1995), 'A European Perspective on the Spatial Links Between Land Use, Development and Transport' in D. Banister (ed.) (1995), *Transport and Urban Development.* E& FN Spon, London, pp. 65-84.

Himanen, V., Nijkamp, P. and Padjen, J. (1993), 'Transport Mobility, Spatial Accessibility and Environmental Sustainability', in P. Nijkamp (ed) *Europe on the Move*, Avebury Gower, Aldershot, pp. 269-289.

Inglehart, R. (1990), *Culture Shift in Advanced Industrial Society,* Princeton University Press, Princeton, N.J.

Jasanoff, S. and Wynne B. (1998), 'Science and Decisionmaking' in S. Rayner and E. Malone (eds) (1998), *Human Choice and Climate Change, Vol.1: The Societal Framework*, Batelle Press, Columbus, OH., pp. 1-87.

Khisty, C. J. and Leleur, S. (1997), 'Societal Planning: Identifying a New Role for the Transport Planner – Part I'. *Innovation*, Vol. 10, No. 10, pp. 17-25.

Kinnock, N. (1995), *Is Road Transport too Cheap? Fair and Efficient Pricing of Transport in Europe: Some Ideas on the Way Forward.* Speech given at the IRU/ACEA Seminar, Paris.

Kinnock, N. (1997a), *The Road Ahead – What Rules for Europe's Transport Revolution?* Speech given at Concert Noble, Brussels.

Kinnock, N. (1997b), *Mobility for All*, Speech given at Conference on Intelligent Transport Sitemaps, Berlin.

Kinnock, N. (1997c), *Transport and Environment,* Speech given at the UN-ECE Conference, Vienna.

Knoflacher, H. (1997), *Landschaft ohne Autobahnen: Für eine zukunftsorientierte Verkehrsplanung.* Böhlau, Wien.

Litman, T. (1996), *Evaluating Transport Equity.* Victoria Transport Policy Institute, Victoria.

Morgan, T. (1992), *Strategies to Overcome Transport Disadvantage*, Social Justice Research Programme into Locational Disadvantage: Trends and Issues, Australian Government Publishing Service, Canberra.

Morris, B. (1993) 'The Car User's Perspective' in D. Banister and K. Button (eds.) (1993), *Transport, the Environment and Sustainable Development* E &F.N. Spon, London, pp. 147-159.

NRMA. (1995), *Rural Transport Issues.* National Roads and Motorists Association Public Affairs Group, Sydney.

Ostrom, E. (1990), *Governing the Commons: The Evolution of Institutions for Collective Action*, Cambridge University Press, Cambridge.

Pearce, D. (1991), *Blueprint 2: Greening the World Economy*, Earthscan, London.

Pearce, D., Marandy, A. and Barbier, E. (1989), *Blueprint for a Sustainable Economy*, Earthscan, London.

Pollitt, C. (1990), *Managerialism and the Public Services: the Anglo-American Experience.* Blackwell, Oxford.

Putnam, R. (1993), *Making Democracy Work: Civic Traditions in Modern Italy.* Princeton University Press, Princeton, NJ.

Rein, M. and Schön, D. (1994), *Frame Reflection: Towards the Resolution of Intractable Policy Controversies.* Basic Books, New York.

Rhodes, R.A.W. (1990) 'Policy Networks: A British Perspective', *Journal of Theoretical Politics*, Vol. 21, pp.292-316.

Richardson, J. and Jordan, G. (1979), *Governing Under Pressure: the Policy Process in a Post-Parliamentary Democracy,* Martin Robertson, Oxford.

Rienstra, S., Stead, D., Banister, D. and Nijkamp, P. (1997), 'Assessing the Complementarity of Common Transport Policy Objectives: A Scenario Approach', *Innovation*, Vol.10, No.3, pp. 273-287.

Sabatier, P. and Jenkins-Smith, H. (eds.) (1993), *Policy Change and Learning: An Advocacy Coalition Approach.* Westview Press, Boulder, Col.

Sabatier, P. (1993), 'Policy Change over a Decade or More' in P. Sabatier and H. Jenkins-Smith (eds.) (1993) *Policy Change and Learning: An Advocacy Coalition Approach.* Westview Press, Boulder, Col.

Schmutzer, M. (1994), *Ingenium und Individuum: eine sozialwissenschaftliche Theorie der Technik und Wissenschaft.* Springer Verlag, Vienna.

Schofield, N. (1993), 'The Role of Government' in D. Banister and K. Button (eds.) (1993), *Transport, the Environment and Sustainable Development* E & FN Spon, London, pp. 117- 124.

Smith, M. J. (1993), *Pressure, Power and Policy: State Autonomy and Policy Networks in Britain and the United States.* Harvester Wheatsheaf, London.

Thompson, M. and Rayner, S. (1998a), 'Cultural Discourses' in S. Rayner and E. Malone. (1998), *Human Choice and Climate Change: Vol. 1 The Societal Framework.* Batelle Press, Columbus, OH.

Thompson, M. and Ney, S. (1999), 'Consulting the Frogs: the Normative Implications of Cultural Theory' in P. Selle, G. Grendstad and M. Thompson (eds.) (1999), *Cultural Theory as Political Science*, Routledge, London, pp. 206-223.

Thompson, M., Rayner, S. and Ney, S. (1998), 'Risk and Governance Part II'. *Government and Opposition*, Vol. 33, pp. 330-354.

Wachs, M. (1979), *Transport for the Elderly.* University of California Press, Berkeley.

Wegener, M. (1995), 'Accessibility and Development Impacts' in D. Banister (ed.) (1995) *Transport and Urban Development*, E & FN Spon, London, pp. 157-161.

7 From NIMBY to Public Debate Participation

SANDRINE RUI

One of the 'barriers' transport policy has to deal with concerns the environmental conflicts surrounding the implementation of infrastructure projects. Since the end of the eighties, the public's increased interest in the decision-making process has driven legislators to imagine new legal procedures to enhance public acceptance. In France this has led to the institutionalisation of the public debate as a formal procedure in the decision-making process; the public debate is complementary to the public inquiry which characterises the traditional consultation framework. The main disadvantage of the latter is that it only allows for citizen participation at a late stage in the project planning phase, i.e. when most technical and other issues relating to the project have already been decided upon. Under the current legislative framework, concerned populations and territorial actors are invited to express their opinion on the project plans early in the decision-making process.

This chapter will show how, despite the real progress in democratising the juridical frame, some difficulties remain. A major one is the difficulty to make citizens participate. Public debates are clearly predominated by institutional actors. Olson (1966) would consider this exemplary of the 'free rider' logic: rationally, inhabitants have more advantages in letting others participate and expect to profit from their actions. In France, this is diagnosed as indicative of the strength of the tradition of representative democracy: citizens prefer to continue to delegate their power of speech despite the fact that there are in the meantime procedures allowing them to express their opinions directly. Both explanations are limited if we consider the strong capacity of this same public to seek confrontation through conflict in specific situations. It is the very principle of public debate, I would contend, that makes the public's participation ambiguous. The public acceptance of projects is sought without prior producing a better institutional acceptance and integration of the public in the debate.

This chapter is organised in three sections. The first section outlines the aim and principles of an exemplary public debate procedure, namely of the 'Bianco circular'. The second section shows why and how the public is kept at a distance from real debates, even when invited to participate. The third section reports on the experiences made by citizens who have participated in such debates as local residents directly affected by the construction of an infrastructure project.

The paper is based on a study of the implementation of TGV projects, in particular of the Lyon-Turin, the Eastern TGV and the Aquitaine TGV; as well as of research on the first experiences made with the 'Bianco circular' procedures.[1]

The Institutionalisation of Public Debate

The 'Bianco' Debate

Since the beginning of the nineties, the French juridical frame characterising the implementation of transport projects has shown a clear tendency towards greater citizen participation.[2] Under the influence of both the ministries of Transport and of the Environment, the 'Bianco circular' introduced a wide consultation procedure early in the process of project planning: territorial representatives, associations, socio-economic actors, each citizen (Circular No. 92-71, p. 1) are invited to express their opinion on the proposed project. These 'Bianco' debates usually last four to five months and are organised by the prefect and the technical services of the State, in co-operation with the regional authorities having a territorial interest in the project. The public can organise or participate in meetings and can also write to the organisers. At the end of the discussions, specifications are drawn up and supplied to the project managers. They, in turn, are expected to take these into account when specifying the technical details of the project in subsequent steps. A follow-up board, made up of experts, is instituted to monitor this, as well as the quality and transparency of information exchange. Several road projects and four TGV projects have benefited from this procedure.

Producing Legitimacy Through Discussion

The new procedure claims to address the 'deficits' of the legislative frame which lead to contest the legitimacy of the projects as well as any decision of implementation (Circular No. 92-71 of 15th December, 1992, p. 1). Generally, this crisis of legitimacy is understood as the result of the increase of public awareness of environmental degradation. This is however merely the entry point to a larger debate which covers political, scientific as well as moral issues.[3] Indeed this crisis of legitimacy is not limited to the transport sector but applies more generally to contemporary democracies and decisions relating to social welfare. This crisis is particularly significant in France where public action has been traditionally determined by a centralised and powerful State. Thus, the emergence of conflicts is at the same time symptomatic of the crisis of the notion of 'public interest'. The invocation of public interest is no longer enough to justify public action and the sacrifices required by some (in favour of the general well-being); nor is it adequate to obtain social acceptance for major public investments. In transport this is shown both by the increase of roadside residents' revolts[4] and by the public support for such actions.[5] Thus beyond this particular situation of conflict, the 'Bianco circular' can be understood as the contemporary answer to an old problem, namely the conditions of producing legitimate decisions: how to base public choice on the will of the collectivity as well as making the decision acceptable to the wider public?

The 'Upstream' Principle

'We realised that when we arrived at the public enquiry phase where we proposed a [fully specified] project, some people (...) asked fundamental questions which should have been asked before.' This is how a representative of the Ministry of Transport justified the introduction of a public debate early in the planning process, or what came to be referred to as the 'upstream' or 'ahead of schedule' principle. The latter does not solely imply a chronological re-arranging of the public debate, i.e. prior to the technical studies, prior to the decision and prior to implementation. It also induces a consideration of 'fundamental' issues – aims, objectives and means – prior to the consideration of technical details and, in that, marks a new intervention logic for major transport projects.

The announcement of this new intervention logic was well received by stakeholders and the public alike. Yet those who have participated in the 'Bianco' debates tend to overwhelmingly report dissatisfaction. In fact, even though the background 'Bianco circular' text is keen on several democratic principles such as transparency, equality and plurality, it remains vague with regard to the method of organising discussions. With reference to what Duran (1999) calls 'constitutive policy', we may conclude that the 'Bianco circular' procedure is above all envisaged pragmatically: the debate is nothing less or more than what the participants make of it. In practice, however, it has not been possible to operationalise this procedure as creating a neutral space for discussions because of the power relations that structure the exchanges. Thus, it often turns out that the public debate feeds rather than helps resolve the underlying conflicts of interest.

From Issues to Roads: The Suppression of the Public

The Normative Valuation of Participants

In principle, the public debate procedure gives the opportunity to each citizen to participate in decision-making. In practice, however, it puts to the test the attribute as such of the 'citizen'. It is a re-make or re-state of the earlier controversies surrounding the civil rights movements and democratisation concerning who is considered a citizen. One of the principal activities of the participants consists in evaluating each other for the purpose of establishing the extent to which any specific participant is entitled to express his or her opinion on the proposed project. Through participant observation and in-depth interviews with participants, it was possible to establish the three criteria of the normative valuation frame dominating this procedure.

- First, in order to test the legitimacy of participation, the nature of interests any citizen or organisation represents or defends are examined. In order to participate, a citizen must be able to display an own interest compatible to the public interest. The valuation concerns the *degree to which the self or represented interests are also (part of) the public interest*. This is undoubtedly a very problematic criterion, above all in France. Given the French 'volontarist' conception of public interest and the hegemonic role of the State and its civil agents in this regard, it would follow that only the latter can in fact be allowed to express a legitimate opinion in the name of the collectivity and the latter's well-being.
- Second, a participant's point of view is only accepted if it is produced on an expert basis. In other words, the *level of competence* is

considered as the source of legitimacy. Experts and technicians are thus endowed with appreciated qualities.

- Third and last, to be legitimate, a participant has to prove that he or she is *representative.* A representative is seen as pursuing collective interests: he or she speaks for a larger group. To do so, he or she is necessarily cut off from own interests, or passions; in other words, he or she is emancipated from personal dependence relations. In the debate, representativeness is then the source of the power of speech. Indeed, institutional representatives (elected or nominated) are expected to take part in the discussions.

This normative valuation frame is directly used by the project managers who organise the discussions. In their opinion, it is useful to 'sort out' the participants. But in the course of the exchanges, everybody appropriates this frame. It therefore acts as a mode of legitimisation and delegitimisation: each participant looks forward to proving that he or she is in accordance with the representation of the 'good participant' by permanently seeking to disqualify the person he or she is speaking to. This process of crossed delegitimisation gives everybody the feeling that, on the one hand, no one is fairly treated, and that, on the other hand, their interlocutors are never up to the issues of the discussions. Therefore, not only do participants in public debates, or those involved in public decision-making processes, have to deal with a bounded rationality as Simon (1959) claims, they also have to cope with a bounded legitimacy.

Roadside Residents as Illegitimate Participants

Roadside residents are the ones who suffer the most from the normative strength of this valuation frame. They are always seen as 'bad participants'. Their point of view is, a *priori,* not acceptable in the public debate and they are not allowed to express themselves on 'fundamental questions'. First of all, their approach is judged biased and partial. In feeling threatened by an infrastructure project that transverses their place of residence, they are seen as pursuing 'narrow-minded' interests. Roadside residents' associations are seen as preoccupied above all by the protection of their yards, and their peace and quiet. In the view of the project managers,[6] they are too involved or too 'close' to the project (metaphorically as well as categorically) to be capable of assuming a global perspective or, more specifically, the public interest perspective. Indeed they are often denied this capability: were local associations, for instance, to propose an alternative transport policy, they would be seen by the organisers as adopting an 'argumentative strategy' devoid of contents. In turn, this is often interpreted as not playing 'fair'.

> There are associations of passionate people who are interested in their passion but not in their proposals, and there are associations which defend very narrow-minded interests, very particular interests they largely paint with green. (Project manager 7)

> People are only interested in their own small problems: will I be concerned? What will my situation be? How much will the compensation be? Instead of developing a general point of view on all the problems a project comes with. (Project manager 3)

Besides, these associations are often disqualified because they are not considered competent. Their interventions are judged unfounded or considered as 'whims'. From the viewpoint of the project managers, these 'whims' are responsible for the rise of infrastructure investment costs, in turn, an additional reason for disqualifying roadside residents from participation: how can an association which is supposedly concerned about the public interest act so irresponsibly when it comes to public spending?

> The previous president of the Val d' Oise department used to say when he talked about road operations that when we presented a project to the public, local associations defended the rule of the three 'I's'. They wanted the project to be 'Invisible', 'Inaudible' and without 'Impact'. He used to add that this rule became then the rule of the four 'Is' because this project would also be 'Impossible'. Because when we add so strong constraints, on an economic level, the project is unrealistic. (Project manager 3)

Finally, local associations are not considered legitimate participants because of the difficulties project managers face in determining whom and how many they represent. Composed of 'individuals of passion', roadside resident associations are denied representativeness *a priori*. Indeed, their capacity to mobilise is often considered by the organisers as primarily the result of the media's benevolence which, in turn, strengthens public opinion support, albeit in a populist fashion, rather than substantially.

> An inhabitant of a small village, without any political or associative representativeness, was on the regional television 48 hours after the public presentation of the project. The media tends to distort the representativeness. [This] is problematic for us. Via the media, opinion spreads like wildfire. (Project manager 9)

> When we have a point of view to defend, we have to evaluate the reactions of the members of the public who have been invited. We must not forget, being responsible, that those who express themselves are not representative of the whole citizenry (...) there are also [those] who did not come to tell [their] opinion. (Project manager 11)

This way of valuing the roadside residents grants them a stigmatised and fixed identity: they are none other than people 'infected' by the 'NIMBY syndrome'. The acronym NIMBY – Not-In-My-Back-Yard – was invented by American planners in the seventies and imported in Europe to refer to the protectionist motivations of project opponents at grassroot level. As a 'syndrome' however, the NIMBY phenomenon says more about the planners' worries than about the reality of the local movement of protest (Jobert, 1998; Trom, 1999).

As a label, the 'NIMBY syndrome' term considers roadside residents' reactions pathological. Indicative of this is how in the course of public discussions, the members of local associations are often called 'anxious' or 'paranoid'. Project managers estimate they do mad things, that they have 'incoherent' discourses and 'irrational' demands. Their collective actions are subsequently interpreted as the expression of a misshapen and foolish mass, highly dependent on manipulations of all kinds.[7] They therefore miss the sense of their own action. The way they are stigmatised is reminiscent of the interpretations of social movements in psychological terms (cf. Le Bon, 1991 [1895]; Tarde, 1989 [1901][8]), a position advocated by planners and politicians alike. For the majority of the latter, environmental conflicts are the result of a lack of mutual understanding and an accident. In other words, they deny the social dimension of these conflicts.

This way of psychologising their behaviour affects the local associations' members. Roadside residents do not deny being 'anxious' yet they insist that they are not sick people who mobilise against a project, but rather people who fight against a project that could make them sick, as transport infrastructure has impacts of different orders. It should also not be forgotten that the 'ground' – the people – are anxious, not least because of the long tradition of secrecy and contempt characteristic of land use planning. In other words, dealing with 'anxious' residents is the price that today's project managers have to pay for yesterday's practices. Reflecting on this, de Champris (1996) writes, 'the NIMBY generally appears on a backdrop composed of slow traumas'. These different traumas are attributed to the choices, practices and wrong attitudes of the public authorities over years. The author notes that the political marketing techniques, such as the unilateral communication practices of the administration, are not only rejected but have also introduced distrust and a critical attitude in the population's minds.

The stigmatisation via the 'NIMBY syndrome' makes problematic any action other than reaction (Goffman, 1963). The discussion between associations' leaders and project managers reveal how much being a roadside resident is experienced as a defect by the former and understood as such by the latter. So, paradoxically, inhabitants justify their interventions in public discussions by confirming that they are 'not concerned by the project'. These tactics follow from a stigmatisation process which is internalised and which prevents participation.

> In public debate or with administration, I am a roadside resident and I am against the project. And I've always had some scruples about admitting that I was a roadside resident. Why? Because I was afraid of being told that I was defending my yard. (Association member 13)

The project manager's reaction is as enlightening:

> Some frankly say they are roadside inhabitants, I appreciate this frankness. (Project manager 19)

Whether roadside participants express themselves in a particular way or in a collective way, they are always disqualified. Indeed, the debate leads to the constitution of a partial public – composed mainly of institutional representatives – and the public at large is kept away from this step of the decision-making process. The public debate pretends to contain the NIMBY reactions 'upstream' and promises to disqualify them 'downstream': one is able to claim that a democratic debate was organised, that a majority consensus was achieved and that it is unfortunate that the opponents did not or could not participate. But the first 'Bianco' debate experiences show that the bet is daring: In the Rhine-Rhone TGV case local associations disregarded by the first round of debate were successful in obtaining a second one five years later under the similar procedure envisaged by the Ministry of Environment; in the Aquitaine TGV case, the residents of Poitou-Charentes mobilised successfully against the project three years after the public debate was completed; and in the Lyon-Turin case, the conflict could likewise not be resolved through the 'Bianco' public debate and opponents are still active. In other words, there is enough evidence to suggest that the conflicts are not resolved by discussions alone early in the decision process. Furthermore, it would seem that the 'upstream' or 'ahead of schedule' principle will not be effective prior to institutionally accepting as legitimate and defining a role for the public in these debates, other and beyond that of a population targeted for persuasion.

From Roads to Issues: How the Public Constitutes Itself

Typically local residents form associations against a transport project once they discover that the project routes transverse their region or location. More often than not, it should be added, they learn about ongoing plans from the media or 'by mistake'. At first local associations will tend to capitalise on the residents' concerns and NIMBY reactions. Soon thereafter, they find out that they must resist the 'NIMBY syndrome' stigmatisation in order to be considered legitimate interlocutors. There are two principal modes of resistance: Local associations tend to present themselves as victims or as citizens. We consider each mode of resistance in turn.

Roadside Residents as Victims

Some associations aim at restoring the roadside resident's image by insisting on their being *victims*. They underline that they are victims in a moral, economic as well as an ecological sense. As victims, they call for solidarity; point to the fact that they could well be seen as representing the majority rather than the minority ('if we take the number of people who are roadside residents today, it becomes the general interest'; Association member 17); and insist that nothing justifies the contempt they suffer from. On the contrary, as victims, roadside residents deserve privileged attention and information and ought to be invited to actively participate in the decision-making process.

> It is not a defect to be a roadside resident, we are not responsible. (...) When one talks about particular interests, he talks about victims. These people, no one has the right to treat them like this. (Association member 6)

> Today in a factory, there are workers who fight for their rights and no one will put them to shame. For the roadside resident, it is the same thing. The roadside resident who discovers a TGV or a road in his yard feels the same as a worker who learns about his redundancy. (Association member 17)

As participants in public discussions, roadside residents that assume the 'victim' status speak in terms of justice and fairness and claim compensation for the damage incurred to them. The problem then becomes that of assessing the damage. This might be straightforward from the technical point of view, but it is far more complicated from the viewpoint of the affected residents. For them, damages are not only linked to the possession (and loss) of material goods. An infrastructure project interferes with their environment, their tranquillity, their mobility. All of the latter are goods in the larger sense and all are defended as rights. Roadside residents are thus very likely to disagree with the modes of compensation established by project managers: they usually do not appreciate that priority is given to expropriated people; that little attention is given to inhabitants that get to suffer from nuisances such as noise pollution and visual inconvenience; and that other victims, for instance companies that see their plans of developing 'green tourism' now destroyed, are simply treated with contempt and offered practically no compensation whatsoever.

> We do not want to be ruined morally and financially. It is our case. Because up to 150m from the tracks, people have financial compensations. But we are at 200m and we have lost everything. (Association member 15)

> When the TGV project was announced, the roadside residents were stricken. The owners who would like to sell their properties to get money cannot do it. (...) Besides, every successive operation is blocked. I have three children. I have property [the respondent is a farmer], but none of them wants it. What can I do? (Association member 10)

> Because of the TGV, some people have lost the licence to run a self-catering holiday cottage. (Association member 22)

In other words, the victimisation logic is always linked to a reflection on the mode of taking into account all the victims, and on the conditions of fair compensation. This way of thinking is the more developed, the less there is some direct compensation deriving from the project in the form of better accessibility or an increase in mobility (Bonnafous, 1993). For local associations, the implementation of a major transport infrastructure project calls for the re-establishment of the solidarity principle and this must take into account the value of what in transport planning are considered 'externalities' and as such of no value or price.

Under the 'victimisation' mode of resistance, the roadside residents' cause is to defend particular own interests. The NIMBY attitude becomes legitimate because the particular interests that are defended are considered entitlements. This logic is however highly risky with regard to collective action. Defending own interests produces divisions within the own territory. It is counter-productive to mobilise against the infrastructure only to have it displaced to the neighbouring location. The alliance around the roadside residents' cause is fragile and is only strong in terms of mobilisation for a short period of time. The potential victims delineate a large population, the actual victims only a small fraction. As some stop being 'roadside' residents, they also tend to give up the fight, i.e. are unlikely to continue to demonstrate solidarity with their neighbours.

Another problem local associations face when they adopt the 'victim' status is that they thus open themselves to comparisons with other victims. In declaring themselves as being in possession of a 'good' to which they are entitled to, they at the same time admit they are socially privileged. The logic of collective action of roadside residents' associations is different from that of those movements who mobilise for claiming something they do not have. In France, the latter are called the *'sans'* ('without') movements: the illegal migrants (who are without residency papers); the unemployed (who are without a job); the homeless (who are without a dwelling). Unlike all these movements, roadside associations are among the 'haves' and not the 'have-nots'; their members tend to derive from the new middle classes that benefit from a high level of instruction and from a protected economic situation (Offe, 1985). Indeed, they are not in the best position to call for national solidarity. Their claims will therefore always remain disputed. Finally, presenting themselves as victims also implies assuming a 'passive' role with regard to action.

Roadside Residents as Citizens

The second way of resisting the stigmatised image of the roadside resident is to identify with the figure of the *citizen* as well as that of the voter and taxpayer. Through these modes of self-presentation, the associations' members underline their sense of belonging to the political community. This, in turn, grants them the right to participate in the decision-making process. It is less the question of compensations linked to the experience of victimisation, more the issue of participation as such that drives these citizens' cause. They argue with reference to democratisation and the enlargement of the public space. The question of compensation is considered the problem of territorial representations, less that of the roadside resident associations, which are thus freed to concentrate their reflections on other more 'global' themes, namely transport policy, the quality of the public service or the side-effects of the consumer society.

Yet this identification with the figure of the citizen is also full of contradictions. First, the accent placed on citizenship leads to the marginalisation of the roadside inhabitant. This attitude reinforces the negative image of the NIMBY logic.

> We think we defend the public interest as well as those who designed the project because we do not have any particular interests. Our fight is a citizen's fight (...) it does not [directly] concern us (...) I mean it is a disinterested fight. (Association member 11)

At the same time participants are at a loss to justify their interest in the project in claiming 'no concern'. As a tax payer, is the participant not fighting against the waste of public money because he or she feels that it is also 'his' or 'her' money? Is he or she not motivated to participate in the public debate because he or she is concerned as a citizen, one or the other way? In other words, is it possible to be a citizen without being a roadside resident?

> I am not a roadside resident of the future motorway. I am (...) a little concerned, but from afar (...). I must say, I became the leader of the association, I became interested in this motorway only when it was 4,5 km away from my home. I was before not interested (...) or less interested (...) I think it is the general case (...) Would we be interested in a motorway plan, in a TGV, in an infrastructure (...) if it were not to pass through our village? (Association member 20)

> Actually, if it had passed 100 km further, I would not have spent 20 hours a week in collective action. (Association member 11)

The citizen figure can be as much of a trap as that of the roadside resident victim. Whilst entitling one to speak out in the public debate, it is a fictitious and normative image that can disqualify those who use it. As d'Iribarne (1996) succinctly puts it, the figure of the autonomous and reasonable citizen becomes the measure to evaluate individuals, yet it can play against those who use it to emancipate themselves. As a citizen, a local resident is always welcomed in the public debate; in fact, if he or she does not participate, this is thought of as a display of the lack of a sense of civil duty. Yet this self-presentation also implies qualities participants are not equally equipped with. A local association leader expressed this clearly:

> How people, citizens who have not studied, who are not '*Ponts et Chaussées*' engineers, how they can have an opinion on the territorial planning policy, it is unbelievable (...) This denies the national education in a large sense. (Local Association Leader)

Local Associations as Social Actors

The figures of the victim and of the citizen to describe modes of participation refer to the liberal and republican conception of citizenship respectively (Walzer, 1997). The republican conception of citizenship cannot be disassociated from the twin ideas of virtue and public spirit. As a citizen, one's duty is to serve the community. Politics is everybody's concern and constitutes the heart of everybody's life. On the other hand, under the liberal conception of citizenship, a citizen is considered a passive holder of rights: citizenship is only the external frame of a person's professional, social and private activities, which constitute the core of his or her social experience. In public debate, participants measure the normative strength of this classical opposition between the republic and liberal conception of citizenship. In the course of public discussions, and taking into account the limits of both modes of self-presentation, they realise that they have a lot to lose by playing one image against the other, one type of liberty against the other. The problem is then to articulate these two faces of citizenship in order to resist and to control their power of self-definition.

In order to solve the tensions between the two faces of citizenship, roadside residents try to constitute themselves as real social actors. They do this through mobilisation, but also, primarily, through coalescing with other structures like trade unions. This leads them to contest the monopoly of knowledge by technicians and project managers. They pull together knowledge competencies and elaborate counter-proposals. They organise themselves in a way that renders them capable of resolving the tension between particular interests and the public interest. Local associations want to defend a mode of appropriation of their territory that is different from that characterising the rationalisation logic of their adversaries, namely the planners.

In order to pass from individual indignation to collective action, a local association has to define itself with regard to the NIMBY logic. They choose to *go beyond the NIMBY logic.* 'Going beyond' can be understood as a way to bring together collective interests with self-interests in order to 'make particular interest coincide with the public interest' (Association member 17). As a basis of the movement's constitution, personal and local concerns are never denied. On the contrary, this activity gives a visibility to collective figures as well as making space for individual experience (Stavo-Debauge, 1999): having experienced how my rights (of integrity, of property, of mobility, of quietness and of public debate or participation) are defied, I may defend the recognition of these very rights for everybody, and for the community. In thus articulating their commitment, local associations become at the same time resistant against the institutionalisation or exploitation, especially by environmental militants.

This *going beyond the NIMBY logic* is not alone the result of organisation and of collective action. For some people, it also constitutes a personal experience. The argumentative work, the confrontation with different points of view, and the recognition by others, allow one to go beyond the first reaction of defence. This work makes sense only because it also represents a personal concern: it is the threat to private property which wakens up the active citizen and which bridges the two faces of civic experience. The very requirements of public debate become the forgetting conditions acquainted with democracy.

> I am always a little shocked by this discussion citizen vs. NIMBY, roadside resident vs. non-resident. I am all of these at the same time. That exists. I started by being a NIMBY, inevitably. But, then, I got a general point of view, I became a regionalist, because I had arguments which came later when I got to know documents and files better. One can change and see things in a more general way when he starts having the TGV in his yard. Maybe it is linked. (Association member 3)

> I realised that being a roadside resident was an opportunity to become a better citizen. (...) When one is not a roadside resident, he cannot be a citizen because he will fight for a reason which will have nothing to do with the project. There is something wrong in the non-resident citizen action (...) Now I will not be afraid anymore to say that I am a roadside resident as well as a citizen. (Association member 12)

When participating in public discussions, local association members do not only aim at learning about the hard job of being a citizen. For lack of identification with a common class (Offe, 1985), roadside residents find a common way through which to defend their singular experiences of the common territory. Whether they are actual owners or whether they estimate themselves as symbolic owners of the concerned territory; whether they live on the territory or far from the territory, they share a certain experience of the space they live in. This shared sense of belonging is expressed in terms of identity but also in rational self-interest terms. The territory is the frame of concrete practices, of regular activities. It is a network of interdependent actors who work collectively to make it exist. It at the same time represents a specific conception of public service and of the civil society. Since it is their territory, inhabitants are particularly conscious of their needs. Therefore, in their view, not only do project managers come and 'massacre' a 'natural space', which has to be protected; not only do they transform relationships, practices, and local economies; they also deny the very experience of the local inhabitants. Indeed for the inhabitants, their territory constitutes a complete and inclusive space with natural, cultural and symbolic limits and frontiers. The latter may overlap with institutional borders, but need not to. And they are not fixed: the inclusive space is at times the 'county', at others the 'valley' or the 'corridor'.

> I live in a village which is in a corridor since we have the Atlantic on one side and the Pyrenees on the other side. (...) This is a corridor which is not even 2 Km wide. In which we can find a seaside road, where we have the railway, where we have National Road 10, where we have the Paris-Madrid train, where we have the A63 motorway. We also have, above our heads, three high-voltage electric lines, one of which is 440,000 volts. And they also want to put a TGV in this corridor! (Association member 10)

> We are in the Rhone-Alps region. It is a region which is largely equipped with infrastructures of transport, whether it is road or railway. I think it is one of the most equipped regions in Europe. We live in a mountainous region, I am a Savoyard, and in this region noise quickly spreads. (Association member 21)

> Dôle is a crossroad planners like because there are now two motorways which are crossing it; there was a project of building a huge outline channel, there is a TGV project, there is a huge chemical industry (the Solvay industry), and what's more, an airport. You see, concerning environment, we gave a lot. So we know a lot about planners. (Association member 21)

Planners and project managers are identified as opponents. Technicians are not mere State representatives, they also control the power of definition. They have the means to impose their vision of the world and of society as well as their own technological choices on the local residents' living space. They can 'transform' the village and in that also denounce the local inhabitants' social power (Thoenig, 1987).

Environmental or planning conflicts do not occur accidentally. They represent conflicts between two social groups which disagree on the modes of appropriation of the common space in the name of common cultural values. In public debates associations always aim at having the social dimension of the conflicts recognised. They claim to participate in the cultural definition of change (Touraine, 1978).

In public discussions, local associations use their territorial experiences to discuss 'fundamental questions'. Their understanding of their living space as a complete – 'finished' – space implies that the room for new infrastructure is not infinite. Not only does the construction of new infrastructure have irreparable impacts; it also occupies a piece of space which could be used for something else or simply left 'in peace'. Above all, they consider that additional development is superfluous. Today's problem, in their opinion, is to balance the side-effects of modernisation, following Beck (1997):

> Modernisation – no longer conceived of in instrumentally rational and linear terms only, but as refracted, as the rule of side-effects – is becoming the motor of social history. (p. 3)

It is from this perspective that we must seek to understand their recurrent demand to develop existing infrastructures, whether they are concerned with a rail or with a road project. Here, they ask to develop two double-track national roads with cycle tracks rather than a motorway; there, they demand the modernisation of existing railways, the use of pendolino train instead of building new tracks for TGV. As counter-proposals, these solutions are often rejected by project managers because of technical reasons. Perhaps much too quickly. Because what needs to be recognised is that in making these proposals local associations admit the need for change, but have another conception of it. For them it is enough to develop or ameliorate the existing infrastructure, a point of view rejected by project managers as 'antic', a way of resisting change, or of making mere modest developments. Yet for local associations, this is what constitutes a 'policy with a promising future' and inevitably what is 'really' or 'more' modern. 'All-motorway' policies or 'all-TGV' policies are instead considered obsolete and iniquitous.

> We were not opposed to the construction of some new lines. We are opposed to the fact that France wants 4700 Km new lines while Germany built 1000 Km – they are not more stupid than us – and while England will, maybe, make 80 Km, and while the United States spectacularly renounced constructing new lines in order to develop existing infrastructures with pendolino. (Association member 14)

The development of existing infrastructure appears to associations also more relevant with regard to the crisis of public spending. They do not understand why the State representatives go on building huge and expensive infrastructures, especially if the financial justification for these projects is opaque. Like project managers they expect the project to abide with land-use planning requirements and to become a public service. But they disagree with the project managers on the means to achieve this goal. While project managers want to join Lyon to Torino and/or Paris to Madrid in the name of setting up a great cities network, local associations consider that they should not forget that parts of the national territory thus run the risk of becoming isolated, economically 'dried up' or 'irrigated'. Besides, the modal choice purported by project managers often leads to the transformation of urban, and consequently, life systems. Populations who had run away from cities are caught up by them. Hence, the very possibility to choose one's own living space fades away. So, far from providing a public service, new infrastructures are often detrimental to large parts of the population. In the opinion of local associations, land use planning cannot ignore the claim for integration of each territory. The competitive logic cannot erase the public service logic, which is the only one which can compensate the social imbalances and the lack of solidarity implied by the first one.

Progress, modernity, solidarity, civil service. Local associations fight against the projects in the name of the same principles which are used to promote them. In their opinion, public debates should offer the opportunity to participate in formulating fair and just choices for society. Hence, environmental conflicts are understood as social and cultural conflicts. Local associations and planners share common values but disagree on the way transport policy may reach them. Yet project managers unlike local associations have the power of definition and this structural inequality makes it very difficult to transform the public debate procedure into a real opportunity to reach consensus. Some local associations see a way out of this problem in reducing the role of technical experts to that of advisers, i.e. they should not participate in public debates as project managers.

> As a 'Pont et Chaussées' engineer, as a member of the Transport administration, you should not participate. You should only participate as a citizen. (...). I am in computers, you are in transport planning. When I am asked a file on computers, I give my technical opinion, it is not my role to decide. Politicians have to decide, citizens have to decide. This is the aim of the public debate. (Association member 20)

The roadside residents' experiences show that the NIMBY reaction has to be taken seriously in public debates, as it is the means of representation and of constitution into a social actor. At present public debates are constructed in such a way as to avoid or bypass conflict not as an opportunity to bring the conflict to the fore and submit it to the procedural frame of decision-making. Through the public debate procedures as currently practised, an attempt is in fact made to protect the debate from the public. This however only helps to postpone contestation, not to resolve it.

A real democratic procedure is one which accepts as given the conflictive dimension of transport policies with regard to previously constituted social relations between local populations and project managers or transport planners. The 'upstream' or 'ahead of schedule' principle for public debates only makes sense if it is thought of not merely as a step 'ahead' of the decision, but as providing the space for the decision as such to be discussed.

Notes

1 The latter involved the organisation of workshops in 1998 with some sixty participants, including local association members, project managers, politicians and mediators.

2 The Ministry of Transport is at the origin of the circular No. 92-71 of 15th December 1992 (Bianco circular). The Bianco circular applies to all major infrastructure projects in transport and lays down the modes and principles of a large and transparent debate. The 'Barnier law' of 2nd February 1995, the author of which was the Ministry of Environment, allows the prolongation of this public debate under the jurisdiction of the National Commission of Public Debate.

3 Since the work of Ronald Inglehart, post-materialist values are often seen as the explanation for the emergence of new social movements (cf. Inglehart, 1977).

4 The French language uses the same term *'riverain'* to refer to the population who lives close to different elements : it is not necessarily a river, as the English term of 'riverside' suggests: it can be a street, a road, a railway line. We use here the term 'roadside' resident which is likewise not entirely correct as the project in question can well be a railway line, but which in English is the corresponding term for *'riverain'*.

5 In 1992, a SOFRES opinion toll revealed that 84 per cent of the French regretted the fact that the viewpoints of roadside residents were not adequately taken into account in the planning of transport infrastructure projects. An equal share considered their mobilisation against the projects legitimate. 65 per cent were of the view that a maximum of concertation was necessary to reach an agreement. Only 29 per cent were concerned that public concertation would paralyse the process of implementation. (cf. Carrère, 1992).

6 Project managers understand the NIMBY reactions. They frequently reported that they would have reacted with the same anger, if in the same situation. This is interesting because it shows a clear evolution: State technicians do not consider the necessity of the projects as a sufficient reason to condemn the selfish attitude of local associations. 'I would like to say that being an EDF (Electricity of France) engineer, I will never say that I would be glad to have a high-tech electric line in my yard. If it was the case, I would fight. I will never promote the beauty neither the aesthetic aspects of a line in the coming evening, in the sunset.' (Project manager 6).

7 In his report, the liaison group KL3 of the World Road Association writes: 'Then, beyond the NIMBY effect, people who are unaware of these problems have a natural tendency to act like self-interested profit maximisers instead of acting like citizens, or again, they may become entirely disinterested in the community interest. This generally leads to greater mobilisation of negative forces than of positive forces, in which private interests take up a united stand to prevent a useful, perfectly acceptable project from seeing the light of day. This becomes absolutely intolerable when the public is manipulated by political or extremist splinter groups, by lobbies or even by mafias.' (World Road Association, *Decision-Making Process for*

Sustainable Transportation, Report under the direction of Christian Leyrit, February 1999, p.25).

8 For a discussion of these authors, see Barrows (1990 [1981]).

References

Barrows, S. (1990 [1981]), *Miroirs Déformants. Réflexions sur la Foule en France à la Fin du XIXe Siècle*, Aubier, Paris.

Beck, U. (1997), *The Reinvention of Politics*, Polity Press, Cambridge.

Bonnafous, A. (1993), 'Systèmes de transport et systèmes de solidarité, un choc de priorités sociale', in Ministère de l'équipement, des Transports et du Tourisme' (ed.), *2001 plus - Le syndrome NIMBY*, Centre de Prospective et de Veille Scientifique, Ministry of Transport, Paris.

Carrère, G. (1992), *Transport Destination 2002 - Le Débat National: Recommandations pour l'Action*, Report to the Ministry of Transport, Ministry of Transport, Paris.

de Champris, A. (1996), *La conflictualité locale et le syndrome NIMBY, nouvel enjeu du management public*, Technical note VIII, Cabinet E.C.s.

Duran, P. (1999), *Penser l'action publique*, LGDJ, Paris.

Goffman, E. (1963), *Stigma*, Prentice Hall, London.

Inglehart, R. (1977), *The Silent Revolution: Changing Values and Political Styles Among Western Publics*, Princeton University Press, Princeton, N.J.

d'Iribarne, P. (1996), *Vous Serez Tous des Maîtres, La Grande Illusion des Temps Modernes*, Seuil, Paris.

Jobert, A. (1998), ‚L'aménagement en politique ou ce que le syndrome NIMBY nous dit de l'intérêt général', *Politix*, No. 42.

Le Bon, G. (1991 [1895]), *La Psychologie des Foules*, PUF, Paris.

Offe, C. (1985), 'New Social Movements: Challenging the Boundaries of Institutional Politics', *Social Research*, Vol. 52, No. 4, pp. 817-868.

Olson, M. (1966), *The Logic of Collective Action*, Harvard University Press, Cambridge.

Simon, H. A. (1959), 'Theories of Decision-Making in Economics and Behavioral Science', *American Economic Review*, Vol. 49, No. 3.

Stavo-Debauge, J. (1999), 'Y a-t-il de nouveaux mouvements militants?', Mouvements, *La Découverte*, No. 3, March-April.

Tarde, G. (1989 [1901]), *L'Opinion et la Foule*, PUF, Paris.

Thoenig, J.-C. (1987), *L'Ère des Technocrates*, L'Harmattan, Paris.

Trom, D. (1999), 'De la réfutation de l'effet NIMBY considérée comme pratique militante. Notes pour une approche pragmatique de l'activité revendicative', *Revue Française de Science Politique*, Vol. 49, No.1.

Touraine, A. (1978), *La Voix et le Regard*, Seuil, Paris.

8 Towards a Prioritisation of Corridor Developments in the East

LIANA GIORGI AND ANNURADHA TANDON

The twenty-first century will witness an expanding European Union with the CEEC countries and the Baltic States as new members. Transport emerges to be one of the key areas for integrating the accession countries. The transport networks will have strong influences on trade development, social and cultural integration, and regional development. Currently with several gaps in the transport system of the Central and Eastern Countries, it is still unclear how the European transport network landscape will develop.

To initiate the closing of the gaps in CEEC/CIS, the TINA process has identified several networks across these countries (EC, 1999). To aid the CEEC/CIS to complete these networks, the ISPA fund has been set up with an outlay of 1040 million Euro a year for the environment and transport sectors. The amount of financial investment needed significantly exceeds this amount and also that which national governments are prepared and able to invest into transport infrastructure. Thus prioritisation of projects is inevitable.

This chapter outlines a method developed by a consortium of European transport researchers in the framework of research funded by the Transport RTD Fourth Framework Programme (Project CODE-TEN)[1] for the evaluation of trans-European networks and their extension to the East, and, more specifically, for the prioritisation of projects along the so-called Helsinki corridors.[2] This method has been given the name the DECODE method.

The DECODE method is a strategic assessment method that subjects to scrutiny the main orientations in transport investment and examines these under different scenarios up to the year 2015.

The main precondition for the use of the scenario approach is to identify the factors or dimensions that are likely to have a major impact on future developments in transport. These are three: external socio-economic developments; policy developments and infrastructure developments. Developments along these dimensions will influence the amount of traffic, the extent of environmental pollution, and the extent of connectivity in Europe.

Network developments must be assessed at the project as well as at the programme and policy levels. This calls for a macro as well as a micro level analysis. The impacts of network development have to be measured at both the national/global level and at the regional level. The presence of many actors and stakeholders for deciding the developments makes the assessment of network developments very complex.

Understanding Key Terms

Below we describe some of the key terms that were used in the development of the DECODE method.

Policy Assessment

Policy assessment often refers to evaluation and monitoring. When applied to monitoring it necessitates knowledge of the policy determination and policy content, hence it is closely related to analysis *of* policy (cf. Parsons, 1995).

The DECODE method is a method for the analysis of policy, whereby it can also be applied to planning. Good practice planning is the step following assessment, i.e. it corresponds to analysis *for* policy and ideally relies on the results of the assessment exercise.

Impact Assessment

Rossi and Freeman (1993) define impact assessment as 'evaluation of whether and to what extent a programme / plan / policy causes changes in the desired direction among a target population'. Impact assessment is one important, albeit not the sole, aspect of policy assessment.

Once impact assessment has been carried out, the question arises as to how to combine impacts to arrive at an overall score or evaluation result. The methods most commonly used for this purpose are cost-benefit analyses, cost-effectiveness analyses and multi-criteria analyses (cf. Sugden and Williams, 1978; Layard and Glaister, 1996).

Scenarios

Scenarios represent a tool used by policy analysts to address the factor of uncertainty. Piers and Sienstra (1999) note that scenarios have different functions but basically they help 'reduce complexity' and in that facilitate discussions about future development. 'They are not predictions, but rather tools for a structured communication about uncertain factors' (p. 4).

How the future image is structured and what it entails differs across approaches. Typically there are two main issues to be addressed: first, the scope of the scenario (i.e. whether it covers one particular dimension alone or whether it provides a more comprehensive image of the future by considering the interaction between related variables); and second, whether it will built on forecasts or backcasts.

The DECODE method uses scenarios that combine information on both external and internal factors to the transport system and is based on forecasts.

Strategic Policy Assessment

Strategic policy assessment is policy analysis which focuses on policies, plans or programmes rather than on specific projects. It is also an approach which seeks to combine tools and perspectives rather than relying on one particular method.

Strategic policy assessment was first developed in the environmental field where it came to be known under the name of 'strategic environmental assessment' (SEA). SEA represents a development of 'environmental impact assessment' (EIA) to address specific strategic questions that cannot be addressed at project level or through an agglomeration or aggregation of the results of numerous project-specific EIAs (cf. EC 1994, 1997a, 1997b).

Transport Corridor

The transport corridor is a *policy, programme or plan* which aims at the overcoming of structural gaps in the extended European space through primarily, investment in multi-modal infrastructure networks. The transport corridor programme for the CEECs was launched by the Crete and Helsinki Conferences of European Ministers of Transport. The corridor maps and backbone network were subsequently elaborated by the TINA[3] Secretariat based on input provided by national governments, under the auspices of the General Directorates for Transport and External Relations (TINA Final Report, 1999).

There are various elements to the notion of corridor that justify strategic assessment and the use of scenarios:

- any one corridor transcends more than one country, is multi-modal in profile and comprises several small scale projects and an elaborated phasing plan;
- together the Helsinki corridors comprise the backbone of a network to cover Eastern Europe as an extension of the Trans-European networks in the West – the impacts of any one corridor are heavily dependent on the developments along other corridors;
- the countries which the corridors transcend are transition countries which only gradually will be integrated into the European Union and which economically, as much as politically, lag behind their West European neighbours. These differences are relevant for assessing implementation plans as well as for the interpretation of impacts.

Drawbacks of the Traditional Methods for Prioritisation

How to decide on prioritisation is a policy problem which is fundamentally more complex than that of deciding on the corridor maps as such.

The traditional approach to project evaluation recommends the use of primarily socio-economic assessment in the form of a cost-benefit analysis in conjunction with financial appraisal. The study area is defined very *stringently* to cover single projects. Local environmental impacts and cross-sectoral impacts (like effects on employment or regional policy) addressed separately to 'refine' policy decisions based on economic and efficiency criteria.

This approach is possibly perfectly applicable to the assessment of projects that target missing links on an already well developed transport network (as in the majority cases of the TEN priority projects in the West). It is potentially problematic for the purpose of prioritisation concerning the extension of the TEN to the CEEC if it is the only evaluation method used.

Considering that all corridor projects are 'priority' projects as they all belong to the Trans-European networks, the application of this traditional approach would imply its use for each single project in order to obtain *comparative* socio-economic assessment estimations. The objectives, in other words, are not to estimate the socio-economic 'value' of the project alone with reference to the do-minimum or do-nothing scenario, but also its value with reference to all other projects.

Besides it being particularly resource-intensive, this exercise is likely to face methodological problems by reason of the difficulties in defining the study area in a stringent way, given that the transport network in Eastern Europe is not as developed as that in the West. In the context of an under-developed network, the impacts of any particular project on the network and vice-versa are more likely to be geographically dispersed and diffuse.

Finally, not least problematic is that this approach assumes that the decision-making is rational, linear, and consistent across national borders. This is far from being the case.

In the context of the co-financing procedures that characterise the pre-accession phase – through the regional funds, for transport in particular ISPA – the accession countries are expected to carry out the socio-economic analyses and financial appraisals of the TINA projects for which they wish to obtain co-financing or full financing. ISPA will in turn evaluate these project proposals and also consider Community objectives prior to reaching a decision.

These procedures leave little room for *strategic assessment*. Common objectives were only taken into account when 'drawing' the corridor maps, and considered primarily the necessities of long-distance travel. Common Transport Policy (CTP) objectives (cf. EC 1992, 1993, 1995a, 1995b, 1999) with regard to the environment, social cohesion or intermodality are only taken into account at the local level. In the absence of common tools for evaluation but also of common input data for estimations, the adoption of the traditional approach to evaluation *as the sole evaluation method* is ironically quite likely to increase the incidence of political decision devoid of scientific content.

The Context of Evaluation: From Projects to Strategies

DECODE is a strategic assessment tool that tries to overcome the problems associated with traditional methods by taking a 'broad' area of study as opposed to a 'strictly' defined area.

The objective of strategic assessment when applied to infrastructure investment programmes is to assess strategies, rather than specific projects, in the context of more general policy and socio-economic developments.

Two questions arise in this connection:

- first, how to analytically combine information on strategic elements, i.e. infrastructure, socio-economic trends and policy to describe aggregate influences on the transport system;
- second, what series of assessment exercises to undertake and how to combine information on impacts at the network level.

With reference to the first question: In the practice of the policy process the specification of an infrastructure strategy is not independent from more general policy and socio-economic developments. For example, the decision to build a highway will not only take into account the transport demand in a particular region but will also consider the existence or not of pricing regimes as well as the actual and potential pressure of environmental groups opposing the construction of highways because of their negative environmental impacts. The forecast of transport volumes used to justify the need for building a highway has to take into account macro-economic developments in the home country as well as in neighbouring countries; as well as the long-term competitive position of the road in relation to other modes of transport which, in turn, is determined – at least in part – by fuel prices and transport costs which are dependent among others on more general developments regarding duties as well as on technological changes.

For the purposes of assessment, i.e. for analytical purposes, it is useful to keep the different steps distinct, whereby this does not preclude that connections are made between the different levels at different stages. One way to do this in a systematic way is through the use of scenarios.

With reference to the second question: transport planning has to consider four separate, albeit interrelated, questions (Leleur *et al.*, 1998), namely:

- Is the project worth the money?
- Can it be further improved in technical terms?
- Does it have a good chance to be agreed upon and decided insofar as it meets more general transport policy objectives?
- Does it have a good chance of being implemented in that it faces few barriers to realisation?

At the level of *project* assessment it is possible to consider these questions in any sequence or even in parallel. Ultimately insofar as the questions are interrelated the answers given to any influence the answers to the others. For instance, if the project is 'worth the money' but does not meet policy objectives it might have to be redesigned to meet the latter which in turn might increase or decrease its chance of realisation. Alternatively a project which meets policy objectives and faces no major barriers to implementation in terms of public acceptability might not be 'worth the money', thus also not possible to finance, unless further improved in technical terms.

The planning context is far more complex in the case of corridor assessment or more generally at the level of infrastructure programme evaluation: there is a plurality of national policy contexts to consider; consequently also a plurality of actors and potential barriers; and not least several projects each of a different size and time scale of implementation. Furthermore, the long-term scale of realisation of corridor infrastructure introduces an element of uncertainty that needs to be considered. Thus, it is wiser to impose a certain order on the 'tests' to be undertaken. In strategic assessment, we would contend, it is better to first address the question of political/policy suitability prior to proceeding to examine the economic efficiency or effectiveness of the project in question or its long-term indirect impacts.

Guiding Principles and Methodological Steps

The DECODE method is based on the following principles:

- the frame of reference is the full network;
- there is no single infrastructure strategy but rather a plurality of these;
- the infrastructure strategies are defined with reference to the full network and considering the actual national policy environments and stakeholder interests;
- there is no single scenario to describe future developments in the policy field and socio-economic trends but rather a set of possible trajectories or future images which logically combine socio-economic forecasts with policy environments at the aggregate level;

- the unit of evaluation or impact assessment comprises the infrastructure strategy as presently evolving set against the scenarios for the future concerning socio-economic and policy developments;
- impact assessment tools have to be refined in order (a) to account for the geographical scope of the network and (b) to allow for the assessment of the spatial distribution of effects.

The following methodological steps can be derived from consideration of the above principles:

- conceptualise and operationalise the unit of evaluation, what in DECODE is called the corridor development alternative;
- estimate traffic flows;
- impact assessment;
- aggregation of impacts.

Steps 2 to 4 are standard procedures in transport planning and evaluation and will only concern us in brief in the following exposition. What pertains to the strategic character of the DECODE method is the notion of 'corridor development alternative'. To the elaboration of this we turn in the following section.

The Corridor Development Alternative

A corridor development alternative is a term especially coined for DECODE and strategic transport assessment. A corridor development alternative represents an image of the infrastructure network under specified socio-economic and policy scenarios. In strategic assessment it is the lens through which the corridor policy programme is examined.

The DECODE method identifies and subsequently puts to the test 'images' of the future which combine information on three dimensions: socio-economic and integration scenarios, policy images and infrastructure strategies. While the specification of infrastructure strategies is an example of a micro-level analysis, the specification of scenarios follows a top-down approach. The interface between the two delineates the (corridor) development alternatives.

The Corridor Development Alternative (CDA) comprises a three-dimensional space.

Figure 8.1 The Corridor Development Alternative (CDA)

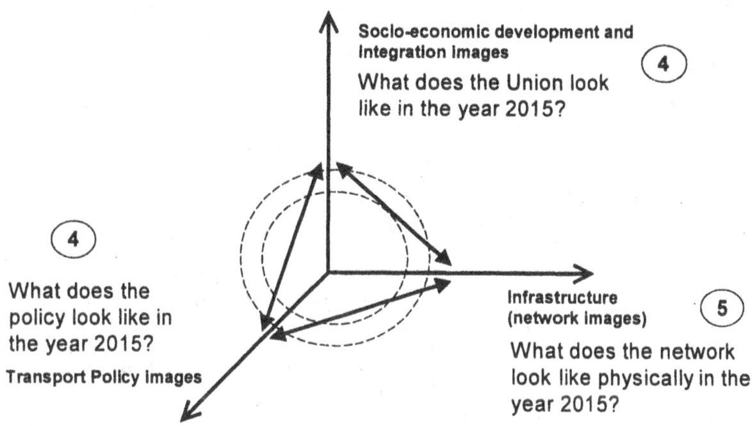

These three spaces together project an image of the socio-economic and integration factors, transport policies and infrastructure strategies. The first space is an image of the socio-economic development and integration. It addresses the question 'what does the Union look like in the year 2015?' The second space is an image of the transport policy in the year 2015. It addresses the question 'what does European transport policy look like in the year 2105?' The third space is an image of the infrastructure, that is the physical network in year 2105. It addresses the question 'what does the network look like physically in the year 2015?'

Image 1: Socio-Economic and Integration Image

The first space is an image of the socio-economic developments and integration. The macro-economic scenarios are developed with reference to socio-economic development and the scope and pace of integration in the context of European integration. Socio-economic scenarios take into account the development of GDP along with demographic projections, motorisation rates, international trade, employment and economic sector development. These are estimated at the regional level, preferably NUTS 2 or equivalent. The integration scenario considers the accession process or the level of integration within and outside the EU. The latter influences economic development as well as traffic flows.

Under the DECODE method, four scenarios were identified by combining the socio-economic and integration factors (cf. CODE-TEN Deliverable 4, 1999; CODE-TEN Final Report, 2000).

Figure 8.2 Socio-Economic and Integration Scenarios

	Quick integration (2005/2010)	Slow integration (2010/2015)
High growth (up to 7%)	**Renaissance**	**Dilution**
Low growth (up to 2,5%)	**Solidarity**	**Fragmentation**

Renaissance scenario This scenario is characterised by high growth and fast integration. It assumes that by the year 2010, most, if not all, of the new accession countries would have joined the EU and that those which do not will be well integrated in the European political and economic space. A 'virtuous circle' will develop facilitating growth and integration, both economic and political. The maximum growth rate under this scenario is seven per cent, the minimum four per cent. Countries more likely to display the maximum growth rates are Hungary and Poland, countries displaying the minimum Bulgaria and Romania.

Dilution scenario This scenario is characterised by high growth and slow integration. Under this scenario reforms will be successful and Europe becomes a free trade zone with extended co-operation agreements driven by market rules and competition as well as globalisation, with a strong influence of new information technologies and multi-nationals. The European Union as an entity with shared political and organisational structures however weakens, thus interventions for cohesion or structural changes are limited. Countries which are slower in implementing liberalisation will be slower in achieving a sustained growth rate.

Solidarity scenario This scenario is characterised by low growth albeit fast integration. The accession process is slower, yet it definitely goes ahead despite comparatively low economic growth rates in both Western and Eastern Europe; in other words, integration is driven by foreign policy and security considerations which at the same time point to the strengthening of the political dimension of the European Union. Structural and cohesion funds become the main vehicle for integration – the volume of financial aid is similar to that transferred to former European peripheral countries or less developed regions. Sectoral policies, including transport, become increasingly subjected to regional development considerations.

Fragmentation scenario This scenario is characterised by low growth and slow or no integration. It assumes likewise a long transition process but also limited support for the accession countries. This also means that Europe loses some of its substance for actual EU Member States. Individual countries will tend to orient themselves towards regional markets. Regions neighbouring the European Union will have the most to gain. Economic reforms continue to be implemented albeit at a slower rate, convergence is realised only in the long run.

Image 2: Policy Scenarios

The second space is an image of the transport policy in the year 2015. The DECODE method uses four 'ideal type' policy scenarios to describe national transport policies and the European Common Transport Policy:

Market approach with infrastructure investment This scenario is characterised by an emphasis on liberalisation and deregulation and on increasing cross-border or international traffic. It also places an emphasis on infrastructure development. As the free market principles are favoured, road pricing for external costs and restricting road traffic are given a lower emphasis. This scenario assumes that the market will decide the kind of projects to be funded, whereby road takes priority.

Management approach with infrastructure investment This scenario lays emphasis on the management of supply and demand hence on regulation or management rather than deregulation, which is in fact what distinguishes this scenario from the previous one. Other goals are the promotion of intermodality and interoperability, the structural goals of increasing accessibility and promoting regional development. Infrastructure development is still considered a means to achieve these goals. Rail projects or a network approach are more likely to be prioritised under this scenario.

Market approach with an emphasis on decoupling This scenario shares a number of features with the first one above with a greater emphasis on deregulation. It however does not place such a strong emphasis on infrastructure development and considers this also as being guided by the market. Instead it is in favour of measures promoting interoperability.

Management approach with emphasis on decoupling In this scenario emphasis is placed on decoupling with the specific objective of promoting environmental sustainability, hence the strategic importance assigned to the application of environmental regulation and the restriction of local traffic. Overcoming structural deficiencies, hence promoting regional development, is still thought of as important, however not at the expense of environmental damage, hence also the absence of increasing accessibility as a significant goal.

Image 3: Infrastructure Strategies

The images of the infrastructure strategies map the physical infrastructure in the year 2015.

When establishing infrastructure strategies at the network level it is important to remember that even if the network transcends national boundaries, national interests continue to play a dominant role. The DECODE method for establishing infrastructure strategies takes this into account. Infrastructure strategies at the network level are established in three consecutive steps:

- *Suitability*: The various projects under consideration in each country are first examined for their degree of policy performance or 'suitability': how congruent are they with national policy strategy and the national transport policy goals?
- *Adaptability*: The second step is to establish again for each project under consideration in each country the degree of its 'adaptability'; this is defined by the likelihood of its implementation, in turn a function of the barriers it is likely to face.

- *Prioritisation of projects*: The third step is to combine information on policy performance and adaptability to identify priority projects in each country and thereafter at the network level.

We consider each of these steps in turn:

Suitability The objective of the suitability test is to examine the extent to which a certain project or programme is in line with the national policy objectives in the field of transport from the point of view of the policy-owner.

The single and/or homogeneous policy-owner in any decision context is, of course, an abstract and analytical construction. For the purpose of the suitability test in DECODE, the policy-owner is defined as that set of actors which influences significantly the agenda setting in national transport policy, the point of reference being policy documents or key discourse texts.

The suitability test employed in DECODE follows the principles of the TENASSESS Policy Assessment Method (see chapter by Bulman and Brown in this volume). Each project is assessed against a comprehensive list of policy objectives which have been previously weighted to reflect the importance attached to each by the national policy-owner.

The question to answer for each specific project is: Can the project as currently proposed (i.e. considering its technical specifications) and from the view of the policy-owner be thought to contribute to the fulfilment of policy goal X? If yes, the project is given an unweighted score of +5; if the answer is no, the project is given an unweighted score of -5. If the policy objective X is not relevant for the project in question, the latter is given a score 0.

The scores are multiplied by the weight for each policy area to provide the score on that policy area. The total project score calculated by adding the individual weighted scores per policy objective and dividing these by the sum of the weights represents how 'suitable' each major project along a corridor is with regard to the national transport policy.

Adaptability The still dominant paradigm in policy analysis – at least with reference to transport evaluation – relies on the technocratic utilitarian view which assumes that it is possible, through the use of the right tools, to measure needs, benefits and costs which, in turn, can provide the basis for achieving an optimal solution. Sociology nevertheless teaches us that it is as important to understand the discourses within which problems are defined and debated and, ultimately, constructed. In other words, if we work on the assumption of communicative rationality rather than rational choice, then we must recognise that the decision process is open with a number of actors having stakes and each with their own discourses.

The objective of the adaptability test in the DECODE method is to identify barriers to the implementation of transport projects, thus to establish the degree of 'adaptability' of any particular project with regard to outside pressures. Earlier research has shown that there is a small set of such barriers in the practice of the implementation of transport policy: there are barriers relating to socio-economic assessment; environmental assessment; the division of competencies with particular reference to regional responsibilities; technical standard harmonisation and financial acceptability (PLANCO, 1998, The Barrier Model).

Analytically, the application of the adaptability test involves first, charting all the projects according to their phase of implementation (conceptual, planning, decision, implementation); and second, identifying for each major project whether any of the afore-mentioned types of barriers are being faced or are likely to occur in the near future.

Prioritisation of projects High suitability scores indicate congruence with national transport policy objectives. High adaptability scores indicate many barriers to implementation.

- Projects with a high suitability score and a low adaptability score are likely to be implemented without major delay and with no change in their design.
- Projects with high suitability and adaptability scores are most likely to require a re-design, thus a delay in their implementation is very likely. Such projects, experience shows, are often 'key' projects in the sense that whether and how they are realised influences the network and the transport system more generally. Their 'key' character in part explains the many barriers or conflicts they face, i.e. their high adaptability scores.
- Projects with low suitability and adaptability scores are difficult to judge regarding their chance or not of realisation. Given their 'low' national profile, their low adaptability might simply indicate little national interest in them. Such projects often get funded in situations where other key projects as described above do not go through.
- Projects with low suitability and high adaptability scores are the least likely to be implemented.

The aggregation of this information at the corridor level throws light on cross-border conditions and the consistency as such of the corridor programmes across different countries. For instance, if a corridor is planned as a multi-modal long-distance link, yet some countries favour road whilst others favour rail, then in an environment of financial insecurity this constitutes what we call a negative boundary condition. This determines not only whether the 'corridor' as such materialises but also the medium- and long-term effects of network development.

The following examples from several of the Helsinki corridors illustrate that presently there are several negative boundary conditions in the actual definition of the corridor development plans (CODE-TEN Deliverable 3, 1999):

Corridor I – Helsinki-Warsaw: Due to the differential emphasis placed on rail and road development by Estonia and Latvia on the one hand, and by Lithuania and Poland on the other, a problematic boundary condition might arise. This, in turn, suggests that there are two possibly competing areas of influence also in relation to the ports: one comprising Poland, Lithuania and Russia in relation to Kaliningrad favouring rail and the corridor branch IA through Belarus, with Gdansk dominating as a port; the other comprising Estonia and Latvia in relation to Moscow and Finland, and favouring the Estonian and Riga ports. Future developments will depend on first, the Russian strategy regarding the opening towards the North; and second, the scope of regional co-operation between the three Baltic States. Otherwise, the environment is emerging as a problem in relation to socio-economic concerns over competition in Latvia and Lithuania.

Corridor II – Berlin-Moscow: In Poland the road links are prioritised over the rail links. However, only the western part of the road connection (i.e. from the German border to Warsaw) is cleared regarding implementation, whereby barriers are expected with reference to the Warsaw section; the situation is less clear regarding the eastern part, mainly due to problems of financing. For Belarus the rail links would appear to be of slightly higher priority, whereas for Russia the reconstruction of the highway (and especially of the bridges) along corridor II is the project of highest national priority.

Corridor IV – Dresden-Thessaloniki/Plovdiv: Corridor IV presents a number of competing priorities between countries as well as between rail and road. The Czech Republic wants to improve in particular the conditions for cross-border road traffic with Germany, thus prioritises the western road parts of the corridor over the eastern and southern road and rail segments – the location of the Plzen bypass is the sole barrier to the completion of these links.

Slovakia is primarily concerned with the construction of the Petrzalka-Parndorf railway line towards Austria which will speed up the traffic between Vienna and Bratislava and enable the re-routing by rail of high-goods vehicles from Devinska-Nova Ves to the Marchegg border crossing. This is in line with Austrian priorities towards the Slovakian border.

In Hungary where both the rail and road connections to the west, i.e. to Austria, are of reasonable standard, the project with the highest suitability scores concerns the upgrading of the rail infrastructure and railway stations on the Budapest – Kelebia line towards the south for connecting to Corridor X. The prioritisation of this project suggests that subject to the change of the political situation in Serbia, it could well be that the 'national' interests of Hungary insofar as international connections are concerned shift away from Corridor IV (east connections) towards Corridor X (south connections).

In Romania the road projects on the western part of the country, i.e. between Nadlac-Bucharest-Constanta are prioritised by reason of the importance attached to the Constanza port for the Romanian transport system. The same is the case with the upgrading of the rail connection between Curtici-Bucharest-Constanta. However considering the sub-optimal situation of the road network in Romania more generally, the road connections are prioritised over the rail connections. The same is true for Bulgaria where in particular the Southern connections to Greece and Turkey and those to Yugoslavia are prioritised.

It is important to keep in mind with regard to both Bulgaria and Romania and Corridor IV that the possible opening of Corridor X would place these two countries in direct competition in terms of channelling the traffic to the east through to the ports in the Black Sea Region; this is also very much dependent on the scope for development of the Black Sea Region and the Aegean for international shipping. Competition has already emerged concerning the location of the second bridge across the Danube.

Corridor V – Venice-Kiev: The Corridor V preference lies with the construction and upgrading of motorways and not so much the development of the rail infrastructure. The exception is Slovakia which is in particular interested in further developing its rail connections to Belarus in relation to Corridor V, and Hungary concerning the Budapest-Cegled-Szolnok link to Yugoslavia.

Corridor V like Corridor I is likely to face negative boundary conditions at least in terms of phasing or timing; this is only partly the result of the competition between ports, and in particular Triest, Koper and Raijeka. Clearly how corridor V develops will depend on the extent to which these three ports collaborate or compete but also, perhaps more importantly, on whether they will be feeding points for the North (i.e. along Corridor X and/or VI) or for the East (i.e. along Corridor V). Whilst this will very much depend on the economic performance of the NIS, it at the same time is likely to influence the modal options for Corridor V.

Corridor VII – Danube: The overcoming of the technical barriers affecting the Danube waterway will be what ultimately determines the scope for development of Corridor VII. Technical barriers in conjunction with environmental concerns have practically stopped infrastructure developments along this corridor over several years.

Corridor IX – Copenhagen-Moscow: Corridor IX is perhaps the one corridor which more than any other is explicitly used to promote national or bilateral cross-border interests: for Denmark it provides the opportunity to legitimise and subsequently proceed to realise land connections with Sweden on the one hand (the Øresund Fixed Link is completed) and Germany on the other (the Fixed Femer Belt is still in the planning stage) despite strong opposition from the population related to environmental issues. Similar is the case in Sweden with regard to the Malmo city tunnel and the upgrading of the railway to Stockholm.

In Finland priority is given to the railway upgrading of the route from Helsinki to the Russian border (and the alternative to Lahti) and the road reconstruction in the same direction. In Russia, the improvement of the cross-border connections to Finland are also considered important; so is the upgrading of the railway infrastructure around St. Petersburg.

Corridor X – Salzburg-Thessaloniki: In Austria the expected increase of traffic from both the East and the South in relation to Corridors IV and X have led to a reassertion of the importance of key railway links between South and East, whereby there is no agreement as to the primary location of these. Railway links with reference to Corridor X are also considered a priority in Slovenia and Croatia, however their realisation is expected to face delays. Both countries instead place an emphasis on the re-construction of the motorways, Slovenia is already well advanced with the implementation of its motorway construction and upgrading programme.

For Hungary and Bulgaria Corridor X provides an opportunity to ameliorate the road and rail links to Yugoslavia. For Yugoslavia both rail and road projects to Hungary on the one hand, and Yugoslavia, on the other, are important. Any developments along Corridor X are largely dependent on the stabilisation of the situation in the Balkans following the Kosovo crisis.

Mapping all priority projects helps establish infrastructure strategies at the network level. The infrastructure strategies are:

- 'All road' strategy: This assumes that all the road projects identified through the TINA process are realised.
- 'Priority road' strategy: This considers that only those road projects considered national priorities by the accession countries themselves and also part of the TINA network are realised.
- 'Network' strategy: This assumes that only those road and rail project considered national priorities by the accession countries and meeting positive boundary conditions are realised.
- 'Do-nothing' strategy: This foresees that no new infrastructure other than the one already under construction is realised.

Combining the Three Dimensions

The corridor development alternatives are formed by combining the three images. In theory it is possible to envisage all external scenarios under all possible policy scenarios and, in turn, for all infrastructure strategies. The number of possible permutations depends on the number of infrastructure strategies defined. Assuming that there are five infrastructure strategies as above, the number of possible permutations is:

5 (infrastructure strategies) X 4 (external scenarios) X 4 (policy scenarios)

Insofar as external developments are not independent from policy developments and also not from infrastructure strategies, it is possible to reduce the number of possible permutations down to a smaller number of more realistic options.

There is inevitably simplification involved in this approach which begins already with the definition of scenarios as categories or 'ideal types' rather than as continua. However this simplification is necessary to keep analytical categories separate.

Under the *renaissance scenario*, we look at all network variants – 'all road', 'all rail', 'network approach' and 'priority road' – set against the do-nothing variant. Under *all external scenarios* we compare the 'priority road' and 'network approach' set against the do-nothing variants in each case.

Estimation of Traffic Flows

With reference to the assessment of the impacts of infrastructure programmes, the first step is to make traffic flow estimations and assignments for each (corridor) development alternative.

Traffic flow estimations derive from observations on the actual relation between transport demand and supply and assumptions as to future developments. In the tool currently in use in DECODE the following variables are used for making traffic estimations:

- population, GDP and employment, actual and forecasted, under the four different socio-economic scenarios;
- growth rates of foreign trade under the four socio-economic scenarios;
- transport costs such as taxes and fees for each of the four policy scenarios.

Traffic assignments abide to the network constraints as defined by the infrastructure strategies under consideration.

Impact Assessment

What impacts are to be estimated depends on the geographical level of coverage and objective of the analysis. The DECODE method does not categorically specify the impacts that should be estimated, but has impact assessment as an integral part of the methodology for strategic policy assessment.

For the purpose of strategic assessment, indirect long-term effects are of particular relevance. In other words, strategic assessment prioritises the measurement of strategic environmental and accessibility impacts next to direct impacts.

Table 8.1 displays the performance indicators used for the impacts under consideration in DECODE.

Aggregation of Impacts

Impacts can be aggregated at the European level, corridor level, corridor development alternative level or at the national level. The most common methodologies for combining impacts are cost-benefit analysis, cost effectiveness analysis and multi-criteria analysis.

The DECODE method uses two methods for the purpose of aggregation of impacts: first, the EUNET method which combines cost-benefit and multi-criteria analysis (cf. Nellthorp *et al.*, 1999) and second, the TENASSESS PAM method which applies the goal achievement matrix, an application of a multi-criteria analysis (see Bulman and Brown in this volume).

Table 8.1 Performance Indicators for Strategic Transport Assessment

Category	Impacts	Indicator(s)	Spatial Disagg[n]
Direct	Investment Cost	Total investment cost of do-something CDA relative to the do-nothing scenario, *millions of euro, 1995 prices and values*	Country
	VOC Savings	Change in total resource VOCs on the network, for freight, in the CDA relative to the do-nothing scenario – considers time savings for freight only *millions of euro, 1995 prices and values*	EU, CEEC I/II/III
	Safety	Change in fatalities on the network in the CDA relative to the do-nothing scenario, *fatalities per annum*	Country
Environmental	Noise	Change in a single proxy score for total noise, across exposed areas, across modes *Km^2 under 55dB(A)*	Country
	Local Air Pollution	Change in area influenced by high CO concentration *Km^2 under 8 mg/m^3 (8 hour average)*	Country
	Regional Air Pollution	Change in NO_x emitted, unweighted *tonnes per annum*	Country
	Global Air Pollution	Change in CO_2 emitted, unweighted *tonnes per annum*	Country
Indirect	Land Take	Financial cost of land take should be included in Investment Costs. Additional external social cost over and above noise and air pollution (ie. Severance; visual intrusion; etc) proxied very roughly by Land Take. *Km^2*	Country
	Accessibility (Economic)	Change in GDP within 4hrs travel time *%*	Country
	Accessibility (Demographic)	Change in population within 4hrs travel time *%*	Country

Source: CODE-TEN Deliverable 6, 1999; CODE-TEN Final Report, 2000

Results and Conclusions

The results of the application of the DECODE method are as follows:

- Under the renaissance scenario of high growth and fast integration, the 'all road' solution is generally inferior, except in terms of accessibility. The 'all rail' approach offers the greatest benefits in terms of safety improvement, air pollution reduction and demographic accessibility. It is also cheaper than the 'network' approach by about 20 per cent, but slightly inferior in terms of vehicle operating costs and time savings, noise reduction and economic accessibility.
- The 'network' approach outperforms the 'priority road' approach under all external scenarios on almost all indicators – the sole exception is demographic accessibility under conditions of high growth and fast integration.
- The 'priority road' approach would have adverse consequences for European transport users overall in terms of vehicle operating costs and time, whatever the growth and integration scenarios.
- Overall accessibility gains under all external scenarios and infrastructure variants are either insignificant or quite small. This however hides the fact that at a more spatially disaggregate level, there is a mixed pattern of gains and losses: in general there are significant accessibility gains close to the corridors with new infrastructure, but significant accessibility losses in adjacent countries which experience traffic growth and hence slower traffic speeds. The spatial disaggregation of the results allows to assess how well each specified corridor development alternative is with respect to the policies from which it was developed.
- Under the favourable conditions of the renaissance scenario the 'network' approach performs very well with respect to its underlying transport policy which gives particular emphasis to intermodality, regional development, accessibility and safety; so does the 'all rail' solution. By contrast, the 'all road' and 'priority road' strategies present more negative and heterogeneous results also with reference to their underlying transport policy.
- When comparing the impacts for the accession countries separately from those for the EU countries, the most significant difference between these two groups is that while the CEEC present positive scores under all possible corridor development alternatives, the EU

shows negative results for the 'priority road' solution under the renaissance, dilution and solidarity scenarios.

- For EU countries, the 'network' approach always performs better than the road alternatives. Regarding the CEEC, the same is true, with the exception of the fragmentation scenario where the 'priority road' solution performs better than the 'network' approach.
- Under most external scenarios, the CEEC find road-based strategies moderately beneficial, whereas Western Europe finds them detrimental. This can be attributed both to the impacts experienced amongst the two groups, with Western Europe suffering particularly from the negative effects of increased road transport, but also the different policy focuses of the two sides.
- Looking at the results from the national perspective confirms the robustness of the 'network' solution. This means that diversification of the investment in different types of infrastructure would appear to have greater success in achieving national transport policy objectives.
- The policy areas of 'increasing cross-border traffic harmonisation', 'intermodality' and 'regional development' explain the better scoring of the 'network' approach as compared to the 'priority road' solution under different socio-economic and integration scenarios.

The second-level prioritisation of projects belonging to the trans-European corridors in the East is only now about to begin. Using DECODE and through expert interviews with the actors concerned we sought to identify those projects that are more likely to be submitted for co-financing to the ISPA Fund.

Whilst acknowledging the importance of project-specific assessment results for evaluation we have suggested that it is important prior to taking any final decision to submit the whole set of projects being proposed to strategic assessment. The DECODE method is one method for carrying out this analysis.

The results suggest that if the Common Transport Policy objectives, in particular with regard to sustainable mobility, are to be taken seriously, and if subsidiarity is understood to also be about the integration of both Community and national interests then it is important to support multimodal solutions, albeit paying close attention to positive boundary conditions, hence intermodality as well as patterns of inter-regional co-operation. Such a strategy can guarantee that even under not so favourable conditions in terms of economic growth or even integration, the impacts of transport infrastructure investment are positive both for the local residents and local economies as well as for Europe as a whole.

Notes

1 The CODE-TEN project involved researchers from INRETS (France), DTT, Technical University (Denmark), SYSTEMA (Greece), PLANCO (Germany), CESUR (Portugal), VTT (Finland), I.T.S, University of Leeds (UK), HALCROW (UK), TRT (Italy), KTI (Hungary), CTC (Bulgaria), INCERTRANS (Romania), University of Gdansk (Poland), TTU (Estonia) and SSCTP (Russia). On behalf of the consortium we would like to thank Michel Beuthe of FUCAM as well as David Banister of the University of London for their input into our work as well as Catharina Sikow-Magny of the EC DG-TREN for her valuable comments to our reports throughout the project's lifetime.

2 CODE-TEN Deliverables 1 to 10, 1998 & 1999; CODE-TEN Working Papers 1999.

3 TINA stands for Transport Infrastructure Needs Assessment.

References

CODE-TEN (1998), *Deliverable P(3) Volume 3 Case Studies – Corridor I, Corridor II, Corridor IV, Corridor V, Corridor VII, Corridor IX, Corridor X; Mediterranean Short Sea shipping; Lisbon-Madrid-Paris Corridor*, ICCR, Vienna.

CODE-TEN (1999a), *Deliverable P(4) Scenarios and Infrastructure Development*, INRETS, Paris.

CODE-TEN (1999b), *Deliverable P(5) Assessment of Spatial and Socio-Economic Impacts*, CESUR, Lisbon.

CODE-TEN (1999c), *Deliverable P(6) Spatial Distribution of Environment & Safety Impacts*, VTT, Helsinki.

CODE-TEN (2000), *Deliverable P(8) Decision Support System*, SYSTEMA, Athens.

European Commission (1992), *The Future Development of the Common Transport Policy - A Global Approach to the Construction of a Community Framework for Sustainable Mobility*, COM(92) 494, European Commission, Brussels.

European Commission (1993), *European Transport Policy in the 90s*, European Commission, Brussels.

European Commission (1994), *Strategic Environmental Assessment – Existing Methodology*, European Commission, Brussels.

European Commission (1995a), *The Common Transport Policy Action Programme 1995-2000*, European Commission, Brussels.

European Commission (1995b), *The Trans-European Transport Network; Transforming Patchwork into a Network*, European Commission, Brussels.

European Commission (1997a), *Case Studies on Strategic Environmental Assessment; Final Report: Volumes 1 & 2*, European Commission, Brussels.

European Commission/ISPRA (1997b), *A Study to Develop and Implement an Overall Strategy for EIA/SEA Research in the EU*, European Commission, Brussels.

European Commission (1999), *Commission Communication to the Council, European Parliament, Economic and Social Committee and Committee of the Regions: The Common Transport Policy; Sustainable Mobility: Perspectives for the Future*, European Commission, Brussels.

Giorgi, L. and Tandon, A. (eds.) CODE-TEN (2000a), *Final Report, The DECODE Method: Theory and Application*, ICCR, Vienna.

Giorgi, L. and Tandon, A. (eds.) CODE-TEN (2000b), *Deliverable P(9) Scientific Report Code-Ten : The DECODE Method for Strategic Transport Assessment*, ICCR, Vienna.

Giorgi, L. and Tandon, A. (2000c), *CODE-TEN Deliverable P(10) Policy Report Code-Ten: The Trans-European Corridors, Policy Recommendations*, ICCR, Vienna.

Glaister, S. *et al.* (1998), *Transport Policy in Britain*, MacMillian Press Ltd., London.

Jansen, G. *et al.* (1998), *CODE-TEN Deliverable R(2) Transport Information System*, PLANCO, Essen.

Layard, R. and Glaister, S. (1996), *Cost-Benefit Analysis*, Cambridge University Press, Cambridge.

Leleur, S. *et al.* (1998), *CODE-TEN Baseline Methodology*, IVTB, Copenhagen.

Nellthorp J., Mackie P.J. and Bristow A.L. (1998), *Measurement and Valuation of the Impacts of Transport Initiatives*, Deliverable D9, (Restricted), EUNET Project - Socio Economic and Spatial Impacts of Transport (Contract: ST-96-SC.037), Institute for Transport Studies, University of Leeds, Leeds.

Parsons, W. (1995), *Public Policy: An Introduction to the Theory and Practice of Policy Analysis*, Aldershot, Edward Elgar.

Piers and Sienstra (1999), 'Review Papers on Scenarios', Paper presented at the PASTEUR Concerted Action Meeting in May, Brussels.

Rossi, P.H and Freeman, H.E. (1993), *Evaluation: A Systematic Approach*, SAGE, California.

Sugden, R. and Williams, A. (1978), *The Principles of Practical Cost-Benefit Analysis*, Oxford University Press, Oxford.

Tandon, A. (ed.) (1999), *CODE-TEN Deliverable P(3) Volume 1: TEN Enlargements: The Corridor Development Plans - Comparative Case Studies*, ICCR, Vienna.

Tandon, A. (1999), *CODE-TEN Deliverable P(3) Volume 2: Project Database*, ICCR, Vienna.

TENASSESS (1997) *Deliverable R(4) - Volumes 1 & 2, Volume 1: The TENASSESS Policy Assessment Methodology (PAM); Volume 2: Demonstration Case Studies*, Halcrow, London.

TENASSESS (1998 & 1999) *Deliverable R(6) - Volumes 1 & 2, Volume 1: The TENASSESS Barrier Model*; Volume 2: *Demonstration Case Studies & Amendments to the Barrier Model*, Halcrow, London.

TINA Secretariat (1999), *Socio-Economic Cost-Benefit Analysis in the Context of Project Appraisals for Developing a Trans-European Network in Bulgaria, Cyprus, Czech Republic, Estonia, Hungary, Latvia, Lithuania, Poland, Romania, Slovakia and Slovenia*, TINA 015/Final. TINA Secretariat, Vienna.

Turro, M. (1999), *Going Trans-European: Planning & Financing Transport Networks for Europe*, Pergamon, Amsterdam.

9 Transition and Integration, TEN-T and Corridors

CHRISTIAN REYNAUD

The political objective of integrating Central and Eastern European countries within the European Union makes it necessary to plan the extension of trans-European networks to ten[1] new candidate countries in the relatively short time-scale of a few years.

Investment is taking place in the corridors defined at the Second Pan-European Congress in Crete (and subsequently specified in more detail at the third Pan-European Congress in Helsinki) in order to improve links between countries or between different regions of the same country in Central Europe: these projects are also a short-term manifestation of the desire for integration.

How can the political objectives and these actions both be achieved, and how can medium-term and long-term programmes be tied in with issues involving short-term commitment? This is a fundamental aspect of any transport policy that works towards an integration which, if successful, would take place in a relatively short space of time, when we remember that the Berlin wall fell less than ten years ago.

Who could have imagined a few years ago that it would be possible to work towards integrating Central and Eastern Europe within a Europe that has taken more than thirty years to build and consolidate itself? Today the project of integration is part of the Treaties of Maastricht and Amsterdam and not merely an element of free trade or the Single Market.

The Treaty of Maastricht was where the concept of the trans-European network was first expressed. Title XII, the wording of which is ambivalent, defines the infrastructure network as the necessary condition for the efficient functioning of the market, insofar as it allows enterprises to better communicate, thus also better competition is in turn, a necessary precondition for innovation. At the same time the network is defined as the expression of an integrated Europe based on solidarity, which cannot alone be achieved through the market.

By the very rationale of the Treaty, these two approaches must now be applied to candidate countries and result in a European Union with a population which will increase by 25 per cent whilst the GCP will only increase by 5 per cent.

The problem was first tackled at the Conference of Crete with the idea that 'corridors' should be extended further East towards the Community of Independent States (CIS). More is involved than just constructing infrastructures. There is also the desire to consolidate ties and co-operation between States in order to develop an investment policy for the short, medium, and long terms. Harmonised criteria were sketched out which took account of the impact of projects on accessibility, development and environmental protection, while ensuring a high level of consistency with the development of national and regional plans.

Transition and integration are expected to walk hand in hand. These two elements can however not be brought together alone through the removal of barriers to market access and liberalisation. The two areas are now bound together in a common process of institutional change which affects both Western Europe and Eastern Europe. In transport, the profound reorganisation of railways and of the concept of public service bear witness to this. This change in institutions will culminate in the advent of a less centralised society where individuals have greater responsibility and exert greater control over their immediate environment. The still somewhat vague concept of a 'citizen's network' is quite closely related to the development of environmentally friendly local policies. In answer to the process of globalisation, which is governed by international competition, we therefore have a common challenge and a renewal of local policies that, in transport, bring together land policy and better management of local trips.

It is beyond the scope of this chapter to cover all these points in detail. My objective is instead to provide a basis for transport planning by reviewing a number of methodological problems encountered when conducting long term transport forecasting in a changing institutional context.

The Nineties: Economic Transition and Social Transformation

Change in Transport and the Economy

In Central European countries economic growth could with few short-term exceptions be sustained throughout the nineties. In the Baltic States it started a bit later but got off to a good and rapid start. Economic recovery was slower in Eastern Europe, namely in Bulgaria and Romania, and the slowest in the CIS countries. There too, however, there are positive signs as of 1997.

Transport reflects and accentuates fluctuations in economic activity:

- immediately following the onset of transition there was a significant reduction in transport paralleling economic regression, albeit to a stronger degree: the reduction in transport was generally much greater than the reduction in economic activity, in fact it was almost twice as great;
- a similar reduction occurred in passenger transport; this was most likely due to the fall of incomes and the increase of unemployment;
- gradually there occurred a complete re-orientation of foreign trade towards EU countries. Currently, roughly between 60 and 70 per cent of the foreign trade of CEECs is with the EU: trade within the CEEC region and with the CIS collapsed within two years, although those countries that signed the Visegrad agreement succeeded in avoiding this falldown to some extent;
- these transformations in transport to a large degree favoured road transport which adapted rapidly to the structural changes. This was to the detriment of rail which was dominant in the previous period. Its share of the market fell from 75 per cent in 1980 to 60 per cent in 1996.

In order to adapt, transport underwent profound structural changes which we shall now describe in more detail.

The Structural Changes

Radical changes cannot be understood without an examination of structural factors. This involves not merely transport but also the activities which generate it. In this connection, it is worth noting the very high consumption of transport in CEECs in relation to added value. This has been four to five times higher than in the EU and was linked to:

- an economy based on heavy industry;
- an economy with costly administrative organisation of flows;
- the aim to achieve industrial interdependence between countries which was costly in terms of transport.

As a consequence, it was possible for economic growth to be accompanied by a drop in freight transport. At the same time, a drop in freight transport can be an indication that rationalisation and re-organisation are taking place.

The above observations are less definite in the case of passenger transport. The rate of car ownership is now much higher than average incomes would lead one to expect. Moreover, there is general agreement that household consumption has fallen less than industrial production and that in the CEECs measured GDP is much lower than real activity. The unmeasured part of the market is often estimated as approximately 30 per cent of the figures listed by the EBRD.

Even allowing for the fact that the statistical tool is in need of rapid improvement; for the tendency before 1990 to overestimate aggregates in order to display better performance; as well as for the propensity towards underestimation after 1990 which reflects the difficulty of adapting to measurement systems, there are nevertheless significant differences with European Union countries with regard to transport. This is accentuated by the fact that the rapidity of change has not always been apparent in economic structures nor in the levels of training and education amongst the population.

The indicators developed by the EBRD to measure transition with reference to firms, the market or the liberalisation of prices, the financial sector as well as the Government and the legal system indicate that considerable progress has been made. The transformations of industry have certainly not ended, but are ongoing. Yet what we need to establish is whether, to what extent, and by when the structures in Central and East European countries will approximate those of the European Union.

It is not unlikely that there will probably be at least as many differences between the different countries of Central Europe as between the countries of the European Union and certain Central European countries, bearing in mind that the differences will continue to be poorly measured by aggregates such as the GDP.

Indicative are foreign trade indicators which show that levels of intra-branch trade between the EU and CEECs are high: the problem is not at all comparable with North-South trade and has impacts on transport. The CEECs are already integrated to quite a high degree within the European economy with levels that are fairly near those of EU countries (of the order of 60 per cent). We can also forecast a revival of regional trade, with the CIS – political stability permitting – or at least between the Visegrad countries: the potential for growth between neighbouring countries in Central Europe is currently assessed at between 20 and 40 per cent. Institutionally, multilateral and bilateral links are forming in the sphere of industrial co-operation, as are links between regions (trans-border links and links between non-adjacent regions).

The main consequences for transport are as follows:

- a facilitation of trade which is still in need of further improvement particularly with regard to border crossings (including between CEEC and CIS countries);
- a development in logistics – the requirements are similar to those of EU countries in the absence of pre-existing structures;
- and, of course, a modification of networks and their use to provide a service.

In connection with companies we can observe:

- a very rapid opening up to SMEs, which may quite soon raise problems with regard to the harmonisation of social conditions in Europe;
- the slower restructuring of large companies, in particular of the railways; and
- limitations with regard to the logistical development of domestic transport.

What is revealed by the EBRD ratings, despite their simplistic nature, is that the most difficult questions are those which require an institutional capability, the problem not being to decide whether a shock treatment is required or not, but to carry out each aspect of transition at the right time. The construction of suitable institutions is the key to success and this is particularly true in the context of building infrastructures requiring long-term national commitment.

With regard to investments the following can be observed: in 1995, national investment accounted for about one per cent of the GDP of CEESs and 4.5 per cent of gross fixed asset formation. There has been a considerable increase since 1993, but the level remains low (about 3 billion EURO, a figure which could double with growth). The contribution through indirect foreign investment (EIB, EBRD) is significant and so is that through EU structural funds: 7 billion EURO prior to joining and an increase afterwards. Still there is a shortfall as ultimate requirements are estimated at between 20 and 30 billion EURO, depending on what is placed on the selected project lists.

However, the issue of investment is not merely one of funding, and any project must fit into a general context consisting of:

- the level of operation of the market and the needs of companies;
- investment choices and the criteria which interest institutions; and
- lastly, tariff rules and the way the sector operates and is organised.

All of these have an effect on infrastructure requirements.

If we consider the progress that has been made in less than ten years, not only with regard to trade and travel but also with regard to the consolidation of democratic procedures, we have to admit that the current situation is more encouraging than originally contemplated (particularly after the initial collapse in production). The deep-rooted support of the population no doubt provides the explanation for this, as well as the best guarantee for the years to come. As a result, it is necessary to be able to take advantage of the opportunities and new flexibilities that are available in the context of recovery in order to ensure continuing progress in the framework of European cohesion.

Transport has allowed these profound changes to take place and it has followed the total re-orientation of foreign trade that has occurred in the space of a few years. The road sector was by far the most adaptable and the winner of transition. Still this should not lead us to underestimate the potential of railways especially for the long-term. Many problems are therefore presented today in similar terms for both European Union countries and CEECs. The re-organisation of railway companies is one such example.

With regard to the construction of trans-European networks, approaches also converge as there is the need to:

- create geographical continuity which is more firmly based on seaboards;
- structure the economic environment and pricing in order to optimise use of infrastructures whilst still protecting the environment;
- and, lastly, support major projects within an institutional framework of consultation which will ensure that mutually agreed long-term decisions will be reached.

Transition Scenarios for a Changing Institutional Context

The move towards a sustainable development policy in transport involves demonstrating the link between carrying out a tangible (infrastructure) project that could be realised in the short term and the fulfilment of more general and more abstract policy objectives which are only achievable in the long term.

The role of institutions, in particular their non-stability or change, is in this regard of fundamental importance. The institutional context involves not only the operation of the market economy (the area of institutional economics to which the EBRD and the World Bank are more sensitive) but also the operation of political institutions (the sphere of political economics). From this arises a problem of clarity of objectives or the matching of objectives to the institutional resources required to achieve them.

In order to shed light on this debate we can refer to a very simple example. In the case of several Central European countries, the desire for liberalisation is stronger the greater the opposition, in the form of inertia, from their institutional framework. This is paradoxical, as the countries with the most liberalisation become those with the least and vice-versa, and the same applies in the area of interventionist policies. There is, in other words, a 'distortion effect' linked with the gap between policy objectives and the institutional reality of a given country or set of countries.

We must therefore find out how to correct for such distortions. It is important to note that such distortions are not limited to transition countries. The institutional context is also changing within the European

Union with the emergence of multinational (or transnational) powers and the progress of regional decentralisation.

Linking the Short Term with the Long Term: Corridor Approaches

The corridor concept is a useful part of such a comprehensive approach, in order to achieve consultation and stimulate the participation of players (the public sector, companies and users) (cf. Reynaud, Chatelus and Chouareff, 1996; Chatelus, 1999).

A) A three level approach The Corridor concept (see diagram) fits with approach to the planning of regional transport infrastructure with three temporal levels. Its principles have been described in the preparatory documents for the Crete Pan-European Congress.

- The first level is the specification of a long term framework with the introduction of multimodal master plans intended to meet all future transport needs.
- At the other extreme of planning, the third level deals with the realisation of concrete projects in the short or medium term (in general about 5 years).
- Located between these two, the second level involves defining priority corridors which enable the transition to be made between comprehensive long term planning and the short term project.

A corridor therefore consists of a coherent set of priority multimodal infrastructures based on a principle infrastructure which provides a means of increasing co-operation between two major areas, for instance Europe and the Mediterranean or the European Union and the CEEC. The objective is not just to improve the infrastructures but also the quality of service and operating systems.

B) An approach for regional infrastructure planning Corridors are also intended to allow infrastructure projects to be planned coherently at regional level. Corridors are multimodal as they combine (to degrees which depend on the geographical context) the two land modes (rail and road), coastal shipping and the principal ports and airports. They provide continuity between adjacent regions and are a response to common priorities and criteria. This approach has been applied in regional infrastructure planning studies for the Middle

East, in the context of the peace process. Four priority corridors have thus been identified in consultation with representatives from Egypt, Israel, Jordan and the Palestinian territories.

The time scale for the construction of these corridors is of the order of fifteen years. They will lead to the gradual development of a continuous framework and regional infrastructures which are joined to the priority infrastructures that feature in national and international plans.

C) Taking account of operating conditions Implementing a Corridor approach in order to identify infrastructure priorities must be accompanied by an increase in the quality of transport systems, which will improve the efficiency of the Corridors. Thus, as was stated at the Lisbon Conference, the quality of transport services must be improved. The efficiency of transport systems also requires trade to be harmonised, facilitated and liberalised in order to reduce non-physical barriers. All the modern logistical and computing techniques that are able to improve transport systems should be promoted in order to maximise the efficiency of the Corridors.

For air and sea transport, traffic management must go hand in hand with, or even take precedence over, infrastructure priorities. This issue affects not only traffic flow but also the safety of users and the population at large.

Using this framework, efforts could concentrate on proposed projects which will then be the object of more detailed studies in the framework of the Corridor.

In this manner it is possible to make the transition from a regional medium-term view to local projects that can be undertaken in the short term (third level) without any loss in coherence at regional level.

Figure 9.1 Methodology of Corridors

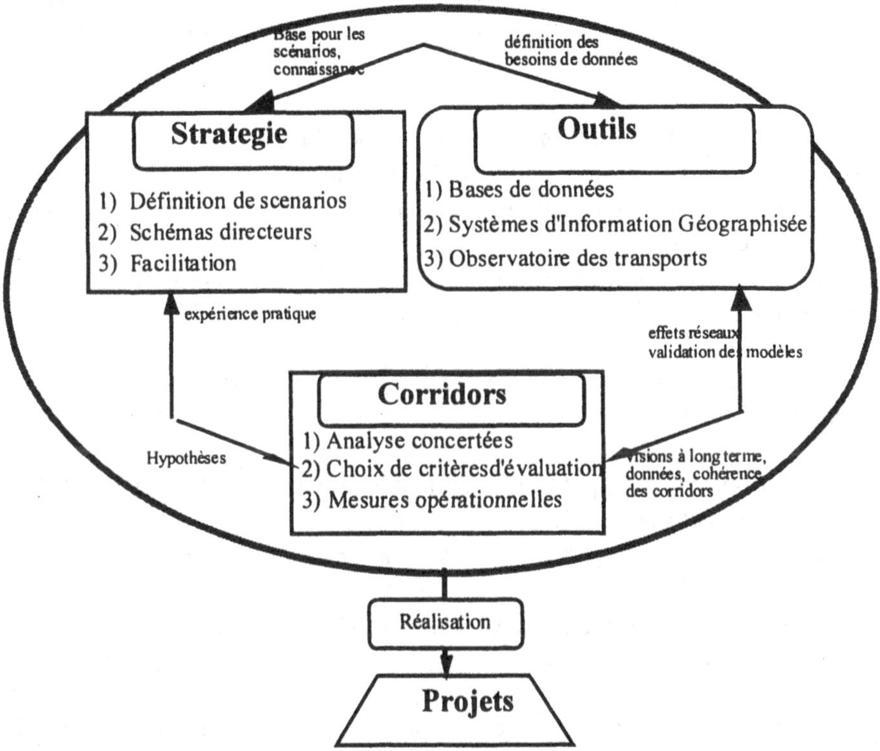

The Scenarios Method

Any scenario is based on a system approach which identifies variables, players and interactions. A traffic projection model (dealing with the link between the socio-economic context and transport activity) may be utilised.

An initial classification differentiates between the economic (and demographic) variables, spatial variables and transport variables between which links are created. Models which make use of spatial data are essential for any consideration of networks and infrastructures.

A major difficulty has proved to be the characterisation of transport policies in scenarios. One possible way is to distinguish between three main types of transport policies, namely between policies aimed at liberalisation, policies aimed at harmonisation and policies targeting the development of TENs.

Another possibility is to classify policies with regard their spatial reference *and* their objectives (cf. Giorgi *et al.*, CODE-TEN Final Report, 2000):

- the international level dominated by a liberal type of regulation;
- the national level, more interested in measures aimed at re-organising the sector and achieving regional equilibrium at national level and social cohesion;
- the local level which concentrates on a land planning policy and management of local transport demand.

These three levels are fairly appropriate for the first segmentation defined in scenarios because:

- regulation by competition dominates international relations (for example road transport);
- the reorganisation of the sector is a major issue at national level (for example rail transport);
- sustainable development is very much linked to local objectives of environmental protection.

The divisions are of course never as clear as this; major environmental issues are also raised at global level, but the means of solving them are more to be found in standards and industrial policies than at the level of the organisation of transport.

A 'Model' of Transition

The introduction of transition and integration in the scenario approach to transport planning adds new dimensions and increases the number of hypotheses to be considered.

With regard to transition and the increase of the GDP in countries in transition, it would seem advisable to define quite a large range of growth rates and central hypotheses within these (cf. NEA, INRETS, IWW, 1999; Reynaud, Mathieu and Siarov, 1999). This is the consequence of uncertainty concerning GDP levels and rates of growth in a period of transition, the still cursory analysis of on-going processes of recovery, and the inaccuracy in the measurement of many socio-economic aggregates. The scale of the differences between EU and Central European countries in transport consumption (tonnes and tonne-kilometres) and car ownership in relation to income and production levels are certainly largely due to these measurement uncertainties.

This being the case, it is apparent from what has happened in the last ten years that transition has not occurred at the same rate in all countries, which to some extent explains the different levels of growth. Whatever the nature of the differences in types of transition, it is nevertheless the case that there are differences of almost five years in the economic recovery of those countries that were affected by an initial phase of decline. The EBRD has shown that quite a good correlation exists between these indicators of transition and the increase in GDP.

When defining scenarios, a distinction must be made between different phases of transition. These correspond to different stages of the transition process: liberalisation (and deregulation), reorganisation and structural reform (and even 'reregulation'), institutional decentralisation.

Integration measured with reference to accession is clearly not independent of the process of transition. Nevertheless, it retains a political aspect, as the EU can encourage transition by speeding up integration, or, on the contrary, delay it in view of the difficulty of reconciling the strategies of enlargement and deepening.

The introduction of integration and transition specific variables in scenarios is possible on the basis of the following observations, which, although necessarily simplistic, satisfy the objective of providing the basis for a satisfactory system model before attempting to consider more complex relationships which are closer to reality:

- the rules of competition and the liberal economy are rapidly adopted by trade and transport in the countries of the East;
- yet reorganisation measures cannot succeed without recognised, stable institutions;
- and, lastly, the decentralisation of decision-making will often take place during a later stage of institutional transition (a stage which is raising doubts in some European Union countries).

Thus, there will be a succession of different phases: short and medium-term liberalisation of the international market, medium and long-term sectoral reorganisation, long and very long-term institutional change.

In order to avoid complicating the formulation of scenarios, and in view of such interdependencies, it is proposed to introduce a translation between the hypotheses of the different scenarios based on a 'rolling' principle that operates both spatially and temporally:

- rolling in time with a rhythm of five years which corresponds to the completion of the different stages of transition described above;
- rolling in space, distinguishing between three sets of countries depending on whether they are likely to join the European Union in the very near or more distant future or merely be associated with it. These countries are located in 'concentric circles' with the European Union at the centre. This type of model by which transition and integration are propagated by geographical contiguity seems to be validated by what has happened in Europe in the last ten years. A duration of five years for this 'wave' of propagation (countries joining before 2005, 2010, 2015 or 2020) would seem reasonable and leads to a considerable reduction in the number of variable combinations to be analysed, without which the scenario approach would be difficult to implement.

Correcting the Effect of Institutional Distortion or 'Institutional Anticipation' on Policy Changes

Once we have this framework for analysing the transport system and the institutional dynamic within which it operates, we can attempt to correct the effect of the 'institutional distortion' mentioned above.

Such correction is essential for any evaluation of policy in countries undergoing rapid institutional change. It also becomes essential within the European Union where exploratory work on the interface of political power between the local and European levels, or subsidiarity, is calling the existing institutional organisation into question.

Three stages of correction are proposed:

- weighting the different transport policy objectives with regard to the different phases of transition. This weighting procedure is based on the hypothesis that a policy objective is only achievable if the country possesses appropriate institutions given that different objectives do not require these institutions to be developed to the same level;

- classifying countries according to the stage that transition has reached. This is similar to the methodology developed by the EBRD. For transport, this classification can be reinforced by a detailed study of the development of road, rail and local transport. This provides additional insight that can moreover reveal disparities between progress in the transport sector and, more generally, progress as described by the EBRD;
- applying the corrective coefficients obtained for each country and for successive dates (2005, 2010, 2015) to the weightings given to transport policy objectives.

When the decisions were being made concerning the reunification of Germany in the early nineties, scenarios were developed for initiating and designing large-scale works. The underlying hypothesis was that the former GDR would catch up in one generation after which travel behaviour in the old and new *Länder* would be similar. This method had the advantage of overcoming shortages of data, providing a strong political message and constructing a coherent framework capable of mobilising resources to achieve objectives.

It is therefore interesting to take a long or very long-term view and wonder about similarities between the European Union and Central European countries with regard to transport in the distant future. Are these societies fundamentally different? In how many generations will convergence, if any, occur? What will be the profile of long-term change once the variously paced phases of recovery and catching up have terminated?

It is certain that geographical proximity (spatial contiguity) will not play a negligible role, which explains why it is in those countries which are the nearest to the EU that transition is taking place most rapidly.

In this context we can imagine two 'time zones' with two different types of development:

- on the one hand rapid growth and integration which will allow Central European counties to catch up within two generations; and
- on the other hand slower growth and transformation which will only lead to this convergence after three generations.

Obviously, those countries where change starts slowly will undergo more rapid acceleration later, as they will benefit from the dynamism of their neighbours.

Conclusions

This chapter has outlined the methodological problems involved in conducting long-term transport forecasting in a changing institutional environment like the one characteristic of transition countries in Central and Eastern Europe in the context of the parallel wider process of European integration.

Whilst significantly more complex, this is a problem not fundamentally different from that of coping with uncertainty in integrated transport planning, i.e. transport planning that considers both the project and policy levels in evaluation and their links. In other words, the proposals advanced here with reference to the evaluation of the trans-European networks and corridors are valid more generally.

A model of transition tailored to transport has been proposed. This builds on two main elements, namely, the consideration of network effects and the use of the scenario approach to forecasting. None of these elements is new to transport planning. The innovativeness of the proposed approach is rather entailed in the use of policy as a structural factor tied to institutions, hence also time-dependant, to analyse and, in turn, operationalise pathways of transition and integration. Such an approach, it is contended, has not merely the advantage of overcoming shortcomings in data or measurement uncertainties; it also provides a basis for discussing and debating proposed institutional reforms and their timing – in turn also the timing of investment.

Note

1 Eleven, counting Cyprus.

References

Chatelus, G. (1999), La méthodologie des corridors en Méditerranée occidentale – Quelles priorités pour les infrastructures régionales de transport au Maghreb? *RTS – Recherche, Transport, Sécurité*, no. 63.

NEA, INRETS and IWW (1999), *Final Report on Traffic Forecast in the Ten Pan-European Transport Corridors of Helsinki*, PHARE – DG VII, Brussels.

Reynaud, C., Chatelus, G. and Chouareff, F. (1996), *Corridor Approach*, Comité sectoriel des infrastructures de transport au Moyen Orient, REDWG, Aman.

Reynaud, C., Mathieu, D. and Siarov, V. (1999), *External Scenarios – Development of Assessment Methodology*, Final Report CODE-TEN, Deliverable [D(7)], INRETS, Arcueil.

10 Transport Policy and Research: What Future?

RONALD J. POHORYLES AND LIANA GIORGI

Introduction

Expert advice has always been sought by politicians. Several studies have looked into the politics of evaluation or expert advise and more generally the applicability of research results in the policy field (cf. Bulmer, 1990; Barker and Peters, 1992; Peter and Barkers, 1993 – following on from work of Weber, Mannheim and Lindblom).

Perhaps the oldest yet still quite popular view of research utilisation is what Bulmer (1990) calls the 'engineering model' which assumes that decision-makers only require information – provided they receive this their decision is simple and straightforward. Yet as Parsons (1995) notes: 'decision-makers confront a range of interpretations or accounts of reality, and thus information is not the kind of value-free thing which the engineering model implies' (p.385). One could add that decision-makers are quite aware of the plurality of information or expert sources and take advantage of this to the full (cf. Wynne, 1997); or as Keynes appreciated 'there is nothing a government hates more than to be well-informed; for it makes the process of arriving at a decision much more complicated and difficult' (quoted in Parsons, 1995, p.393). In other words, the science and policy interaction is as much about the politics of science as it is about the science of politics.

Nevertheless, the process of Europeanisation is posing anew the fundamental question of the applicability of research results for a very simple reason. For the European project to materialise, it is necessary to obtain not only the support of national governments, but more generally of the policy apparatus in each country, of the research communities and of the European citizens. After all, research of a European added value cannot ultimately be 'applied' or exploited unless recognised as of added value by the Member States. The recognition of this mechanism has led the Commission to place much emphasis on dissemination. Unintentionally, one could almost argue, the European project is strengthening the reliance of policy on research and information.

The aim of this chapter is to illustrate the use of a particular survey technique, namely the Delphi method, for establishing a consultation procedure among experts, members of the transport policy community across Europe, on the subjects of transport policy and research. Such a survey was carried out in the framework of the TENASSESS project funded by the Transport RTD Fourth Framework Programme and had the following objectives:

- to explore the scope and barriers to research exploitation of European transport research;
- to test a tool for simulating discussion on policy developments in the field of transport based on input supplied through research.

This chapter is organised as follows: in the first section we review the methodology employed providing details on the sample, the questionnaires and the fieldwork. In the second section we discuss the subject of research exploitation and applicability in view of our findings. In the last section we report on the results of the simulated discussion on trends and developments in national transport policies and the Common Transport Policy (CTP).

Methodology

A Panel Survey with Delphi Elements

The Delphi survey tool was developed in the fifties by the Pentagon for the purpose of arriving at predictions on military goals. Its success led to its adoption in numerous other fields. A Delphi survey has the following characteristics:

- it is a survey of experts;
- as a result, it typically relies on small samples;
- it is a longitudinal panel survey, i.e. it comprises several waves and relies on the same sample of respondents;
- the answers to the questions of wave n are used as input to wave n+1. One usual way to do this is to present respondents with the aggregate results and ask them to comment on the trend outlined.

Thus a discussion is simulated which in conjunction with other information sources can assist in the making of predictions, for instance on implementation time frames; the reaching of consensus; or the identification of innovative solutions to a particular problem.

The TENASSESS survey incorporates the above elements, is however not a Delphi-survey in the strict sense of the word. The questionnaires and the themes varied in part across waves, and the results of each wave were fed to experts in a generic way. This we think was a more useful way to simulate a discussion and contributed to keeping the interest of the respondents.

In the first wave of the survey, respondents were presented with a set of policy statements and were asked to indicate their degree of agreement. In the second wave, some of these statements were elaborated and respondents were asked to judge the probability for achieving the specified goal; to indicate which type of measure would be mostly necessary; and to judge the importance of the European level in this process. Finally, in the third wave the aggregate results from the first and second waves were elaborated in a comprehensive statement describing the trend and respondents were asked to indicate agreement or disagreement vis-à-vis the statement as a whole and with reference to its individual components.

Table 10.1 Policy Statement from First Wave (Example)

The process of transport planning in your country faces further democratisation and the participation of all interested parties. Specifically, the public has the opportunity to directly participate in decision-making processes. [Indicate agreement or disagreement on a five-point scale]
Example [statement 1.17; second wave]

	INCREASING THE POSSIBILITIES FOR ACTIVE PARTICIPATION OF LOCAL ACTORS AND THE PUBLIC IN THE DECISION-MAKING PROCESS							
		very high 1	2	3	4	very low 5		don't know
1.	How do you judge your expertise concerning this goal?	☐	☐	☐	☐	☐		☐
2.	How do you consider the importance to achieve this goal?	☐	☐	☐	☐	☐		☐
3.	How high do you estimate the probability to achieve the objective set out							
	Concerning... a. the political will?	☐	☐	☐	☐	☐		☐
	b. public acceptability?	☐	☐	☐	☐	☐		☐
	c. organisational aspects?	☐	☐	☐	☐	☐		☐
	d. available financing?	☐	☐	☐	☐	☐		☐
	e. technical/technological development?	☐	☐	☐	☐	☐		☐
4.	Which of the following instrumental categories is the most important to achieve this objective?	a) investment ☐		b) pricing ☐		c) regulation ☐		
5.	How important do you consider the contribution of your institution to the achievement of this goal?	☐	☐	☐	☐	☐		☐
6.	How important do you consider common action on the European level to achieve this objective?	☐	☐	☐	☐	☐		☐
		2000	2005	2010	2020	later	neve r	don't know
7.	When do you expect this goal to be achieved?	☐	☐	☐	☐	☐	☐	☐

Table 10.2 Elaborated Policy Statement Third Wave (Example)

Increasing the possibilities for active participation of local actors and the public in the decision-making process

A. A goal of medium priority.
B. Barriers to the implementation of this goal are mainly of an organisational and financial nature. Barriers may also be expected to emerge in the political field.
C. Regulations comprise the primary tool for achieving this goal.
D. Action at EU level is a facilitator to the process but not the major promoter.
E. This goal could be achieved by 2010.

1. Would you agree that statements A to E characterise the factual trend in relation to this goal? Yes ☐ No ☐

2. Of the statements A to E, which in your opinion do not accurately reflect the actual trend in this field? *Please circle accordingly.*

A B C D E

3. Would you yourself agree with this development? Yes ☐ No ☐

4. Please indicate which statements A to E you disagree with. *Please circle accordingly.*

A B C D E

5. Comments: Please elaborate on the reasons for your disagreement and/or suggest alternatives.

The third wave questionnaire also included a question that ranked the policy objectives in terms of priority on the basis of the aggregate results of the first wave and asked the respondents to react to this by providing their own ranking.

The simulation of a policy-relevant discussion was not the sole objective of the TENASSESS survey. The second major objective was to obtain information on the availability, use and applicability of information sources and, in particular, of research. A major section of the second wave questionnaire as well as of the fourth wave questionnaire was dedicated to this subject. The next section outlines analytically the topics explored by TENASSESS questionnaires.

Topics Explored

The TENASSESS survey used four questionnaires.

First wave questionnaire The first wave questionnaire was short and included a set of 39 *policy statements* grouped in ten categories (in parentheses the number of statements per category):

- decision-making process and structure (11);
- the internal market (5);
- transport demand and intermodal competition (3);
- pricing, taxes and charges (3);
- system and network development and the TEN (4);
- environmental protection (3);
- safety standards (3);
- social policy issues (2);
- external links with third countries (2);
- financing (3).

Second wave questionnaire This had four main sections: the first section was called '*strategic policy issues*' and contained 18 policy goals with a set of seven standard questions on each. The questions asked the respondent to judge their expertise in the field; to rate the importance of this specific goal achievement; to assess the barriers to implementation; to indicate the type(s) of policy instruments necessary to achieve this goal; to assess the importance of common action on the European level for achieving this objective; to assess the importance of the respondent's institution in achieving this goal; and to estimate when this goal could be expected to be achieved. The 18 policy objectives were filtered out of the set of 39 policy statements of the first wave using input from the responses of the first wave and other research on national transport policy prioritisation and the Common Transport Policy (cf. Giorgi, L., 1996, TENASSES Deliverable 1).

The second section asked a set of questions on *information sources*: the frequency of use; the type of technology; the usefulness of various information sources including at the European level; and the time spent on searching for relevant information in the field of transport.

The third section explored the reasons that prevent an easy access to information as well as the *barriers to its applicability*; asked a set of questions on the areas in which research is needed and used; tapped knowledge of European research programmes; and inquired into the types of institutions consulted for obtaining transport-related research results and information.

Finally the fourth section asked a set of questions on the *efficiency and effectiveness* of co-operation networks at European, national and regional levels.

Third wave questionnaire This questionnaire fed back to the respondents the results of the first and second wave questionnaires on the subject of policy in the form of elaborated policy goals with components on the importance of each; the barriers to its implementation; the role of the European Union; the type of policy-mix necessary for implementation; and the time frame of the latter. Respondents could in their turn indicate whether they agreed with the emerging trend as described on the whole and for each policy component. Two additional questions explored the ranking of policy goals; and their interrelations.

Fourth wave questionnaire The final questionnaire explored research themes per transport mode or sector and user needs. It sought to identify the future research priorities.

All four questionnaires were made available in four European languages, namely, English, French, German and Spanish.

The Sample

The address database for the survey included 446 experts. These were contact persons at the various institutions identified in the course of the overview of national transport policies as relevant actors.

The sample included respondents from most European Union countries but the distribution was uneven: thus whereas the address list for France included 120 experts, the one for Britain included 76, the one for Austria 27 and the one for Belgium 3. This mainly is a reflection of the differences in size and institutional structure in the countries under investigation. Admittedly however for some countries our sample could not be considered as complete as we did not carry out in-depth country analyses for all fifteen EU Member States: this was the case for Belgium, Sweden, Finland, Portugal and Ireland.

The Fieldwork

The fieldwork was carried out in four consecutive waves:

- the first wave questionnaire was sent out in May 1997;
- the second wave questionnaire was sent out in January 1998;
- the third wave questionnaire was sent out in May 1998;
- the fourth wave questionnaire was sent out in January 1999.

All 445 experts were contacted the first and second time round. The sample for the third and fourth waves was reduced to those who had answered the first and/or second wave questionnaires and those who had not but who had contacted to inform us that the reason was lack of time or change of job or position – in the latter case we asked the respondent to indicate who had taken their position and contacted the new person.

The questionnaires were followed by fax and telephone reminders – two such reminders (at regular intervals of two weeks) were sent to all those who had not replied within six weeks of sending the questionnaire. Where possible, these reminders were made on location and in the language of the respondent.

Table 10.3 displays the response rates per wave.

Table 10.3 Response rates to TENASSESS Delphi Survey (in absolute)

Country	Sample	Written refusals	Net response* (W1)	Net response (W2)	Net response (W3)	Net response (W4)
FR	120	2	39	40	28	8
DE	80	17	11	18	15	8
UK	76	8	26	25	14	6
ES	36	0	6	5	3	3
DK	32	0	6	6	6	2
GR	29	14	6	6	5	0
AT	27	4	6	9	7	1
IT	22	0	1	3	1	1
NL	11	0	2	1	2	1
SE	9	1	3	3	2	2
BE	3	0	2	1	1	0
EIB	1	0	1	1	1	1
Total	446	46	109	118	85	33

*Note: Net response corresponds to the number of questionnaires which could be used in the analysis, in absolute figures

Source: TENASSESS Survey

The gross response rate (i.e. considering written refusals as a response) for the first wave was 34 per cent; for the second 37 per cent. The net response rate was 24 and 27 per cent respectively; it was highest in France and the UK (33 per cent) and lowest in Germany (14 per cent for the first wave but 22 per cent for the second). (We do not consider here the response rates of countries like Sweden, Belgium or the Netherlands where the sample was far too small and not representative.)

The longitudinal response rate was 72 per cent for the second wave but only 39 per cent for the fourth wave, i.e. panel attrition was quite high. This is also why the results of the fourth wave reported in the sections that follow should be treated with caution.

Mail surveys are notoriously known to produce low response rates. The average response rates for mail surveys is known to lie around 10 per cent. The achievement of 37 per cent (gross) and 27 per cent (net) in the TENASSESS survey is thus a comparatively good result.

The longitudinal response rate for the third wave was quite good. The high panel attrition through to the fourth wave however suggests that four waves might be one too many for this type of an expert survey.

Information, Research and Knowledge as Resource

Types of Information Sources

Following Parsons (1995), we can classify the information sources in decision-making, including with reference to the exploitation of research results, according to two dimensions: first, whether formal or informal; second whether internal or external:

- formal and internal sources include governmental inquiries, think-tank reports and reports from internal government experts;
- formal and external sources include reports from the legislature, formal consultations as well as commissioned research;
- informal and internal sources include informal discussions and informal use of advisers; and
- informal and external sources include publications as well as participation in conferences and workshops.

In the TENASSESS survey we asked respondents to assess the frequency of use and usefulness of specific information media that would fall under the above classification scheme. Table 10.4 displays the ratio of respondents reporting frequent use and among the latter, a high degree of usefulness.

Table 10.4 Frequency and Usefulness of Information Sources

Name	Type	% using often	% find very useful
Personal contact	Informal	77	88
Journals	Informal / External	74	77
Official documents	Formal / Internal	68	69
Books	Informal / External	56	60
Reports	Formal / External	54	76
Conferences	Formal / External	46	58
Seminars (external)	Formal / External	43	66
Seminars (internal)	Formal / Internal	31	49

Note: In descending order according to ratio of frequent use

Source: TENASSESS Delphi Survey

All information media are used to a considerable degree. Informal means of communication are still the most preferred – personal contact is used by three quarters of the respondents and is also the one evaluated as the most useful. This is not surprising if one considers that the majority has little time available to review existing literature and research: 61 per cent of the respondents spend less than five hours per week collecting information on transport-related research, a further 31 per cent less than ten hours. Professional journals and official government documents rank second and third respectively as information sources; in terms of usefulness, research reports are, however, considered more important even if their rate of uptake is significantly lower.

Speed and the New Communication Technologies

The speed of retrieving information is an important criterion of usefulness. In 1997 63 per cent of the respondents had an internet access, thus it was not surprising to observe two years later that an equal number ranked Web Sites as the most efficient dissemination mode for European research projects. Executive summaries of research reports and journal publications ranked second and third respectively.

More generally the survey results suggest that the new communication media are useful for speeding personal communications and for downloading publications. Their use for the latter purpose however lags behind general access to the internet: thus only 40 per cent of those with access to the internet used it for downloading official government documents; and 20 per cent for downloading of reports. The use of the electronic media for the organisation of conferences is further behind (11 per cent) – whilst low in comparative perspective this percentage is quite high if one considers that the technologies for this purpose are not yet as advanced.

Who Supplies Information and Modes of Information Acquisition

The source of information can also be assessed from an institutional perspective. Table 10.5 displays the incidence of consultation of different types of organisations for the purpose of gathering information on transport-related research.

Table 10.5 Organisations Consulted for Obtaining Information

Type of organisation	% consulting this organisation
Research institutes	63
Government	54
Universities	49
Consultancies	40
Non-Governmental Organisations	27
Chambers, Interest Groups	22
Industry	19

Source: TENASSESS Survey

A factor analysis of the responses revealed an interesting pattern in the use of multiple information sources. There are four typical modes of information acquisition:

- seeking information primarily from governmental institutions in conjunction with industry and interest groups;
- using consultancies and chambers or interest groups as the primary sources of information;
- relying on academic research, mainly research institutes and universities, to obtain information;

- relying on universities in conjunction with governmental institutions for information.

The results are interesting because they suggest that dissemination strategies must take into account the plurality not only of users and products of research (Giorgi and Pohoryles, 1999; Sansom *et al.*, 1999) but also the differences in modes of information acquisition. These differences reflect the heterogeneity of the targeted audience for transport research, itself a function less of personal styles of communication and more of the variation in inter-organisational structures.

Barriers to the Access of Information

Asked to assess the reasons that prevent an easy access to information, respondents identified three as of particular relevance: 'lack of information where and how to obtain results', 'lack of a dissemination strategy' and 'complex ordering procedures'. All other possible obstacles mentioned in the questionnaire, including language barriers and confidentiality, were judged as far less important. Table 10.6 displays these results analytically.

Table 10.6 Barriers to Access to Information

Barrier	% considering this important
Lack of information on how to access	79
Lack of dissemination strategy	51
Complex ordering procedures	30
Information available through informal channels only	21
Confidential results	21
No results published	17
Not available in print	15
Not available on-line	14
Language barriers	9
Out-of-print	6

Source: TENASSESS Survey

Lack of Knowledge of European Research

Not knowing how to access information in conjunction with the perceived weak dissemination strategy on the part of the Commission explains the lack of knowledge of European transport research: in early 1997, 43 per cent of the respondents were not aware of any European research results of the EURET and APAS programmes or of the Fourth Framework Programme of the Transport RTD Programme at European level. This compared to 19 per cent not knowing of any results deriving from national transport research programmes or projects.

Among those aware of the European research programmes, the judgement on the availability of these results is far from positive: less than one quarter judged the availability as good.

The lack of awareness of European research programmes is not specific to the field of transport. A (relative) majority of respondents is likewise not aware of some of the main European information sources like the EUROPA Web Site, the CORDIS Database or the European Office of Publications. The same is true among those with internet access, albeit not as significantly (Table 10.7).

Table 10.7 Knowledge and Use of European Information Sources

Sources	All respondents		Respondents with Internet	
	% not heard	% not used	% not heard	% not used
CORDIS Database	49	25	39	26
EUROPA WWW	43	28	32	29
EURO Abstracts	49	25	39	30
CORDIS Newsletter	53	26	43	31
EURO Info Centre	46	27	36	32
EUR-OP	59	23	57	26

Source: TENASSESS Survey

Collaboration Between Science and Policy Communities

Considering the above it is not surprising that respondents evaluate the collaboration between the scientific and policy communities at the European level as seriously lacking with regard to the formulation, evaluation, dissemination and exploitation of research. In particular, dissemination and exploitation get 'bad marks'.[1] Table 10.8 compares the shares of bad marks for European and national science-policy interaction.

Table 10.8 Evaluation of Collaboration Networks at European & National Levels (% Giving a Bad Evaluation)

Area	European level	National level
Research agenda setting	33	20
Research evaluation	35	25
Research dissemination	54	35
Research exploitation	69	50

Source: TENASSESS Survey

The majority of the respondents still considers that the *agenda setting* and the *evaluation* of research proposals are characterised by a good degree of collaboration between the scientific and policy communities – this needs to be underlined. The opposite is the case for *dissemination* and *exploitation*, at least at the European level. The comparatively better marks granted to national research programmes is indicative of the prevailing dominance of national research in the European Union with respect to impact.

A more positive note is provided by the fourth-wave survey results. Despite it comprising the smallest sample due to panel attrition – a fact which calls for caution in the interpretation of statistical significance – the evidence is positive. Thus two years later, one third of the respondents claim that their awareness of European transport research has increased. Four out of ten also perceive improvements in the field of collaboration between the research and policy sides in terms of the formulation of the research agenda, two out of ten in terms also of dissemination.

The problem would appear still to be one of exploitation. As one respondent noted in his/her comments to the open section of the questionnaire, 'the high-level agenda [at European level] appears now to be better understood ... the problems relating to an effective implementation seem however no closer to a solution'.

Barriers to Research Exploitation

There are many barriers to research exploitation, some relate to the research supply side, some to the policy demand side. In the TENASSESS survey we asked respondents to assess those barriers that relate to the science and policy *interaction*.

A factor analysis of the responses revealed eight factors explained most of the variance in the respondents' answers. These factors reflect the interrelations among the various barriers and provide insight into the real causes for the low impact of research. Table 10.9 displays the results analytically:

Basic instead of applied Exclusively theoretical research studies tend to be too long and too complex. Even if relevant such studies are unlikely to have an impact on the policy discourse.

User-unfriendly Research results which cannot be generalised are often also difficult to exploit. The difficulty with identifying the more generic application of research results often has to do with their presentation which, overall, is judged as user-unfriendly.

Not policy-relevant The exemplification of research results through empirical findings or case studies is important for exploitation – in transport this concerns primarily the geographical scope for application.

Badly structured Badly structured research reports tend to be repetitive; in some ways bad structure appears to reflect high ambitions and little understanding of the limitations of research.

Unclear on goals Lack of clarity of the client's goals is often the reason for the lack of co-ordination between the client and the researcher; equally possible is that the failure to establish co-ordination between the client and the researcher leads to the inability to well reflect on the client's goals in the research reports.

Not integrated in state-of-the-art Research studies which display little reference to previous studies in the field, i.e. which do not elaborate the consistency or lack of consistency between actual and previous results, are likely to be evaluated as not being part of the mainstream scientific discourse and in turn as far too complex in terms of policy relevance.

Table 10.9 Barriers to Research Exploitation

Research is ... as reflected by ...	% are of this opinion
Basic instead of applied	33
Theoretical orientation	
Length (too long)	
User-unfriendly	29
Lack of generic application	
Lack of user-orientation	
Presentation style (not clear)	
Not policy-relevant	24
Contents (not policy-focused)	
Geographical scope (inadequate)	
Badly structured	22
Repetition	
Presentation	
Lack of scope	
Unclear on goals	21
Lack of clarity of client's goals	
Lack of co-ordination with client	
Not integrated in state-of-the-art	20
Lack of consistency of studies	
Specific orientation	
Difficult to understand	17
Complex themes	
No common scientific language	
Too technical	17
Technical orientation	
Outdated	

Note: The factor loadings are expressed as percentages of those indicating agreement with the first (and strongest) item on each factor

Source: TENASSESS Survey

Difficult to understand Studies which deal with complex themes are often difficult to understand, especially for those who do not share the scientific language of the researcher, a typical problem with multidisciplinary research.

Too technical Technical research studies run the risk to quickly become outdated, thus it would seem important that their practical implications are elaborated and implemented quickly. However the presentation style in which they are often written prevents this from materialising.

The above results highlight that a comprehensive evaluation of the impacts of research needs to consider both dissemination and exploitation and, with reference to the latter, the problems of reporting as well as the quality of contents. As one of our respondents noted:

> The EU has intensified information dissemination through workshops and gatherings that indeed help networking among research groups. But one may add that some research is taken up in a 'Darwinistic' manner which appears to suit the European system well but which is not always to the benefit of good research; in some cases the EU demand for dissemination is energetically followed but on the basis of very limited results.[2]

Towards a European Research Agenda

In wave four of the TENASSESS survey we asked respondents to identify main research areas in the various sectors of transport, namely, road, rail, air, waterborne, intermodal, urban and strategic. Through an open question we also asked respondents to provide us with specific examples.

Table 10.10 displays the four main research areas identified by our respondents for each transport sector, which are relevant for future policy decisions.

Intermodality and combined transport is clearly one of the most salient themes at present. It is among the four most frequently mentioned areas for all mode specific transport sectors with the exception of air. Within the sector for combined transport itself, pricing ranks first – the Commission's Communication on Intermodality (1998) indeed agrees that pricing conditions comprise the main barrier to the implementation of the transport system approach that governs intermodality.

Table 10.10 Main Research Areas by Sector

Sector	Main research areas
Road sector	Environmental impacts
	External costs
	Pricing
	Intermodality / Combined transport
Rail sector	Intermodality / Combined transport
	Deregulation & Competition
	Financing and PPP
	Pricing
Air sector	Environmental impacts
	Deregulation & Competition
	Traffic Management
	Safety
Waterborne sector	Intermodality / Combined transport
	Deregulation & Competition
	Modal Shift
	Spatial impacts
Intermodal sector	Pricing
	Combined transport
	Deregulation & Competition
	Modal shift
Urban sector	Spatial impacts
	Social impacts
	Environmental impacts
	Deregulation & Competition
Strategic sector	Deregulation & Competition
	External costs
	Policy co-ordination issues
	Pricing

Source: TENASSESS Survey

The second most salient theme is that of *competition and deregulation*. The Transport Acquis (1999) is dominated by directives on the subject of market access with the aim of promoting competition and supporting deregulation. There has been comparatively little research that has directly looked into the impacts of this strategy in the framework of the Fourth Framework Programme (Pohoryles and Giorgi, 1998, TENASSESS Deliverable 5) even though the topic was indirectly addressed in a number of research projects. The respondents to the TENASSESS survey would appear to be of the opinion that more research is needed in this field.

The study of *environmental impacts* is ranked as first priority for the air and the road sectors and third for the urban sector. This is not surprising: it is well known that the air and road are the most environmentally polluting of the transport modes. The salience of this theme for urban transport reflects the dominance of road transport for short-distance travel much to the detriment of public transport (cf. Communication of the Commission on the Citizens' Network, 1998). However the study of environmental impacts has not been a top priority in the air sector of the level of the European research programmes (Giorgi and Pohoryles, 1996, TENASSESS Deliverable 5).

Social and spatial impacts are considered a priority for research only in the case of the urban sector. This is surprising given that much of European research over the last several years was launched under the motto of promoting 'sustainable mobility'. This could suggest that the distributional aspects of transport development are considered as deriving from other policies, or not yet sufficiently understood. As one of our respondents put it: 'The economic and social impacts of transport are understood in a very distorted way by policy-makers; more analysis [and dissemination] is necessary to achieve harmonisation'.

Specific research needs mentioned by the respondents are as follows:
In the *road sector*:

- the establishment of standards for construction material;
- the elaboration of policy recommendations for noise-levels;
- the analysis of the impacts of pricing policies on promoting combined transport;
- the evaluation of traffic reduction policies;
- the analysis of potential for improving combined transport with respect to rail.

In the *rail sector*:

- the elaboration of standards for signalling and gauges;
- the elaboration of standards for basic amenities provided in trains, including for disabled passengers;
- the analysis of combined transport solutions for passengers;
- the revisiting of safety standards;

- the re-assessment of the environmental impacts of rail transport.

In the *air sector*:

- the elaboration of air reduction policies;
- the assessment of the environmental impacts of air transport and ways to overcome them;
- distance-dependency of air fares.

In the *intermodal sector*:

- the development of multi-modal planning methods;
- the investigation of options for promoting combined transport road – rail; as well as road – water;
- database on relevant issues concerning intermodal transport;
- analysis of pricing barriers;
- analysis of the implications of intermodality for sustainability considering that it need not necessarily support a modal shift.

In the *urban sector*:

- benchmarking of urban systems with a view towards promoting sustainability;
- comprehensive ticketing options;
- analysis of the impact of transport investment in reducing social exclusion.

In the *strategic sector*:

- analysis of institutional impacts;
- social science research on policies and organisational aspects;
- social impacts;
- the relation of transport to other sectors.

No doubt the above is not an exhaustive list of transport-related research themes. What however it shows is that questionnaires of the type used in the TENASSESS survey can assist in the setting and refinement of the research agenda at European level.

Summary of Findings

This section has looked into the use and applicability of research, and more generally information, in the transport sector. Summarising the findings we could note the following:

- Informal means of information are the most widespread in terms of use.
- Research reports and publications are useful information sources. However, the limited time available to policy makers is a limiting factor in terms of use or uptake.
- This no doubt partly explains the increasing significance of modern communication technologies for obtaining information: Web Sites are the one most important tool for gaining an overview of European research projects. They can however not substitute for more detailed literature surveys.
- Institutionally there are different modes of information acquisition. These reflect the heterogeneity of the users of research and the variation in inter-organisational structures across policy communities. Also true is that those who use knowledge in policy-making use more types of providers.
- Lack of information on how and where to obtain research results and information is the most significant barrier to the access to information.
- The lack of a comprehensive dissemination strategy is also the main reason behind the comparatively low knowledge of European research results.
- Dissemination and exploitation are the two fields where more collaboration between science and policy is needed. The latter works better at the national level than at the European level.
- A better science-policy interaction can contribute to the overcoming of the barriers to research exploitation. There are many practical ways in which this can be achieved and reflected in the outputs of research: more clarity in the clients' goals or programme's objectives; elaboration of concise exploitation plans in the case of technical studies; use of examples or case studies; a good balance between generic and specialised information; references to previous research results; and a concise structure.
- Intermodality and deregulation are the two most salient research topics for European transport research.
- In some cases, the knowledge and information needs of policy-makers are not met by the existing research programmes. This is for instance

the case of the environmental impacts/solutions with regard to air transport.

Trends in Transport Policy: A Simulated Discussion

This section reports on the emerging trends in transport policy as judged by experts, respondents to the TENASSESS survey.

First, we address the question of policy goal prioritisation and interrelations and the differences in this respect between own evaluation and the perception of the Union's views – the divergence between the two for some policy areas raise questions about the scope and pace of harmonisation but also about the information policy of the European Commission.

Secondly, we discuss the main trends in transport policy as perceived by the experts. The statements which the experts were invited to evaluate addressed a range of issues: the decision-making process and structure; the relation between national transport policies and European (common) transport policy (CTP); the main themes of concern in transport policies; the Tran-European Networks (TEN); the issue of pricing; the integration of environmental concerns; the social dimension; and last but not least the problematic question of financing and its implications.

European Policy Objectives for the Future

Both the first and second wave questionnaires of the TENASSESS survey entailed a series of questions on strategic policy issues in transport. On the basis of the analysis of the responses at the aggregate level, it was possible to elaborate the trends and strategies in the field. These were, in turn, presented to the respondents with the third wave questionnaire with the request that they re-consider them in conjunction with the information provided. On the basis of this final input it was possible to revise once again the strategies for the future and the reference scenarios in the field of policy.

We may distinguish between goals of high priority and goals of medium priority as well as between goals for which EU action is considered pivotal and goals for which EU action is considered a facilitator. Below we elaborate each of these goals (in parentheses the percentage of respondents agreeing with the various policy components).

Goals of *high priority and for which EU action is pivotal* include interoperability, fiscal harmonisation and the reduction of environmental pollution:

Realising the interoperability and interconnectivity of all national transport networks in the Member States of the EU

- A goal of highest priority (82).
- EU action is important for the achievement of this goal (88).
- Barriers to the implementation of this goal are mainly of a financial and organisational nature (80).
- A policy mix is necessary for the implementation of this goal, albeit prioritising investment over regulation (90).
- Provided the relevant measures are taken, this goal could be achieved by the year 2010 (76).

Harmonisation of fiscal regulations in the transport sector in Europe

- A goal of highest priority (83) with action at EU level considered the major promoter for its achievement (91).
- Barriers to the implementation of this goal cut through all policy arenas and policy fields. At the level of policy arenas, barriers are likely to emerge in the political field, with reference to public acceptability but may also concern organisational aspects. Barriers may also be expected with reference to financing as well as the level of technological development (91).
- A policy mix would appear relevant for the implementation of this goal, involving primarily regulation measures and pricing (91).
- Provided the relevant actions are taken, this goal could be achieved by the year 2005 (77).

Reducing the transport-related CO2 emissions by 15 per cent (base year 1990) by the year 2010

- A goal of highest priority (82) with action at EU level being very important (89).
- Barriers to the implementation of this goal mainly relate to the lack of political will to enforce it; otherwise, they are mainly of an organisational and financial nature (89).
- Characteristic is that not all appropriate measures have been implemented in all countries to enforce this goal (94).

- A policy mix is necessary for the implementation of this goal, prioritising regulation over pricing and investment measures (88).
- One of the most important measures in the field of regulation would be the enforcement of strategic environmental assessment (to replace mere EIA) for all transport infrastructure projects (80).
- Expected year of achievement (provided all relevant measures are taken): 2010 (83).

Policy goals of *high priority but not requiring major EU action* are safety and intermodality:

Reducing the fatalities and injuries in road transport by 50 per cent (with 1993 as a base year) by 2010

- A goal of highest priority (78); action at the EU level is a facilitator to the process of implementation but not the major promoter (91).
- Barriers to the implementation of this goal are mainly of an organisational and financial nature (79).
- Regulations comprise the primary tool for achieving this goal (68).
- This goal could be achieved by the year 2010 (79).

Establishing integrated, multimodal transport networks, both passenger and freight, through high-performance modal interfaces

- A goal of highest priority (82); Action at the EU level facilitates implementation (88).
- Barriers to the implementation of this goal are mainly of a financial and organisational nature (88).
- A policy mix is necessary for implementing this goal, albeit prioritising investment over regulation (87).
- This goal could be achieved by the year 2010 (78).

Policy goals of *medium priority but requiring EU action* for implementation are: the internalisation of external costs through the polluter-pay principle; the Trans-European Networks (TEN); and the development of external links with Central and East European countries.

Internalising the external costs of transport (through the polluter-pay principle) to increase the operational transport efficiency as well as to reduce negative environmental impacts

- A goal of medium priority (86), action at the EU level being the main promoter (84).
- Barriers to the implementation of this goal are mainly of an organisational and financial nature, barriers may also be expected to emerge in the political field as well as in the field of public acceptability (82).
- A policy mix involving regulation and pricing measures is necessary for the implementation of this goal (93).
- This goal could be achieved by the year 2010.

Stimulating a positive economic development in Europe by realising the TEN

- A goal of medium priority (92); EU action is the main promoter (92).
- Barriers to the implementation of this goal are mainly of a financial origin. Organisational barriers also play an important role (97).
- A major problem regarding this goal is that it would not appear to contribute to regional cohesion, tending instead to increase the disparities between core and peripheral regions (83).
- Investment is the primary policy tool for implementing this goal (86).
- The could be implemented by the year 2010 (90).

Developing efficient external transport links with the CEEC and the NIS

- A goal of medium priority (86), EU action being the main promoter (90).
- Barriers to the implementation of this goal are mainly of a financial nature; organisational barriers may also emerge (92).
- Investment comprises the main tool for achieving this goal (91).
- The links could be completed by the year 2020 (91).

Policy goals of *medium priority and not requiring active EU action* are the promotion of active citizen participation; reducing the need for public financing; and moving competencies to the regions.

Reducing the need for public financing in transport by attracting private capital

- A goal of medium priority (94) with EU action facilitating implementation (93).
- Barriers to the implementation of this goal are mainly of a financial and organisational nature; however, the level of technological development as well a that of public acceptability are major concerns (91).
- A policy mix would appear relevant for the implementation of this goal, involving primarily regulation measures followed by investment and pricing measures (94).
- The goal could be realised (insofar as it becomes usual practice) by the year 2005 (79).

Increasing the possibilities for active participation of local actors and the public in the decision-making process

- A goal of medium priority (83), with EU action being a facilitator (91).
- Barriers to the implementation of this goal are mainly of an organisational and financial nature; barriers may also be expected to emerge in the political field (86).
- Regulations comprise the primary tool for achieving this goal (80).
- This goal could be achieved by the year 2010 (91).

Moving competencies to the regions in order to enable more effective decision-making processes with regards to transport issues

- A goal of medium priority (85), where the EU has a facilitating role to play (92).
- Barriers to the implementation of this goal are of a financial, organisational and technological nature (90).
- A policy mix would appear relevant for the implementation of this goal, including investment and regulation (93).
- This goal could be achieved by the year 2005.

There is finally one policy goal which could be classified in *neither of the above four categories* by reason of the polarisation it brings forth.

Completing the liberalisation and deregulation of transport service operation and infrastructure provision in the Member States of the EU

- A policy goal which is still under debate across Europe with significant national variation across the Northern-Southern divide (92).
- Action at the EU level is the main promoter of this goal (97).
- Barriers to the implementation of this goal relate to all policy arenas and fields: primarily to issues of financing, organisation and public acceptability; secondarily to aspects relating to technological development and political will (96).
- Regulations are considered the primary policy tool for implementing this goal (92).
- This goal could be achieved by the year 2010 (86).

The following observations could be made:

It is not infrastructure investment that is considered the highest priority for contemporary transport policy, but rather interoperability and intermodality, fiscal harmonisation and the promotion of sustainable mobility through the overcoming of negative environmental effects and the increase of safety.

Not all of the above goals are perceived as being dependent on EU action for implementation – thus only goals that require major regulatory reforms (like fiscal harmonisation or the reduction of CO2 emissions) or major technological investments (like interoperability) are thought to be driven by EU action. The promotion of intermodality, on the other hand, benefits from EU action but is not dependent on it. The exception would appear to be safety regulations.

Regulation measures (alone or coupled with investment) are the most frequently mentioned types of measures for the implementation of transport policy goals. Pricing measures are much less frequently mentioned – only with reference to environmental goals, the reduction of public financing and fiscal harmonisation – and always as secondary to regulation and/or investment.

The most frequently mentioned future reference year for the implementation of transport policy goals is the year 2010. Only fiscal harmonisation, the promotion of better co-ordination with regions and the attraction of private capital for transport investments are flagged out for

2005; the development of the pan-European networks to link Western and Eastern Europe is not expected to materialise to the full before 2020.

The barriers to the implementation of the above policy goals are multiple. Among them financial and organisational barriers are the most important.

Where To in Transport Policy: An Overview of Trends

The answers to the questions of all three questionnaires are revealing in many respects both where they indicate convergence of opinion and where they show divergence or polarisation. Each of the tables that follow display the percentage of respondents agreeing or disagreeing with the policy statements; the last column sums together those respondents who claimed a moderate position with those who refused to answer – with two telling exceptions to be discussed below, the 'don't know' answers were overall a minority and did not exceed 3 per cent.

On the subject of the decision process and structure there are two clear trends (Table 10.11):

- 61 per cent of the respondents were of the opinion that the role of the regions is increasing with regard to transport policies – this finding is in line with the case studies of major infrastructure projects carried out in the framework of TENASSESS and reported in chapter 2 of this volume. The case studies exemplified how the regional dimension is exerting a strong influence on the success or failure of the implementation of major transport infrastructure projects.
- 75 per cent of the respondents agree that there is a lack of measures for performance in relation to transport policy objectives. Indeed a desk review of national transport policy documents showed that despite the detailed formulation of transport policy and/or infrastructure plans in the majority of European countries, strategic thinking stops short of elaborating measures for evaluating performance be it in terms of efficiency or in terms of effectiveness.

On other issues, the trend is less clear. Thus while the relative majority is of the opinion that national and regional transport policy plans are important, there is still a strong minority which rejects this view and an equally strong minority which is ambivalent on the subject. The same is true of citizen participation as well as the question of the effectiveness of conflict resolution mechanisms.

Furthermore, even though the absolute majority is of the opinion that transport planning is already now incorporated in the wider framework of spatial and environmental planning, the views expressed on the subject of the effectiveness of environmental legislation (see later tables) call for a relativisation of this view.

Table 10.11 Decision Process and Structure

Decision process and structure	**Agree**	**Disagree**	Between/DN
National / regional transport policy documents carry a lot of weight as general orientation guidelines.	49%	23%	28%
Transport planning at national level is incorporated in the larger framework of spatial and environmental planning.	55%	21%	24%
There is an increasing role assigned to the regions in transport policy.	61%	26%	13%
The process of transport planning faces further democratisation with increased opportunities for citizen participation.	47%	39%	14%
There exist sufficient resolution mechanisms for conflicts about competencies in transport policy among different administrative levels.	42%	34%	24%
There is a lack of performance measures to assess the success or failure of transport policies.	75%	12%	13%

Source: TENASSESS Survey

Hesitancy would be the right word to describe the relation between national transport policies and European transport policy or CTP. Thus while close to fifty per cent of the respondents are of the view that national transport policies and European transport policy display similar trends and tendencies, an equivalent number does not think that CTP has a strong impact on national transport policies, transport remaining largely an issue of national concern. Indeed half of those respondents that recognise common trends in their national transport policies and in European transport policy are of this view. The implications of these perceptions for the notion of subsidiarity are not without relevance (Table 10.12).

Table 10.12 National Transport Policies and CTP

National transport policies and CTP	Agree	Disagree	Between/DN
National transport policies and the European transport policy display the same trends and tendencies in terms of objectives	46%	25%	29%
The European Transport Policy has considerable impact on national transport policies	41%	34%	25%
There is no Common Transport Policy. Despite efforts, transport policy remains a national issue	47%	29%	24%

Source: TENASSESS Survey

The recognition of the similarities between national transport policies as well as between the latter and CTP are reflected in the clear statements on the contents of contemporary transport policy in Europe (Table 10.13):

- 75 per cent of the respondents agree with the statement that the major dilemma in contemporary transport policy is the inherent conflict between economic growth and environmental protection. Despite the incorporation of environmental concerns in transport policies, this conflict is still far from having been resolved. It is in fact often a major barrier to the implementation of infrastructure projects, also in those countries which can claim a high level of environmental consciousness with reference to their political culture (see Ollivier-Trigalo in this volume).
- The second major theme for debate would appear to be that of privatisation and deregulation. Even though the relative majority agrees that these are accepted policies, there is a strong minority that rejects this view.
- Striking is the agreement on the role of transport for overcoming structural inequalities at the regional level via economic development. 76 per cent of the respondents consider transport as contributing to

regional and national economic development and to the welfare of citizens. All the more surprising is therefore that 50 per cent of the respondents refused to express an opinion as to whether there is an unavoidable association between transport volume growth and economic growth.

- Finally, 79 per cent of the respondents agree that a systems approach to transport is distinct from the contemporary mode-specific approach and that it is lacking in the contemporary European transport policy landscape. A clear majority, albeit a smaller one, is of the opinion that too much emphasis is placed on long-distance freight transport; less on local short-distance transport.

Table 10.13 What is Transport Policy About?

General contents of transport policies	Agree	Disagree	Between/DN
The thematic conflicts within transport policy can basically be reduced to one pair of contrasting arguments: policies concerned with reducing the negative impacts of transport for the environment and society; vs. policies to enhance economic development by improving transport flows.	75%	18%	7%
Privatisation and deregulation of the transport market are accepted policies. There are only arguments about the pace.	47%	36%	17%
Transport infrastructures are vital to regional and national economic development, and thereby contribute significantly to welfare.	76%	8%	16%
Economic growth and wealth depend on the growth of transport volume.	29%	21%	50%
Transport policy (at the European level) is still oriented too much towards specific modes. A general system approach is missing.	79%	9%	12%
Transport policy focuses too much on large infrastructure development for freight long haulage, too little priority is given to the local level where most transport volume is generated.	53%	32%	15%
A common legislation is necessary to back up further improvement of safety standards in transport throughout Europe.	78%	12%	10%

The views on the *Trans-European Networks (TENs)* fall on the negative side. 65 per cent of the respondents are of the opinion that the

TENs are the result of a national licitation process, rather than a sound concept of governance. 48 per cent are also of the opinion that regional cohesion, one of the main objectives of the TEN implementation, has not been met by the specific selection of TEN priority projects. Fewer think nevertheless that this will increase the disparity between core regions and peripheral regions (Table 10.14).

Table 10.14 The Trans-European Networks

The Trans-European Network (TEN)	Agree	Disagree	Between/DN
The TEN are the result of a national licitation process rather than a sound concept of government. The TEN lack a clear-cut evaluation of their economic, environmental, intermodal and integration effects.	65%	11%	24%
Regional cohesion is supported by the development of the TEN.	22%	48%	30%
TEN are contributing to an increasing disparity between economic core regions and peripheral regions.	28%	37%	35%

Source: TENASSESS Survey

Turning to the subject of pricing we can again observe wide-ranging consensus as to the importance of this policy goal. Indeed 64 per cent of the respondents are of the opinion that priority should be give to pricing measures over the TEN and that the user-pay principle needs to be more forcefully implemented. A majority is also of the view that the subsidising of railways is not in line with the rules for fair competition. The discrepancy between this proportion and the one on pricing more generally is indicative of the many problems being faced with the implementation of pricing measures (Table 10.15).

Table 10.15 Pricing and Transport

On the subject of pricing	Agree	Disagree	Between/DN
Priority should be given to progress with fair and efficient prices in transport over the development of TEN infrastructure.	64%	13%	23%
Currently some transport users pay too much relative to their cost, some pay too little. This is not only unfair but also inefficient. The user-pay principle needs to be strengthened.	64%	20%	16%
The political and financial support of the development of the railways does not comply with the rules of fair competition between the modes.	54%	36%	10%

Source: TENASSESS Survey

In line with the earlier finding regarding the recognition of environment as the major challenge for contemporary transport policy developments, 69 per cent of the respondents note the necessity to elaborate clearer policy goals in this field. Only 34 per cent are of the opinion that the existing measures will achieve the goal set by the EU ministers of environmental affairs about reducing C02 emissions by 15 per cent till 1990. Two measures are recognised as important for bringing the policy debate forward (Table 10.16):

- first, to introduce strategic environmental assessment as a compulsory measure for the evaluation of policy programmes or infrastructure plans;
- second, to consider environmental taxation as a means for internalising external costs in transport.

Table 10.16 Integration of Environmental Concerns

Integration of environmental concerns	Agree	Disagree	Between/DN
The measures implemented allow to achieve the goal of a CO2 reduction by 15% till 2010 (base 1990) as agreed by EU ministers of environmental affairs.	34%	45%	21%
The environmental impacts of transport infrastructures are not assessed sufficiently. SEA should become compulsory at an early stage.	**66%**	**22%**	**12%**
It is not that important to determine the magnitute of the aggregate externalities in transport with any great accuracy. What is important is to define clear environmental policy objectives and to gear the choice of instruments accordingly.	**69%**	**19%**	**12%**
The internalisation of externalities concerns not a general increase in taxes / charges, but a shift of emphasis towards environmental taxation.	**76%**	**13%**	**11%**

Source: TENASSESS Survey

Equity is next to environmental protection the other cornerstone of sustainable mobility. The majority of the respondents – 57 per cent – think that this is unlike that of environmental protection not sufficiently considered in deliberations concerning transport policy. An even greater number – 63 per cent – think that it is necessary to insist on more detailed assessment of the distribution effects of CTP (Table 10.17).

Table 10.17 Equity and Transport

On the subject of equity ...	Agree	Disagree	Between/DN
The issue of equity is not considered sufficiently in contemporary transport policy.	57%	27%	16%
Further assessment is necessary of who are the social groups winning or losing from transport policy developments in Europe.	63%	21%	16%

Source: TENASSESS Survey

Financing is one of the most important barriers to the implementation of major transport infrastructure projects (cf PLANCO, 1998, TENASSESS Deliverable 6). European transport experts agree: 84 per cent think that the inflated influence of the Treasury on public financing is becoming a major decision criterion for the implementation of transport infrastructure projects. Even though public-private partnership is one new mode of financing, the high risks involved in infrastructure investments lead private and subsequently public investors to opt for cost efficient solutions. Case studies have shown that this is indeed one solution to the problem; hence also phasing or the splitting of the project (Table 10.18).

Table 10.18 Financing and Transport

On the issue of financing ...	Agree	Disagree	Between/DN
With the (forthcoming) European Monetary Union and the (national) government struggling to fulfil the convergence criteria, the Treasury has a major influence on all aspects of transport investments.	83%	7%	10%
The availability of funds has become the main decision criterion for the realisation of transport initiatives.	84%	4%	12%
Due to the high risks involved in infrastructure investments, private involvement will opt for cost efficient solutions and over-dimensioned projects will be avoided.	62%	23%	15%

Source: TENASSESS Survey

Goal Prioritisation

Despite the apparent agreement on the trends in national and European transport policies, there is a considerable degree of disagreement over the prioritisation of specific policy objectives. Transport experts across Europe were asked to prioritise a set of twelve policy objectives and also to give their perception of the latter's prioritisation at the level of the Common Transport Policy. A number of interesting observations can be made (Table 10.19).

The divergence between the own ranking of policy goals and the perceived ranking at the level of CTP is significant for seven objectives: namely, safety, intermodality and interoperability, fiscal harmonisation, the TEN, the external links (to the CEEC), and citizen participation.

- Thus whilst 87 per cent of the respondents consider safety to be among the top 5 priority goals, only 29 per cent consider this to be a priority goal at CTP level. This is consistent with the findings reported earlier in this section.
- Different is the case for intermodality: 84 per cent rank intermodality among the top 5 priority goals, and 53 per cent think it is a priority goal at the European level as well. Similarly for interoperability: 62 per cent consider this a priority goal; 76 per cent a priority goal for CTP.
- 43 per cent consider fiscal harmonisation as among the top 5 priority goals, yet 75 per cent think that this same goal is a top priority for CTP.
- And while only 30 per cent view the TEN as a top priority goal, 61 per cent are of the opinion that it is a priority goal for CTP. External links are neither considered an own priority nor one for CTP. Nevertheless, it is interesting to observe that whilst 9 per cent would rank this as among their own top priority goals, 29 per cent think it is a top priority for CTP.
- Promoting citizen participation is not a priority goal for most respondents (23 per cent) – yet even fewer (9 per cent) consider it a priority at European level.

Table 10.19 Prioritisation of CTP Policy Objectives

Policy objectives	% think is a top 5 priority	
	Own	CTP
Reducing fatalities and serious injuries	87	29
Promoting intermodality	84	53
Promoting interoperability	62	76
Reducing CO2 emissions	54	57
Effecting fiscal harmonisation	43	75
Enforcing the Polluter-Pay Principle	45	57
Promoting economic development via TEN	30	61
Promoting citizen participation	23	8
Effecting deregulation & privatisation	20	24
Moving competencies to regions	16	17
Promoting Public-Private Partnerships	12	13
Promoting establishment of external links	9	23

Note: Ranked in descending order according to 'own priority'

Source: TENASSESS Survey

Whereby one can read the above differences in opinion regarding the prioritisation of policy goals as an indication of the divergence between national transport policies and CTP, another factor at work could well be the lack of comprehensive information about CTP. This is important to keep in mind when elaborating dissemination strategies at European level.

Goal Interrelationships

Another interesting finding concerns the interrelation between policy objectives. One major problem in the development of policy assessment methodologies relates to the so-called problem of 'double counting' which is a result of such interrelationships. In our survey European transport experts were provided with a matrix and asked to mark the two-way relationships between policy goals with a '3' to indicate 'strong interrelationship', a '2' to indicate a moderate interrelationship, a '1' to indicate a weak interrelationship and a '0' to indicate no interrelationship. The table below (Table 10.20) displays the average marks for each policy goal (out of a maximum of 100).

Table 10.20 Goal Interrelationship

Policy objectives	Degree of relationship
Promoting intermodality	41
Effecting fiscal harmonisation	32
Enforcing the Polluter-Pay Principle	32
Enforcing the Polluter-Pay Principle	32
Promoting interoperability	27
Reducing CO2 emissions	27
Promoting Public-Private Partnerships	27
Promoting establishment of external links	23
Promoting economic development via TEN	23
Promoting citizen participation	18
Effecting deregulation & privatisation	14
Reducing fatalities and serious injuries	9
Moving competencies to regions	9

Source: TENASSESS Survey

Depending on their degree of association, transport policy objectives could be classified in three main categories:

- the first category includes policy goals the outcome of which influences more generally developments in transport policy and in particular the implementation trajectory of other transport policy goals. Here are included the policy goals of intermodality, fiscal harmonisation and the polluter-pays principle;
- the second category includes policy objectives moderately dependent on others for their successful implementation – interoperability is one such goal; so are public-private partnerships, the setting of standards for reducing emissions as well as the TEN and corridor infrastructure programmes;
- finally, policy objectives with a low degree of interdependence are the promotion of citizen participation, the allocation of political responsibility to regions, deregulation as well as safety. These goals could be thought of as horizontal or cross-sectional: the significance of the first three derives from the way in which they influence the decision process; safety is important under whatever conditions.

The degree of interdependence between policy objectives is a two-fold measure: first, it is an indicator of the difficulty in implementation of any particular goal; second, it is a measure of the intensity of impacts to be expected with regard to the transport system as a whole.

Conclusions

This chapter has looked into the views on policy among transport experts in Europe. From the methodological viewpoint the results show that the method employed – a panel survey with Delphi elements – is a reasonable tool for surveying expert opinion, obtaining feedback on research results, as well as for simulating policy-relevant discussions.

The results suggest that there is a considerable convergence of opinion on the priorities of transport policy as well as on the problems and challenges being faced. The earlier emphasis on infrastructure investment has been replaced by a more comprehensive systems approach which stresses a new policy mix for achieving the goals of sustainable mobility and growth.

Notes

1 Also indicative are the item non-response rates to these questions that follow the same trend.

2 Following on from this, another comment made by one of our respondents is also relevant: 'Both policy-makers and the scientific community have recognised that limited funding needs careful targeting. The higher profile given to transport and the environment has helped in this respect'.

References

Barker, A. and Peters, B. G. (eds.) (1992), *The Politics of Expert Advice: Creating, Using and Manipulating Scientific Knowledge for Public Policy*, Edinburgh University Press, Edinburgh.

Bulmer, M. (1990), 'Successful Applications of Sociology' in Bryant, C. G. A. and Becker, H. A. (eds.), *What has Sociology Achieved?*, Macmillan, London.

Giorgi, L. and Pohoryles, R. J. (1999), *Project Definitions and Classification*, Project Report SITPRO [D(1)], ICCR, Vienna.

Halcrow Fox (1999), *Final Report* SITPRO, London.

Parsons, W. (1995), *Public Policy: An Introduction to the Theory and Practice of Policy Analysis*, Edward Elgar, Aldershot.

PLANCO (1999a), *The Barrier Model*, Project Report TENASSESS [D(6)], *Technical Annex A: Amendments to the Barrier Model*, ICCR & PLANCO, Vienna & Essen.

PLANCO (1999b), *The Barrier Model*, Project Report TENASSESS [D(6)], *Technical Annex B: Application and Testing of the Barrier Model*, ICCR & PLANCO, Vienna & Essen.

PLANCO (1999c), *The Barrier Model*, Project Report TENASSESS [D(6)], *Technical Annex C: Public Acceptance*, (Contribution of FACTUM, AT), ICCR & PLANCO, Vienna & Essen.

Pohoryles, R. J. and Giorgi, L. (1998), *Interconnection Among Tasks: A Guide to the Fourth Framework Strategic Transport Research Programme*, Project Report TENASSESS, [D(5)], ICCR, Vienna.

Sanson, T., Pearman, A., D. Matthews, B., Nellthorp, J. (1999), *The SITPRO Methodology*, SITPRO (Study of the Impacts of the Transport RTD Programme) Deliverable 2, Halcrow Fox, London.

TENASSESS Consortium (1997), *Country Profiles: National Transport Policies*, Project Report TENASSESS, [D(1)], Technical Annex, ICCR, Vienna (Country Profiles Austria, Germany, France, Italy, UK, Spain, Denmark, Netherlands, Finland, Sweden, Greece, Belgium, Luxembourg).

Wynne (1996), *Risk, Environment and Modernity*, Sage Publications, London.